Catholic Realism
and the Abolition of War

Catholic Realism
and the Abolition of War

David Carroll Cochran

ORBIS BOOKS
Maryknoll, New York 10545

ORBIS BOOKS
Maryknoll, New York 10545

Fathers and Brothers
MARYKNOLL

Founded in 1970, Orbis Books endeavors to publish works that enlighten the mind, nourish the spirit, and challenge the conscience. The publishing arm of the Maryknoll Fathers and Brothers, Orbis seeks to explore the global dimensions of the Christian faith and mission, to invite dialogue with diverse cultures and religious traditions, and to serve the cause of reconciliation and peace. The books published reflect the views of their authors and do not represent the official position of the Maryknoll Society. To learn more about Maryknoll and Orbis Books, please visit our website at www.maryknollsociety.org.

Library of Congress Cataloging-in-Publication Data

Cochran, David Carroll.
   Catholic realism and the abolition of war / David Carroll Cochran.
      pages cm
   Includes bibliographical references and index.
   ISBN 978-1-62698-074-7 (pbk.)
   1. War—Religious aspects—Catholic Church. 2. War—Moral and ethical aspects. 3. Just war doctrine. 4. Violence. 5. Violence—Religious aspects—Catholic Church. 6. Pacifism. 7. Pacifism—Religious aspects—Catholic Church. I. Title.
BX1795.W37C63 2014
261.8'73—dc23

                                                    2013025080

For Christine

Contents

Acknowledgments   ix

Chapter 1:   The Argument in Brief   1

Section I: War and Catholicism

Chapter 2:   Christianity, the Just War, and Pacifism   7

Chapter 3:   The Domestic Parallel   15

Chapter 4:   Contemporary Catholic Doctrine   20

Chapter 5:   The Neoconservative Backlash   32

Section II: The Immorality of War

Chapter 6:   Killing the Innocent: Civilians   43

Chapter 7:   Killing the Innocent: Soldiers   60

Chapter 8:   Policing, War, and Force   77

Chapter 9:   Lawlessness, Disorder, and Dehumanization   83

Chapter 10: Lies and Illusions   94

Section III: Abolishing Institutionalized Violence

Chapter 11: War as an Institution   109

Chapter 12: Trial by Ordeal and Combat   114

Chapter 13: The Duel   121

Chapter 14: Slavery   133

Chapter 15: Lynching   149

Chapter 16: Realism and Moral Progress   161

Section IV: Ending War

Chapter 17: The Path to Abolition   171

Chapter 18: Global Political Authority   177

Chapter 19: Democracy, the Rule of Law, and Nonviolence   183

Chapter 20: Development, Trade, and International Integration   191

Chapter 21: Conflict Resolution and Peacekeeping   198

Chapter 22: A Last Word: Terrorism   205

References   212

Index   237

Acknowledgments

In addition to Jim Keane and everyone at Orbis, my thanks to the following persons, who in ways large and small, direct and indirect, knowingly and unknowingly, helped form this book:

Anne Cochran, Andy Auge, Benn Darr, Bernie Giese, Beth Driscoll, Bill Joensen, Bob Beck, Brian Cochran, Cari Colletti, Carol Oberfoell, Chad DeWaard, Cheryl Jacobsen, Chris Budzisz, Christine Cochran, Cindy Smith, Clarke Cochran, Donna Bauerly, Jenna Lea, JimCollins, John Eby, John Waldmeir, Joyce Meldrem, Kathy Bishara, Kevin Koch, Kristin Anderson-Bricker, Lee Cochran, Lisa Sowle Cahill, Margaret Cochran, Mark Kehren, Mary Ellen Carroll, Matt Shadle, Rick Anderson, Stacia McDermott, Stephen Cochran, and Suzanne Ward.

1

The Argument in Brief

War's two great lies are its righteousness and its inevitability. It is neither. War is never morally permissible, and while it is deeply rooted in human history, it is not an inescapable part of the human condition. Like other forms of institutionalized violence once thought both just and unavoidable, we can and should abolish it completely, leaving a world still marked by conflict and violence, but nonetheless better off for war's absence.

War predates Christianity, so from the beginning Christians have struggled to reconcile its continued existence with the teachings of the gospels. While a small minority of Christians have always been pacifists, rejecting all war, the dominant Christian framework has long been the just war tradition, which accepts that war, while often terrible, is sometimes necessary to defend a just and peaceful order. These two traditions have counterparts in other world religions, and secular versions of each exist as well.

Advocates of the just war consider their position one of moral realism. The world as it is, inescapably torn by sin and discord, requires political power backed by force to uphold order and protect the innocent. Throughout its long history, this argument has relied on a parallel to policing and individual self-defense. Just as governments have the duty to protect their citizens from murderers and thieves, and individuals have the right to fight off attackers in the night, rulers are permitted to take their nations to war when necessary. Just war adherents consider pacifists, who are often suspicious of conventional political power and focus more on radical discipleship or countercultural models of living, to be hopelessly utopian, blind to the reality of evil and the necessity of force to overcome it. Peace, justice, and public order don't happen on their own; sometimes we have to fight for them.

The just war tradition has been especially central in Catholic teaching on war and peace. This teaching, however, has undergone significant changes since the Second Vatican Council, becoming more critical of war, endorsing nonviolence, and calling for international cooperation to eliminate war's underlying causes. These changes have sparked a backlash among a group of influential neoconservative thinkers in the United States. By their account, contemporary Catholic teaching has forgotten its traditional understanding of war's crucial role in protecting social order, become too squeamish about its use, and succumbed to a dangerously utopian form of sentimentality.

A narrow space for justified war still exists in Catholic doctrine. Its neoconservative critics would expand that space, returning the tradition to a more permissive position on war. But they have it backward. The Catholic tradition's own moral principles reveal why the remaining space for a just war should be closed entirely, why war is, by its very nature, inherently immoral. There is no such thing as a just war.

At the heart of Catholic ethics is the absolute prohibition on intentionally killing the innocent. War inevitably violates this prohibition in two ways. The first is noncombatant deaths, which account for at least half of war's casualties across its history. Indiscriminately massacring civilians is routine in both ancient and modern warfare; wars in which one or more sides respect the principle of noncombatant immunity are the exception rather than the rule. Even when modern militaries try to minimize civilian deaths, the nature of combat, with its highly lethal weaponry, its low threshold for killing, and its unique rules of engagement, means deliberately exposing innocent people to morally unacceptable levels of deadly risk as a direct means to military success. This inevitably kills shocking numbers of them, and it systematically violates the moral limits on lethal force embodied, for example, in domestic policing and individual self-defense.

Slaughtering soldiers is the second way war intentionally kills the innocent. Even as it sanctions their deliberate killing, the just war tradition itself acknowledges their innocence for the wrongdoing that purportedly justifies war in the first place, which is why it prohibits killing soldiers when they are wounded or surrendering, or punishing them afterward for being on the unjust side of the conflict. Like the young Pope Emeritus Benedict XVI, drafted into Hitler's army during the Second World War, ordinary soldiers are not responsible for the wars they fight in. Most serve in good faith or under compulsion, and the just war tradition has long acknowledged the basic moral equality of all soldiers in a conflict, regardless of the decisions their leaders make. The way innocent soldiers on all sides of a war butcher each other is fundamentally different from the use of force by police officers or individuals acting in legitimate self-defense. As such, it cannot conform to Catholic doctrine's strict conditions for justifying killing.

Rejecting war does not mean Catholicism must give up its traditional emphasis on social order and the need for conventional political power to protect it, including that backed by force. The world as it is still needs laws and their effective enforcement to uphold peace and justice, and policing remains legitimate here precisely because it differs from war. Indeed, given the lawlessness, destruction, famine, disease, shattered families, mistrust, abuse, and dehumanization war unleashes, it is more likely to threaten a just and peaceful order than protect it.

Like any long-standing and deeply unjust practice, war perpetuates itself through falsehood. This is evident in the noble causes it claims to champion, in the adventure and glory it promises the young, in the propaganda it thrives on, and in its systematically ignoring or explaining away the enemy's suffering, especially their dead. War even suffers from its own form of utopianism. Again and again, its advocates place unrealistic faith in its abilities, consistently overestimating its effectiveness compared to alternatives.

War's falsehoods are so powerful because it is a form of institutionalized violence. It relies on a background set of ideas, roles, and behaviors that are accepted as common sense: "War is natural and unavoidable." "It is simply the way the world works." "To think otherwise is unrealistic and naïve." Like other forms of institutionalized violence, however, war is a social invention rather than something innate in the human condition. This in no way denies its long history and frequency across cultures. It is only to say that while human beings have the basic capacity for violence, this capacity can, like the capacity for nonviolence, take a variety of institutional forms, none of which are inevitable.

We know this because we have other examples of institutionalized violence once considered natural, unavoidable, and simply part of the way the world worked. Among these were trials by ordeal and combat, vendettas and duels, slavery, and lynching. Each of these enjoyed wide social acceptance and moral legitimacy in terms remarkably similar to war. They were thought inevitable given the nature of the world, especially human sinfulness. They were thought necessary to uphold a just order, ensure peace and security, and protect the innocent from those bent on mayhem. Their opponents were condemned as unrealistic, utopian, and dangerous, blind to the realities of evil and unwilling to do what was necessary to defeat it.

Yet today we look back and ask how people could ever have done such things and accepted their absurd justifications. Such a transformation was possible only through a gradual and uneven process of changing both social attitudes and public policies. Abolishing these forms of institutionalized violence meant transforming norms, using political power to enforce them, and developing new kinds of institutional legitimacy and authority. It took the hard work of moral persuasion and conventional political action. This did not produce perfect peace and justice. Each institution's end left behind plenty of offenses against life and dignity. But it did, on balance, make the world a more humane place. As Catholicism's combination of optimistic humanism and moral realism about sin and injustice makes clear, moral progress does not require moral perfection.

This is why abolishing war is not unrealistic. Like other forms of institutionalized violence, a reinforcing cycle of changing social attitudes and political institutions can reduce and eventually eliminate it. While difficult, such a process is not impossible. It requires significant change, but not a transformation in human nature or a conversion of the world to radical religious discipleship. Such a process remains committed to social order and the need for conventional political power to enforce it. It will not leave the world free of conflict, injustice, and violence—only significantly better off without war.

What might such a path away from war look like? We can get a good idea by examining the progress we have already made. Data on war actually show a long-term decline, one that has accelerated in the last half-century. While complex, the factors behind this decline are precisely those emphasized by contemporary Catholic teaching on war and peace. Rather than the utopian illusions its neoconservative critics see, a growing body of social scientific evidence confirms that this teaching offers a realistic template for further dismantling war as an institution. This process centers on action by the international community to use the increasing political authority dispersed across a range of global institutions to spread and more effectively enforce norms against war. Its tools include support for democracy, the rule of law, human rights, nonviolent action, economic and human development, trade, international integration, conflict mediation and resolution, postconflict peacekeeping, and more effective global policing. As this varied and complex list shows, there is no simple and easy formula for abolishing war. That would be utopian. But a patient, consistent, and multidimensional global effort can weaken and ultimately consign war to humanity's past, where future generations can study it alongside slavery, dueling, or other forms of institutionalized violence as historical rather than contemporary evils.

SECTION I

WAR AND CATHOLICISM

2

Christianity, the Just War, and Pacifism

"Render therefore to Caesar the things that are Caesar's; and to God, the things that are God's" (Matthew 22:21 D-R). Has there ever been a less helpful answer to such an important question? From the birth of Christianity to today, followers of Jesus have struggled to reconcile membership in the Christian community with its call to discipleship and the promise of God's kingdom, and membership in ordinary society, with its own leaders, roles, and expectations. The struggle endures because the teachings of Jesus in the gospels seem ambiguous enough to justify very different answers. Over two millennia, the balance Christians have struck between what they owe Caesar and what they owe God has taken just about every conceivable form.

The use of violence by public authorities makes this balancing dilemma particularly acute. Here Christians face the "hard teachings" of Jesus (found, for example, in Matthew 25, Luke 6 and 17, and Mark 11). Those who follow Christ are to turn the other cheek, love their enemies, put away their swords, give their possessions to those who demand them, forgive those who wrong them, and return love for hate. The meek, the persecuted, the peacemakers: these are the ones favored by God. But Jesus does not explicitly apply these teachings to government officials in their public roles—magistrates, judges, and soldiers charged with restraining lawbreakers, punishing the guilty, compensating the wronged, or protecting the community from external enemies. In his interactions with such figures, such as the centurion in Matthew 8:5-13 or the royal official in John 4:46-54, Jesus neither endorses nor condemns their public roles.

In his advice to the earliest Christian communities, St. Paul continues this pattern. In Romans 12, he tells followers of Jesus to bless those who persecute them, set aside vengeance, minister to their enemies, and conquer evil with goodness. But immediately afterward in Romans 13, he tells them to subordinate themselves to public officials, whose authority comes from God and who rightly punish wrongdoers with the sword. So the question of the Christian's relationship to the coercive power of the state—its claim to the legitimate use of violence by its agents—is one of the oldest and most fundamental in the Christian tradition.[1]

The earliest Christians, living in the first few centuries after Jesus, had, in the words of Archbishop Charles Chaput, "mixed feelings" about the state.[2] While usually recognizing its necessity for public order, most followed the advice of Origen and other early church fathers to decline public office and refuse service as magistrates or soldiers. The role of soldier was especially problematic, given the shedding of blood it entailed, as well as the practice of swearing an oath to the emperor, which many considered idolatry.[3] Christianity was also still a relatively small and marginalized sect, as apt to be persecuted by public officials as recruited for government service. The larger reason, however, that early Christians eschewed state institutions and offices was that their focus lay elsewhere. They lived in expectation of the kingdom. Their main concern was sustaining the Christian community, one with a distinctive way of life untainted by the ways of this world, in preparation for Christ's imminent return. Theirs was a life of discipleship focused on Christ's promise of heavenly salvation rather than citizenship focused on the earthly affairs of state.[4]

As centuries passed without Christ's return, and Christianity moved from the margins to the center of the Roman world, culminating, after Constantine, with its establishment as the religion of the Empire, it gradually became more comfortable with political power and participation in government institutions, including those using violence. Most dramatic in this shift is the eventual Christian sanction for war. St. Ambrose, the influential fourth-century bishop of Milan, endorsed the use of military force against barbarian invaders then threatening the Empire. He drew on biblical evidence, such as wars authorized by God in the Old Testament, and classical Roman justifications, found in writers such as Cicero, of wars to maintain peace, protect the innocent, uphold alliances, and punish wrongdoing.[5]

This emerging justification for war under some circumstances reached its fullest expression in the early church with Ambrose's student St. Augustine, the father of just war theory.[6] Augustine used Old Testament wars in his justification, but he also took the "hard sayings" of the New Testament seriously. Rather than avoiding gospel calls for mercy, forgiveness, and love, including for enemies, Augustine made them central to his just war thinking. For Christians, these become internal dispositions that require different types of action in different circumstances. In the believer's personal interactions, their meaning is more direct and literal—the practice of nonviolence, forgiveness, ministering to those in need, and so on. But in the political realm, they may actually require that public authorities use force to protect the innocent and punish wrongdoers. Crucial here is Augustine's concept of two "cities." The city of God embodies the promise of God's kingdom—untainted by sin, ruled by love, and marked by perfect peace. But this vision is not yet fulfilled in the earthly city where Christians still struggle with the realities of sin, conflict, and injustice. God's kingdom is still very real for Augustine, but it lies further away in eschatological time, creating a space in which Christians must live in the earthly city. On his account, the earthly city "seeks an earthly peace" whose end is a "well-ordered concord of civic obedience and rule."[7] Practicing love in the earthly city means its rulers, acting as public officials rather than as private individuals, must sustain this "temporal peace" by upholding "the tranquility of order."[8] For Augustine, it is sometimes necessary to go to war to protect this peaceful civic order and punish those who threaten it. This is how, in the words of J. Bryan Hehir, Augustine "legitimized the use of force as a means of implementing the gospel command of love in the political order."[9] A just war is fought not to destroy peace and love but to uphold them.

The just war tradition Augustine launched became the dominant lens through which Christians viewed war for the next sixteen centuries, a dominance that continues to this day. Building on Augustine's foundation, St. Thomas Aquinas, Francisco de Vitoria, and Francisco Suárez fleshed out the theoretical conditions under which wars are just. More specific rules and practices—religious prohibitions on war at certain times of the year, barring clergy and other protected groups from combat, and codes of chivalry—also contributed to the tradition's development. After the Reformation, most Protestant churches, following the lead of Martin Luther and John Calvin, incorporated just war principles into their own teaching, and Protestants from Hugo Grotius in the seventeenth century to Paul Ramsey in the twentieth made key contributions to just war thinking. And, of course, the just war framework also draws on contributions from religious traditions beyond Christianity, secular-based theories, and the development of international law.[10]

While specific formulations of the just war can vary, they usually share several common features. *Jus ad bellum* principles guide the decision to go to war. Most important is a just cause, which has ranged from protecting the innocent from attack, to vindicating a country's lost rights, to punishing wrongdoing, to collecting national debts. The decision to launch such a war must be made by government authorities rather than private citizens, be a last resort, and truly be motivated by right intentions rather than serving as a cover for unjust motives. Given the suffering war unleashes, there must be a strong probability of success, so the suffering is not in vain, and proportionality of results, so that the good achieved outweighs that suffering. Most formulations also recognize that since in most conflicts neither side is completely blameless, the moral merit on the one side must outweigh that on the other, and many include a requirement that the war be launched with a sense of regret instead of nationalistic celebration.

Just war theories also include *jus in bello* principles, which guide how wars are fought once under way. The fact that a war is justified does not mean all actions in it are morally permitted. The two key restraints here are discrimination, which prohibits intentionally targeting non-combatants, and proportionality, which prohibits inflicting death and destruction beyond what is necessary to achieve the war's legitimate ends. Most accounts also forbid certain specific actions in war: mistreating or executing prisoners, desecrating holy places, targeting medical facilities or personnel, ignoring flags of truce, and the like.

As this overview illustrates, the just war framework is highly rule based. It offers moral guidance by applying a set of broad criteria to particular concrete situations. It expresses its core principles in universal terms, as precepts derived by reason, accessible to all, and applicable across time and place.

In relying on this framework, Christian just war proponents are rarely prowar in the sense that they think it a good thing. Many, in fact, are deeply troubled by war and see just war principles primarily as a way to minimize it. They are united, however, in their belief that war is some-times necessary to uphold peace by protecting justice and Augustine's "tranquility of order." Aquinas, for example, argues that "those who wage war justly aim at peace" by protecting the common good and the just order it embodies.[11] Writing seven centuries later, John Courtney Murray claims there "is no peace without justice, law, and order," and these will, under some circumstances, require military force to protect. For him the just war position expresses "a will to peace, which, in the extremity, bears within itself a will to enforce the precept of peace by arms."[12] In most accounts of just war theory, repudiating war entirely and forever is utopian and potentially dangerous; it mistakes the way the world actually works. At the center of the just war framework, then, is an assertion of moral realism. It recognizes the importance of peace, justice, and order, but also the necessity of war to protect these values given the nature of human existence, one marked by covetousness and discord.

In coming to terms with the world as it actually is, the just war tra-dition endorses conventional state action, including, at times, violent coercion. It is comfortable using political power since this is the only possible way to secure certain morally worthy ends. If others will use political power to wage wars that threaten peace and justice, then it is sometimes necessary to use political power to wage wars aimed at defeating such threats. This is why just war theorists from Augustine to Paul Ramsey are frequently called "Christian realists." Theirs is "an account of politics that is non-utopian in the interest of keeping the political within humane limits."[13]

While the just war framework is the dominant lens through which Christianity has viewed the morality of war for centuries now, its association with Catholicism is especially close. This lies partly in its development within the church long before the Reformation, and partly in Catholicism's incorporating it so thoroughly into its theology and doctrine, but it is also rooted in its fitting so well into the Catholic tradition's ethical and political orientation. Catholicism grounds its social teaching largely in natural law, producing moral principles that are universally valid and accessible to all through reason. Like the just war framework, it offers moral principles that people can readily accept without being Christian believers themselves. The Catholic tradition is also comfortable with political power, considering it necessary to create and protect a just order in the world as it is. The *Compendium of the Social Doctrine of the Church* calls political authority "a positive and irreplaceable component of civil life," pointing to the "necessity of political institutions" for "attaining the common good" and upholding "an ordered and upright community life."[14] And, of course, the Catholic Church has a long history of being itself a sovereign state, one that while not having much of an armed forces anymore, does still maintain formal relations with other countries, a worldwide diplomatic corps, and membership in a range of global intergovernmental organizations.

* * *

In spite of its dominant position, the just war tradition's support within Christianity has never been unanimous. There have always been those who, following the example of the earliest Christians, refused to sanction any war. While always small and subject to significant diversity among its advocates, the pacifist tradition has offered a continuing challenge to just war assumptions across the centuries. A small number of religious orders and movements kept it alive in the medieval church, but Christian pacifism really reemerged with the Reformation, as several Protestant sects—Quakers, Mennonites, Church of the Brethren, Hutterites—sought to live Christ's teachings, including nonviolence and love for enemies, in more radically direct and consistent ways. These communities have maintained a small but influential place for pacifism within Protestantism down to the present, even as figures such as Dorothy Day helped reintroduce pacifism to Catholicism in the twentieth century. Like the just war tradition, pacifism also has sources outside Christianity, drawing on other religious traditions, especially Eastern ones such as Jainism and Buddhism, and modern secular versions.[15]

As Lisa Sowle Cahill demonstrates, most Christian pacifists, including recent Catholic advocates, don't simply differ from just war theory in their conclusions about war, but in their ethical orientation as well. Rather than relying primarily on universal norms appealing to reason and accessible to Christians and non-Christians alike, Christian pacifism usually begins with a more intense and personal commitment to living as a follower of Jesus. This sense of discipleship is crucial. Rather than adjusting the gospel to fit the world as it is, believers focus instead on being the kind of distinctive Christian community that prefigures God's kingdom, which often means living a life at odds with the world as it is. In Cahill's words, "Minority pacifist groups throughout the history of the Christian church have taken the eschatological or kingdom thrust of the gospel seriously by setting an agenda of radical practice and witness for the discipleship community."[16] Stanley Hauerwas, one of today's most influential pacifists, argues that a "genuine Christian pacifism, that is, pacifism that is determined by the reality of Christ's cross, assumes we must be peaceful not because such peace holds out the hope of a world free from war but because as followers of Jesus we cannot be anything other than peaceful in a world inextricably at war."[17]

This style of pacifism often contains a strong "strain of anarchism," an urge to separate from the corrupting influences of society, especially the institutions of state power that rely on violence.[18] It is the life of the individual pacifist or community of believers that matters, not engagement with the fallen world beyond. Other expressions of pacifism, again including some beyond Christianity, are more hopeful, retaining the importance of modeling a different kind of life, but also trusting that such action can help heal a world riven by violent conflict.[19] It is precisely the witness offered by pacifists to a radically alternative way of living that can convert a fallen world to a new and peaceful path. Notice, however, that unlike the just war tradition, both of these emphases within pacifism—based as they are on the life of small, countercultural minorities—are far less comfortable with conventional politics and the world as it is. The separatist impulse is to avoid the institutions of the state as hopelessly tainted by violence, while the engaging and healing impulse is to carry on the work of moral witness outside corrupt mainstream institutions to radically transform the world and human relationships within it.

Pacifism's uncompromising approach to war and its tendency toward intense moral conversion, communities of radical witness, and suspicion of conventional political power has never won over more than a small number of people. Most find it irrelevant and unrealistic at best, and foolish, self-indulgent, and potentially dangerous at worst. James Turner Johnson considers pacifism too "idealistic" since it underestimates threats posed by "the forces of injustice and evil" in the world.[20] Robert George argues that "war is always horrible; but sometimes the alternatives are even more horrible." While expressing respect for the commitment of pacifists, he warns, "Let us not delude ourselves into supposing that justice never requires resistance to evil doers by military force."[21] Michael Howard, in his history of antiwar thinking, observes of pacifists, "And if they do so renounce the use of force while others do not, then not only their own survival but that of their value-system can be at a very high risk."[22] Perhaps the political commentator Charles Krauthammer sums up public perceptions of pacifism best, calling it "a form of moral foolishness, tinged with moral vanity" that is "supremely impracticable." He continues: "People who hold such beliefs are deserving of a certain respect. But they are not to be put in positions of authority. One should be grateful for the saintly among us. And one should be vigilant that they not get to make the decisions upon which the lives of others depend."[23]

Notes

[1]For an excellent overview of this question in the Christian tradition, one that informs the rest of this chapter, see Cahill 1994.

[2]Chaput 2008, 64-65.

[3]Hollenbach 1983, chap. 1.

[4]Johnson 1987, chap. 1; and Cahill 1994, chap. 3.

[5]Christopher 1999, chap. 2; and Massaro and Shannon 2003, 9-10.

[6]For good overviews of Augustine's just war theory, see Cahill 1994, chap. 4; and Christopher 1999, chap. 3.

[7]Augustine 1950, book 19, chap. 17.

[8]Augustine 1950, book 19, chaps. 26 and 13.

[9]Hehir 1980, 16.

[10]For the development of the just war tradition from its diverse sources, see Johnson 1987; Massaro and Shannon 2003; Cahill 1994; Hehir 1980; Christopher 1999; Yoder 1984; Himes 1991; Syse and Reichberg 2007; Miller 1991; Elshtain 1992; Nardin 1996; and Walzer 1992.

[11]Aquinas 1947, 2-2.40.1.

[12]Murray 1959, 10 and 16.

[13]Hauerwas 1988, 170-71.

[14]Pontifical Council for Justice and Peace 2004, nos. 168 and 393-94.

[15]There are many sources within the pacifist tradition, and a range of views on the legitimate use of violence, but they are all united by the position that war is morally impermissible under any circumstances. See Holmes and Gan 2005; Yoder 1992a; Cahill 1994; Johnson 1987; Teichman 1986; Cady 1989; Ceadel 1987; Holmes 1990; and Norman 1988.

[16]Cahill 1994, 151.

[17]Hauerwas 1988, 153-54.
[18]Deats 1980, 75. See also Koontz 1996.
[19]On these two strands within pacifism, see Johnson 1987.
[20]Johnson 1987, xiii.
[21]George 2011.
[22]Howard 2008, 118.
[23]Krauthammer 2006, 315.

3

The Domestic Parallel

Considering pacifism's absolute opposition to war utopian and dangerously naïve, those within the just war tradition claim to offer a more
realistic moral framework. While war should be avoided if possible
and its destructiveness minimized, a willingness to meet threats to the
just social order and the innocent lives within it by military force when
necessary is only common sense. One of the most powerful arguments
that just war advocates use when making this case is the parallel to
domestic security. Just as force is sometimes necessary to protect the
community and its members from internal attackers—murderers, thieves,
rapists, rioters—force is sometimes necessary to protect against external
enemies as well.

There are two elements to this domestic parallel. The oldest and
most important is policing. The authority of public officials to make
war is a "kind of extension" of their power to use violence for internal law and order.[1] In this way, the just war tradition, in the words of
Gerald Schlabach, "gets much of its credibility by imagining war to be
like police action," where innocent persons are protected, public order
upheld, and lawbreakers punished.[2] The second and related element is
that of individual self-defense. In the absence of an effective police presence, individuals have the right to use force to protect themselves and
their loved ones from unjust attacks (the "armed intruder in the night"
scenario). In a like way, countries may rightfully use force to protect
themselves from unjust attacks by other countries, especially since the
international community lacks a common effective policing body to
keep the peace among states.[3]

These domestic parallels, especially the policing one, have been particularly important to just war arguments within the Catholic tradition.
While he believes the gospels prohibit a private individual from killing in
personal self-defense, Ambrose does endorse the duty of public officials
to protect the community through both policing and war. In his *On the*

Duties of the Clergy, he praises the virtue of courage that "in war preserves one's country from the barbarians, or at home defends the weak, or comrades from robbers."[4] Augustine follows Ambrose in prohibiting killing in private self-defense, which is motivated by self-love, while approving killing by public officials in defense of the public order, which is motivated by love of others, including those against whom force is used (just as a father punishing his child acts from love).[5] He argues that "when the soldier kills an enemy or the judge or official puts a criminal to death," he acts legitimately, under his responsibility to uphold peace.[6]

While Aquinas departs from Augustine and endorses force, including lethal force if necessary, in private self-defense, he continues to justify war through a parallel to policing, endorsing the right of "public authority acting for the common good" to intentionally kill "as in the case of a soldier fighting against the foe, and in the minister of the judge struggling with robbers."[7] Pointing to Romans 13, Aquinas writes in *Summa Theologia,*

> And as the care of the common weal is committed to those who are in authority, it is their business to watch over the common weal of the city, kingdom or province subject to them. And just as it is lawful for them to have recourse to the sword in defending that common weal against internal disturbances, when they punish evildoers . . . so too, it is their business to have recourse to the sword of war in defending the common weal against external enemies.[8]

Here he echoes John of Salisbury, who a century earlier in *Policraticus*, invokes the image of rulers, charged by God to uphold justice and the civic order, wielding swords in each hand—one for domestic law enforcement and the other for military force.[9] In his defense of just wars, Vitoria also gives the sword in Romans 13 a dual purpose: "To draw the sword and use arms against internal wrongdoers and seditious citizens is lawful . . . Therefore it is lawful also to use the sword and arms against external enemies."[10]

The domestic parallel appears just as strongly in modern Catholic arguments for the just war and against pacifism. A catechism for priests in the 1930s declares that civil authorities, acting in domestic law enforcement, may kill when necessary to "punish the guilty and protect the innocent," continuing in the next section to claim, "In like manner, the soldier is guiltless who, actuated not by motives of ambition or cruelty, but by a pure desire of serving the interests of his country, takes away the life of an enemy in a just war."[11] Pope Pius XII, in a Christmas message soon after the end of the Second World War, states, "A person threatened with unjust aggression, or already its victim, may not remain passively indifferent . . . All the more does the solidarity of the family of nations forbid others to behave as mere spectators, in an attitude of apathetic neutrality."[12] The *New Catholic Encyclopedia*, which draws on entries going back about a century, maintains that "absolute pacifism" is "irreconcilable with Catholic doctrine" because "public authorities . . . would fail in an essential duty were they to offer no forceful resistance to violent aggressors from within or without."[13]

Catholic philosophers and theologians make similar claims. In her defense of the just war and critique of pacifism, Elizabeth Anscombe argues that "society without coercive power is generally impossible" and that the "same authority which puts down internal dissention, which promulgates laws and restrains those who break them if it can, must equally oppose external enemies."[14] John Finnis, advocating a self-defense–based just war ethic that necessarily "wholly excludes pacifism," claims that "the structure of the action of political societies can be the same as that of individuals' act of self-defense," and he compares legitimate war to the right to "resist forcibly the entry of squatters into my family house."[15] In his arguments for the just war's superiority to pacifism, Brian Stiltner writes, "If a Christian wants to practice nonviolence as a personal ideal for himself or herself, that is fine. But as long as there are 'bad guys' in the world, we will need governments to use their police powers domestically and military power internationally to protect people from harm and bring evildoers to justice . . . To think otherwise is irresponsible."[16]

Outside the Catholic tradition, secular accounts of why war is justified under certain conditions also rely heavily on the domestic parallel. Michael Walzer's influential just war framework rests on a "comparison of international to civil order," considering "aggression the international equivalent of armed robbery or murder," and just war an exercise in "law enforcement" by the attacked state. He argues that "a people can defend its country in the same way as men and women can defend their homes."[17] Paula Smithka and James Sterba both argue that anyone who accepts the right of individuals to defend themselves against unwarranted attacks must also acknowledge the right of nations to do the same with military force.[18] And Jan Narveson, in his classic argument against pacifism, writes,

> It appears, then, that to hold the pacifist position as a genuine, full-blooded moral principle is to hold that nobody has a right to fight back when attacked, that fighting back is inherently evil, as such. It means we are all mistaken in supposing that we have a right to self-protection . . . It appears to mean, for instance, that

we have no right to punish criminals, that all of our machinery of criminal justice is, in fact, unjust. Robbers, murderers, rapists, and miscellaneous delinquents ought, on this theory, to be let loose.[19]

Pacifists, for their part, are significantly more divided than just war advocates on the correspondence between domestic security and war.[20] Some forms of pacifism reject, or are at least deeply suspicious of participating in, state police functions. Many Christians in the Anabaptist tradition, for example, consider any use of government violence, in policing or in war, a violation of the gospel. Such groups are often the most separatist, focusing on their own communities of nonviolent discipleship and avoiding the larger institutions of the state. Others distinguish between policing and war, accepting the former under certain conditions while rejecting the later by pointing to fundamental differences between the two. Quakers, for example, often draw this distinction. Indeed, some of the earliest Christians agreed to participate in the Roman army as long as their duties were restricted to internal policing rather than warfare.[21] Similar differences arise when it comes to individual self-defense. Some pacifists, Tolstoy and John Howard Yoder for instance, reject killing in personal self-defense, while others like A. A. Milne endorse it when necessary, even while condemning the killing in war as of a very different kind.[22] Taken as a whole then, pacifism is far more ambivalent and inconsistent on the parallel of domestic security to war, and this is one reason the parallel is such a powerful part of the dominant just war tradition's arguments.

Notes

[1]Teichman 1986, 38-40.

[2]Schlabach 2007a, 70. See also Winright 1995 and 1999.

[3]For the importance of this justification to just war arguments, see Rodin 2002.

[4]Ambrose 391, book 1, chap. 27. On his condemning killing in private self-defense, see Megivern 1997, 32.

[5]Cahill 1994, chap. 4; Holmes 1989, chap. 4; and Johnson 2005, 16-17.

[6]Augustine 1964, 9.

[7]Aquinas 1947, 2-2.64.7.

[8]Aquinas 1947, 2-2.40.1.

[9]John of Salisbury 1979, 73-74.

[10]Victoria 1995, 166.

[11]McHugh and Callan 1934, 421-22. Today's *Catechism* also connects killing in individual self-defense to the right of public authorities to repel aggression in both domestic law enforcement and war. See *Catechism of the Catholic Church* 1994, nos. 2263-65 and the cross-references for nos. 2266 and 2308.

[12]Pius XII 1961, 37.

[13]McReavy and Meehan 2003, 747.

[14]Anscombe 1970, 43.

[15]Finnis 1996, 34 and 21-22.
[16]Clough and Stiltner 2007, 71.
[17]Walzer 1992, 55-63.
[18]Smithka 1992; and Sterba 1992.
[19]Narveson 1970, 69.
[20]See Cahill 1994, chap. 8; Winright 1999; Yoder 1992a; Schlabach 2007a, 77-79; Clough and Stiltner 2007, 44-50; and Deats 1980, 81-83.
[21]Egan 1980, 176; and Massaro and Shannon 2003, 8-9.
[22]Tolstoy 2005; Yoder 1992b; and Milne 2005. See also Cochran 1996.

4

Contemporary Catholic Doctrine

The just war framework remains the dominant lens through which modern Catholic teaching addresses war. This teaching has, however, seen dramatic shifts in emphasis and tone over the last century. Building on initial changes in the decades before it convened, the Second Vatican Council famously called for "an evaluation of war with an entirely new attitude."[1] Popes since the council have fleshed out this revised understanding in encyclicals and other Vatican documents, while national conferences of bishops have echoed similar themes in their own statements.[2]

While traditional just war theory assumed war was a regular and often necessary part of normal statecraft, early twentieth-century popes began condemning it in stronger terms, questioning its utility, and offering themselves as mediators in armed disputes. Following the Second World War, Pius XII eliminated punishing evil and vindicating rights as just causes, leaving only resisting unjust aggression, which he still considered sometimes necessary to uphold a just order. Even here, however, he stressed the caveat that the gravity of the aggression must outweigh the turmoil unleashed by the war. Kenneth Himes writes, "Evident in Pius XII's thought is the high regard Roman Catholicism has for order, in this case international order. The chaos of war might be worse than some measure of injustice in the social order."[3] For Pius XII, then, upholding a just order in some cases requires going to war, but in other cases it requires forgoing war, even in the face of some level of injustice.

This emphasis on the demands of a just and peaceful order, on both the domestic and international levels, remains central to Catholic teaching following the Second Vatican Council as well.[4] Benedict XVI speaks of "the ceaseless pursuit of a just ordering of human affairs," and, according to the U.S. Bishops, "Peace is the fruit of order."[5] Contemporary Catholic doctrine still recognizes the possibility of a just war if necessary to protect the peaceful order from those who threaten it by unjust aggression.[6] The Second Vatican Council states, "As long as the danger of war remains and there is no competent and sufficiently powerful authority at the international level, governments cannot be denied the right to legitimate defense once every means of peaceful settlement has been exhausted."[7] And John Paul II famously points out, "We are not pacifists, we do not want peace at any cost."[8]

But while statements such as these still appear in contemporary Catholic teaching, condemnations of war and calls for its abolition are far more frequent and prominent. The Second Vatican Council declares that God "urgently demands of us that we free ourselves from the age-old slavery of war," which is leading humanity toward destruction.[9] Addressing the United Nations, Paul VI, pointing to "the blood of millions, countless unheard-of sufferings, useless massacres, and frightening ruins," declares "never again war, never again war!"[10] And John Paul II calls on humanity to "proceed resolutely toward outlawing war completely."[11]

These types of condemnations mark a shift in Catholicism's understanding of order and moral realism when it comes to war. Now it is war itself that is more likely to threaten Augustine's tranquility of order, to destroy rather than uphold peace and justice. For Paul VI, an international system of amassing weapons and fighting wars "institutionalizes disorder and thus becomes a *perversion of peace.*"[12] Now the tradition's moral realism is turned on war itself, not simply accepting it as part of the world as it is, but seeing war clearly for what it does to the world: perpetuating cycles of violence, creating more problems than it solves, and unleashing the scourges of suffering, injustice, hatred, and chaos.[13]

John Paul II offers the most consistent and powerful teaching on this theme. In 1991's *Centesimus Annus*, he writes, "No, never again war, which destroys the lives of innocent people, teaches how to kill, throws into upheaval even the lives of those who do the killing and leaves behind a trail of resentment and hatred, thus making it all the more difficult to find a just solution of the very problems which provoked the war."[14] Two years later, in the annual papal peace message, he declares,

Recourse to violence, in fact, aggravates existing tensions and creates new ones. *Nothing is resolved by war; on the contrary, everything is placed in jeopardy by war.* The results of this scourge are the suffering and death of innumerable individuals, the disintegration of human relations and the irreparable loss of an immense artistic and environmental patrimony. War worsens the sufferings of the poor; indeed, it creates new poor by destroying means of subsistence, homes and property, and by eating away at the very fabric of the social environment.[15]

In another annual peace message, he says,

> Recent history clearly shows the failure of recourse to violence as
> a means for resolving political and social problems. War destroys,
> it does not build up; it weakens the moral foundations of society
> and creates further divisions and long-lasting tensions. And yet the
> news continues to speak of wars and armed conflicts, and of their
> countless victims. How often have my Predecessors and I myself
> called for an end to these horrors! I shall continue to do so until it
> is understood that war is the failure of all true humanism.[16]

A key factor driving these denunciations of war in contemporary
church doctrine is a growing focus on *jus in bello*. Beyond the reasons
that may or may not justify going to war in the first place, the Catholic
tradition has become increasingly concerned with the destruction caused
by the actual conduct of war, especially death and deprivation suffered by
noncombatants.[17] The indiscriminate nature of many modern weapons
and the rise of total war are especially prominent in this line of teaching.[18]
Invoking the need to give up recourse to arms, John XXIII states that
"this conviction owes its origin chiefly to the terrifying destructive force
of modern weapons . . . in this age which boasts of its atomic power,
it no longer makes sense to maintain that war is a fit instrument with
which to repair the violation of justice."[19]

Similarly, John Paul II argues, "It is not hard to see that the terrifying
power of the means of destruction—to which even medium and small-
sized countries have access—and the ever closer links between the peoples
of the whole world make it very difficult or practically impossible to limit
the consequences of a conflict."[20] The U.S. Bishops point to John Paul
II's statement that "the scale and horror of modern warfare" render "it
totally unacceptable as a means of settling differences between nations"
and bluntly declare that "modern warfare threatens the obliteration of
human life on a previously unimaginable scale."[21]

These assertions about the indiscriminate nature of modern war and
its weaponry have led some to claim that the Catholic tradition now effectively forbids all war.[22] In the wake of the 1991 Gulf War, an editorial
in *La Civilta Cattolica*, a Rome-based Catholic paper with close ties to
the Vatican, asked, "At this point can anyone speak any longer of a 'just
war'? Or do we not rather have to say a 'just war' is impossible because,
even when a just cause is present, the wrongs that wars produce by their
very nature are so grave and dreadful that they can never be justified in
the light of conscience?"[23] On the eve of the 2003 Iraq war, Archbishop
Renato Martino, president of the Vatican's Pontifical Council for Justice
and Peace, suggested that war might occupy a place similar to the death

penalty in modern Catholic teaching: just in theory but unjust for all practical purposes in today's world.[24] And two years before he was to become Pope Benedict XVI, then-Cardinal Joseph Ratzinger commented that "today we should be asking ourselves if it is still licit to admit the very existence of a 'just war.'"[25]

This may well be where Catholic doctrine is heading, but it is not there yet. While the church's official teaching documents clearly denounce war, they do not rule it out categorically. The current position is best described as a "stringent" version of just war teaching, one that is aware of war's horrors and skeptical of its morality but still leaves room for its just use under certain conditions.[26] Catholic teaching may now have, in the words of the U.S. Bishops, a "presumption against war," but it does not rule out war completely.[27]

Alongside its continuing reliance on the just war framework, however, Catholic teaching has also become much more accepting of pacifism and nonviolent witness.[28] While rejecting all war as unjust was long considered unacceptable for Catholics, the Second Vatican Council marks a shift in church doctrine by endorsing conscientious objection and recognizing pacifism as a valid option for individual believers. John Paul II praises those who reject war on principle and instead embrace nonviolence, crediting them rather than military force for bringing an end to the Cold War and offering a creative alternative to war: "Those who built their lives on the value of non-violence have given us a luminous and prophetic example. Their example of integrity and loyalty, often to the point of martyrdom, has provided us with rich and splendid lessons."[29] The U.S. Bishops now refer to the just war framework and the pacifist embrace of nonviolence as Catholicism's "dual tradition," one often in "tension" but sharing "the strong presumption against the use of force" and a "common goal: to diminish violence in this world."[30] It is important to recognize, however, that pacifism is still a junior partner in this arrangement. It represents a subjective moral option for particular persons, ones whose witness to nonviolence is inspiring, but not a universal norm binding on persons and governments generally.[31]

* * *

Another major shift in the Catholic approach to war after the Second Vatican Council is the addition of an affirmative peacemaking agenda. According to the U.S. Bishops, this new "vocation of peacemaking" is now a mandatory and essential dimension of our faith.[32] Here the Catholic tradition's emphasis on engaging the world by working for universal norms through political means looks beyond the question of when war may be necessary to also embrace the broader challenge of fostering "a

positive conception of peace, based on a vision of a just world order."[33]
As the Second Vatican Council states in *Gaudium et Spes*,

> Peace is not merely the absence of war; nor can it be reduced solely
> to the maintenance of a balance of power between enemies; nor is
> it brought about by dictatorship. Instead, it is rightly and appro-
> priately called an enterprise of justice. Peace results from that order
> structured into human society by its divine Founder, and actualized
> by men as they thirst after ever greater justice.[34]

Similarly, for John Paul II, "True peace therefore is the fruit of justice,
that moral virtue and legal guarantee which ensures full respect for rights
and responsibilities, and the just distribution of benefits and burdens."[35]
In this way, Catholic teaching connects peace to its larger commitment
to political and economic justice.[36]

The bridge for this connection is the concept of development, which
according to both Paul VI and John Paul II must be "authentic," meaning
it must go beyond simply economic growth to address "all the dimensions of the human person."[37] Development in the Catholic tradition is
the cultivation of social settings in which persons can truly flourish free
of political oppression and economic deprivation.[38] For Paul VI,

> It is not just a question of eliminating hunger and reducing poverty.
> It is not just a question of fighting wretched conditions, though
> this is an urgent and necessary task. It involves building a human
> community where men can live truly human lives, free from dis-
> crimination on account of race, religion or nationality, free from
> servitude to other men or to natural forces which they cannot yet
> control satisfactorily. It involves building a human community
> where liberty is not an idle word, where the needy Lazarus can sit
> down with the rich man at the same banquet table.[39]

Development targets the root causes of war, terrorism, and other forms
of political violence.[40] It addresses, in the words of John Paul II, the "real
and serious grievances" behind them—the "injustices suffered, legitimate
aspirations frustrated, poverty, and the exploitation of multitudes of
desperate people who see no real possibility of improving their lot by
peaceful means."[41] So when Paul VI calls development the "new name
for peace," he is grounding the Catholic understanding of peace in the
tradition's commitment to championing a broader set of political and
economic priorities in today's world.[42]

Those political priorities center on the spread of democratic values and practices. While historically suspicious of democracy, the Catholic Church has emerged since the Second Vatican Council as a global leader in advocating the cause of democracy around the world.[43] Benedict XVI, for example, calls in *Caritas in Veritate* for the worldwide "consolidation of democratic regimes capable of ensuring freedom and peace."[44] For the Catholic tradition, the common good depends upon active participation by citizens, the rule of law, and a flourishing civil society, all of which entail a robust set of political and civil rights—freedom of expression and conscience, especially in the practice of religion; the right to vote and hold office; freedom of association in forming civic groups, political parties, and unions; the right to due process and equal treatment under the law; the right of women to full participation in society; and prohibitions on discrimination against cultural minorities.[45] According to John Paul II, "Authentic democracy is possible only in a State ruled by law," one with a solid foundation in the explicit recognition of human rights.[46] He calls on countries around the world to "replace corrupt, dictatorial and authoritarian forms of government by democratic and participatory ones" to ensure "the 'health' of a political community—as expressed in the free and responsible participation of all citizens in public affairs, in the rule of law and in respect for the promotion of human rights."[47]

On the other side of the development coin, economic priorities center on addressing global inequality and the suffering of the world's poor. The Catholic tradition consistently calls attention to the gap between rich and poor, both globally and within countries; to the realities of poverty, hunger, and disease in the developing world; to the injustices of economic exploitation, especially for particularly vulnerable groups such as women and children; to those denied what Catholic doctrine considers basic human rights to food, shelter, health care, education, and employment; to how war and the arms trade exacerbate these evils; and to the need for international development efforts, particularly by the world's wealthier countries, aimed at eliminating them.[48] Decrying excessive economic inequalities that feed conflict and leave people "scandalized because some countries with a majority of citizens who are counted as Christians have an abundance of wealth, whereas others are deprived of the necessities of life and are tormented with hunger, disease, and every kind of misery," the Second Vatican Council calls for economic aid and development to create an "authentic economic order" upholding justice for all.[49] John Paul II writes, "Our world also shows increasing evidence of *another grave threat to peace*: many individuals and indeed whole peoples are living today *in conditions of extreme poverty*. The gap between rich and poor has become more marked, even in the most economically developed nations."[50] In *Centesimus Annus* he demands "a *concerted worldwide effort to promote development,* an effort which also involves sacrificing the positions of income and of power enjoyed by the more developed economies."[51]

Notice how these positions on political and economic development give more substance to the concept of a just order that is still central to the Catholic understanding of war and peace. Augustine's tranquility of order now comes with specific requirements: democracy, the rule of law, human rights, and a just distribution of wealth broad enough that all can lead lives of dignity and meet their basic needs. Contemporary Catholicism's peacemaking agenda holds this vision of a just order as its goal, arguing that building it, and overcoming the threat war poses to it, requires a continuing political commitment to international cooperation and institution-building.

In *Caritas in Veritate,* Benedict XVI writes that peace and development depend "*on a recognition that the human race is a single family* working together in true communion."[52] Similarly, the U.S. Bishops state, "Geography and political divisions do not alter the fact that we are all one human family, and indifference to the suffering of members of that family is not a moral option."[53] Catholic teaching after the Second Vatican Council frequently features such calls for international cooperation. While a globalized and interdependent world brings new challenges, it also creates the potential to forge closer ties of solidarity, to set aside war in favor of negotiation, and to develop structures for mutual collaboration in the interest of the global common good.[54] Pointing to the "need for a solidarity" brought by "radical interdependence," John Paul II urges nations in *Sollicitudo rei Socialis* to set aside "war and an unacceptable exaggerated concern for security, which deadens the impulse toward united cooperation by all for the common good of the human race."[55] This echoes John XXIII's call in *Pacem in Terris* for replacing "armed force" with "mutual trust" and "vigorous and sincere co-operation."[56] Putting what Paul VI calls "an overall policy of worldwide collaboration" into practice requires, in John Paul II's words, "a real international system" with "international structures capable of intervening through appropriate arbitration in the conflicts that arise between nations."[57]

Catholic teaching matches these general calls for peaceful global cooperation with more specific commitments to a full array of international organizations, institutions, and initiatives dedicated to development, peacemaking, and conflict resolution. These include mediation and diplomacy efforts; intergovernmental organizations and regional security regimes; nongovernmental organizations and grassroots civil society groups; international courts; truth and reconciliation commissions; microfinance initiatives; and international agreements limiting the arms trade, banning particular weapon systems (from landmines to nuclear arms), increasing development aid, guaranteeing human rights, assisting refugees, preventing human trafficking, and protecting the environment.[58] The tradition is especially supportive of international law.[59] Urging countries to uphold "the *force of law*" over "the *law of force*," John Paul II declares, "Peace and international law are closely linked to each other: *law favors peace*."[60] And Benedict XVI calls for the "growth of a global juridic culture" embodying "international norms," saying, "It bears repeating: power must always be disciplined by law, and this applies also to relations between sovereign States."[61]

While acknowledging that the organization doesn't always live up to its mandate, Catholic teaching also regularly endorses the United Nations as a crucial institution in the work of global peace, justice, and human rights.[62] According to John Paul II, the United Nations, "even with limitations and delays due in great part to the failures of its members, has made a notable contribution to the promotion of respect for human dignity, the freedom of peoples and the requirements of development, thus preparing the cultural and institutional soil for the building of peace."[63] And the U.S. Bishops write, "We regret the apparent unwillingness of some to see in the United Nations organization the potential for world order which exists and to encourage its development."[64]

Catholic teaching's endorsement of international law and the United Nations connects it to what is perhaps the most ambitious element of its peacemaking agenda. Recall the Second Vatican Council's statement that under certain conditions "governments cannot be denied the right to legitimate defense" as long as "no competent and sufficiently powerful authority at the international level" exists to resolve disputes and prevent war.[65] The Council goes on to urge the world community to reach the point "when all war can be completely outlawed by international consent," something that "requires the establishment of some universal public authority acknowledged as such by all and endowed with the power to safeguard on the behalf of all, security, regard for justice, and respect for rights."[66] This ideal of a global political authority is a consistent element in contemporary Catholic doctrine.[67] While limited in crucial ways—democratic norms, transparency, human rights, and the continuing subsidiarity functions of national governments and global civil society—it envisions a substantial exercise of political power by international governing institutions. According to the U.S. Bishops, just as feudalism gave way to the state system, "we are now entering an era of new, global interdependencies requiring global systems of governance."[68] John Paul II asks, "Is this not the time for all to work together for *a new constitutional organization of the human family*, truly capable of ensuring peace and harmony between peoples, as well as their integral development?"[69] And, in a remarkable section in *Caritas in Veritate*, Benedict XVI calls for "*a political, juridical and economic order*" with "real teeth" to manage global problems such as war, economic crises, poverty, hunger, environmental destruction, and migration. On his account, such "a greater degree of universal ordering" requires "*a true world political authority*," one "regulated by law" and "universally recognized." To have "the authority to ensure compliance with its decisions from all parties," it must be "vested with effective power to ensure security for all, regard for justice, and respect for rights."[70]

Here the Catholic tradition is still concerned with engaging the world through political methods to secure universal values, but its focus has shifted dramatically. While the traditional just war framework looks to individual governments and considers war an unfortunate but often morally acceptable part of routine statecraft, Catholicism after the Second Vatican Council looks to the international order, seeing global political institutions as the way to achieve peace, justice, and the elimination of war.

Notes

[1] Second Vatican Council 1965, no. 80.

[2] For good overviews of these shifts, see Himes 2008 and 1991; Christiansen 1999a; Curran 2002; Massaro and Shannon 2003; Whitmore 2005; and Shadle 2011, chaps. 7-8.

[3] Himes 1991, 331.

[4] See, for example, Benedict XVI 2009a, no. 67; Paul VI 1967, no. 76; Second Vatican Council 1965, nos. 78-79 and 88; John XXIII 1963, nos. 2-10; John Paul II 2002, nos. 2-3; Pontifical Council for Justice and Peace 2004, chap. 9; and United States Conference of Catholic Bishops 1983, nos. 234-36.

[5] Benedict XVI 2009a, no. 78; and United States Conference of Catholic Bishops 1983, opening summary.

[6] See, for example, *Catechism of the Catholic Church* 1994, no. 2308; Pontifical Council for Justice and Peace 2004, nos. 500-04; John Paul II 1993b; United States Conference of Catholic Bishops 1983, nos. 73, 75-78, and 316-17; and United States Conference of Catholic Bishops 2001.

[7] Second Vatican Council 1965, no. 79.

[8] John Paul II 1991d.

[9] Second Vatican Council 1965, no. 81.

[10] Paul VI 1966, 54.

[11] John Paul II 1991b, 531.

[12] Paul VI 1977, 246 (italics in original).

[13] See, for example, John XXIII 1961, nos. 205-06; Second Vatican Council 1965, nos. 77, 79, and 80; Paul VI 1975, no. 37; John Paul II 1991a, nos. 18 and 23; John Paul II 2000, nos. 3 and 8; John Paul II 2002, no. 10; John Paul II 2005, no. 4; John Paul II 1991c; and Pontifical Council for Justice and Peace 2004, chap. 11.

[14] John Paul II 1991a, no. 52.

[15]John Paul II 1993a, no. 4 (italics in original).

[16]John Paul II 1999, no. 11.

[17]See, for example, Second Vatican Council 1965, nos. 79-80; John Paul II 1999, no. 11; Pontifical Council for Justice and Peace 1994; United States Conference of Catholic Bishops 1983, nos. 101-04 and 217; United States Conference of Catholic Bishops 1995; and United States Conference of Catholic Bishops 2001.

[18]See, for example, John XXIII 1963, no. 112; Second Vatican Council 1965, nos. 79-80; John Paul II 1987, no. 24; and United States Conference of Catholic Bishops 1983, nos. 101-04.

[19]John XXIII 1963, nos. 126-27.

[20]John Paul II 1991a, no. 51.

[21]United States Conference of Catholic Bishops 1983, nos. 219 (footnote #94) and 15.

[22]See, for example, Egan 1993, 61-62; and Douglass 1968, 155.

[23]*La Civilta Cattolica* 1991, 453.

[24]Allen 2003.

[25]*Zenit* 2003.

[26]Christiansen 1999a.

[27]United States Conference of Catholic Bishops 1983, nos. 70, 83, and 93; and United States Conference of Catholic Bishops 1993.

[28]See, for example, Second Vatican Council 1965, nos. 78-79; World Synod of Catholic Bishops 1971, no. 65; John Paul II 1995a, no. 27; United States Conference of Catholic Bishops 1983, nos. 73-74, 78, 111-17, 120-21, and 222; and United States Conference of Catholic Bishops 1993.

[29]John Paul II 2000, no. 4. See also John Paul II 1991a, no. 23.

[30]United States Conference of Catholic Bishops 1993.

[31]Himes 1991.

[32]United States Conference of Catholic Bishops 1993.

[33]United States Conference of Catholic Bishops 1983, no. 234.

[34]Second Vatican Council 1965, no. 78. See also Paul VI 1967, no. 76.

[35]John Paul II 2002, no. 3.

[36]See also John XXIII 1963, nos. 31-35; and Second Vatican Council 1965, nos. 26 and 85.

[37]Paul VI 1967, no. 14; and John Paul II 1987, no. 1.

[38]See, for example, John XXIII 1963, nos. 122-23; Second Vatican Council 1965, no. 60; Paul VI 1967, nos. 10, 15-17, 20, and 34-35; World Synod of Catholic Bishops 1971, no. 15; Paul VI 1971, no. 41; John Paul II 1987, nos. 15-16, 29-30, 32-33, and 35; John Paul II 1991a, no. 29; and Benedict XVI 2009a, nos. 11, 18, and 23.

[39]Paul VI 1967, no. 47.

[40]United States Conference of Catholic Bishops 1993. See also Pontifical Council for Justice and Peace 2004, nos. 513-14; John Paul II 1991a, no. 18; and United States Conference of Catholic Bishops 2001.

[41]John Paul II 1991a, no. 52.

[42]Paul VI 1967, no. 76.

[43]Curran 2002, 152.

[44]Benedict XVI 2009a, no. 21.

[45]See, for example, John XXIII 1963, nos. 11-30, 39-43, 52, 61, 67-69, 94-97, and 139; Second Vatican Council 1965, nos. 12-22, 26, 29-31, and 73-76; World Synod of Catholic Bishops 1971, nos. 9, 22-26, 39-58, and 63; Paul VI 1971, nos. 13, 17, 22, and 24; John Paul II 1987, nos. 15, 26, 33, and 38; John Paul II 1991a, nos. 19, 21-22, 29, and 44-48; Benedict XVI 2009a, nos. 34-42, and 57; John Paul II 1989;

John Paul II 1995b; John Paul II 1998, no. 5; John Paul II 1999; John Paul II 2003a, nos. 4 and 8; John Paul II 2004, nos. 5-6; Benedict XVI 2007, nos. 7 and 12; Benedict XVI 2009b, no. 12; and Pontifical Council for Justice and Peace 2004, chap. 3 and nos. 189-91, 393-95, and 406-17.

[46]John Paul II 1991a, nos. 46-47.

[47]John Paul II 1987, no. 44.

[48]See, for example, John XXIII 1961, nos. 157-74; John XXIII 1963, no. 64; Second Vatican Council 1965, nos. 64-66 and 72; Paul VI 1967, nos. 9, 25, 33, 45-53, and 58-59; World Synod of Catholic Bishops 1971, nos. 9 and 13; John Paul II 1987, nos. 10, 14-15, 19-23, 28, 39, and 43; John Paul II 1991a, nos. 18-19, 28, and 35-36; Benedict XVI 2009a, nos. 21-23, 29, 32, 42, 45-47, and 58-66; John Paul II 1993a, no. 3; John Paul II 1998, no. 6; Benedict XVI 2009b; Pontifical Council for Justice and Peace 1994; and United States Conference of Catholic Bishops 1993.

[49]Second Vatican Council 1965, nos. 83, 85, and 88.

[50]John Paul II 1993a, no. 1 (italics in original).

[51]John Paul II 1991a, no. 52 (italics in original).

[52]Benedict XVI 2009a, no. 53 (italics in original).

[53]United States Conference of Catholic Bishops 1993.

[54]See, for example, John XXIII 1961, nos. 200-06; John XXIII 1963, nos. 93, 98-99, 118, 126, and 129; Second Vatican Council 1965, nos. 23-28 and 33; Paul VI 1967, nos. 43 and 77; Paul VI 1971, nos. 43 and 45; John Paul II 1987, nos. 17 and 38; John Paul II 1991a, nos. 51-52; John Paul II 1995a, no. 41; Benedict XVI 2009a, nos. 7, 9, 33, and 42; John Paul II 1998, no. 6; John Paul II 2000, no. 6; John Paul II 2002, nos. 3 and 8-10; Benedict XVI 2009b; and United States Conference of Catholic Bishops 1983, nos. 200 and 272-73.

[55]John Paul II 1987, nos. 22 and 26.

[56]John XXIII 1963, nos. 113-14.

[57]Paul VI 1967, no. 52; John Paul II 1987, no. 39; and John Paul II 1991a, no. 27.

[58]See, for example, John XXIII 1961, no. 49; John XXIII 1963, nos. 103-08 and 112-13; Second Vatican Council 1965, nos. 77, 83-84, 86, and 90; Paul VI 1967, nos. 33 and 77; World Synod of Catholic Bishops 1971, nos. 21-22 and 65-71; Paul VI 1971, no. 21; John Paul II 1987, nos. 24, 26, 34, and 43-45; John Paul II 1991a, nos. 21, 27-28, 52, and 58; Benedict XVI 2009a, nos. 21, 24-25, 27, 32, 41, 46-52, 58, 61, 67, and 71-72; John Paul II 1990; John Paul II 2000, nos. 7, 10, and 11-12; John Paul II 2004, nos. 6-7 and 9; Benedict XVI 2008, no. 14; Benedict XVI 2009b, no. 6; Benedict XVI 2010; Paul VI 1977; Pontifical Council for Justice and Peace 1994; John Paul II 1991b, 530-31; Pontifical Council for Justice and Peace 1994; John Paul II 2003b; Pontifical Council for Justice and Peace 2004, chaps. 9-10 and no. 506; United States Conference of Catholic Bishops 1983, nos. 239, 242 and 265; United States Conference of Catholic Bishops 1993; and United States Conference of Catholic Bishops 1995.

[59]See, for example, John Paul II 1991a, no. 52; Benedict XVI 2009a, no. 67; John Paul II 2000, nos. 11-12; John Paul II 2004, nos. 6 and 9; Paul VI 1977; and John Paul II 1991b, 530-31.

[60]John Paul II 2004, no. 5 (italics in original).

[61]Benedict XVI 2008, nos. 11 and 13.

[62]See, for example, John XXIII 1963, nos. 142-45; Paul VI 1967, no. 78; World Synod of Catholic Bishops 1971, nos. 63 and 65; John Paul II 1987, no. 26; John Paul II 1991a, no. 21; Benedict XVI 2009a, no. 67; John Paul II 2000, no. 11; John Paul II 2003a, no. 5; Benedict XVI 2007, no. 13; Paul VI 1966; Paul VI 1977; United

States Conference of Catholic Bishops 1983, nos. 242 and 267-68; and United States Conference of Catholic Bishops 1993.

[63]John Paul II 2004, no. 7.

[64]United States Conference of Catholic Bishops 1983, no. 97.

[65]Second Vatican Council 1965, no. 79.

[66]Second Vatican Council 1965, no. 82.

[67]See, for example, John XXIII 1963, nos. 137-41 and 144; Paul VI 1967, no. 78; World Synod of Catholic Bishops 1971, no. 65; United States Conference of Catholic Bishops 1983, nos. 96 and 241; and United States Conference of Catholic Bishops 1993.

[68]United States Conference of Catholic Bishops 1983, no. 242.

[69]John Paul II 2003a, no. 6 (italics in original).

[70]Benedict XVI 2009a, no. 67 (italics in original).

5

The Neoconservative Backlash

Not surprisingly, the dramatic shifts in Catholic doctrine's increasingly restrictive view of the legitimacy of war have sparked opposition. The dominant voices in this backlash have been American, and, while they include some Protestants, the most forceful are a group of Catholic neoconservative intellectuals and activists, the most prominent of whom is George Weigel.

An odd dimension of this critique deserves initial mention. Many critics of Catholicism's "new attitude" toward war are self-described "orthodox" or "faithful" Catholics on a range of other issues—abortion, euthanasia, same-sex marriage, a male-only priesthood—and they frequently criticize their opponents on these issues as "dissenters" from authoritative church teaching. Their own opposition to church teaching when it comes to war is therefore a bit awkward. Sometimes they directly criticize papal encyclicals and other Vatican statements, but more often they attack proxies. James Schall, for example, ignoring John Paul II's "No, never again war" statement in *Centesimus Annus*, instead heaps scorn on religious peace protestors with banners that say "War, Never Again."[1] At times Weigel gently scolds encyclicals and Second Vatican Council documents for being "murky" or suffering from "ambiguities," but he saves his sharpest criticism for other sources—editorials in liberal Catholic journals, nuns protesting war, left-leaning politicians, and peace-oriented clerics and intellectuals—who end up making precisely the same points.[2] Even stranger is Weigel's habit of trading on his reputation as a church insider and papal confidant to claim the Vatican secretly agrees with him, even when it makes clear statements to the contrary. He asserts, for example, that Vatican officials quietly disagreed with 1983's landmark U.S. Bishops statement *The Challenge of Peace*, in spite of its closely following two decades of papal teaching and receiving approval from Rome; that John Paul II was not actually opposed to the Iraq war and was even secretly grateful to the United States for invading, despite his public statements to the contrary; and that he can discern those things in Benedict XVI's *Caritas in Veritate* that are authentic Catholic teaching and those things, slipped in by meddlesome Vatican bureaucrats, that don't reflect the now-retired pope's actual beliefs (these distinctions line up surprisingly well with Weigel's own political views).[3]

Much of the backlash against contemporary Catholic teaching by American neoconservatives is rooted in debates over American foreign policy. Before the Second Vatican Council, government officials could expect little criticism of U.S. military decisions from either American bishops or Rome. Even actions such as intentionally destroying entire cities full of civilians in the Second World War, which clearly violated Catholic teaching, raised little protest. John Ford's now well-known article on the immorality of obliteration bombing, originally published in 1944, was largely ignored at the time, and John Courtney Murray later regretted the failure of the church to object more forcefully to civilian targeting such as "the atrocities of Hiroshima and Nagasaki."[4] Even as late as 1966, Boston's Cardinal Cushing would dismiss criticism of the war in Vietnam by saying American soldiers were "making peace the hard way, but the only way it can be made in a hard world."[5]

In the decades following the Second Vatican Council, however, the larger changes in Catholic teaching on war inevitably produced a more critical view of American military policy.[6] Statements from Rome and the U.S. Bishops now emphasized international understanding, negotiation, multilateral institutions, disarmament, reduced military spending, nonviolence, and eliminating the roots of war. All of this led to more outspoken criticism of American actions during Vietnam, the nuclear standoff with the Soviet Union, proxy wars in the developing world (especially Latin America), and the war on terrorism following the attacks of September 11, 2001. This critical stance culminated most recently in the almost universal condemnation of the Iraq war from Catholic leaders in the United States and Rome, including John Paul II and then-cardinal Joseph Ratzinger, soon to be named Benedict XVI.[7] This trend has dismayed modern Catholic teaching's neoconservative opponents, most of whom are longtime advocates of a large and active American military presence in the world. From fighting communism during the Cold War to fighting terrorism today, they emphasize unilateral American power, aggressive and frequent military force, and a vital role for war in securing freedom and security. Most were enthusiastic advocates for the U.S. invasion of Iraq.

For Weigel and his fellow critics, the modern shifts in Catholic doctrine's judgments of war amount to "a great forgetting of the classic just war tradition among those who had long been assumed to be its primary intellectual custodians."[8] Richard John Neuhaus calls "the public witness of the Catholic Church" at the time of the Iraq war "confused and weakened" because it ignored the older just war framework developed by Augustine, Aquinas, Vitoria, and others.[9] Weigel, too, blames Catholic opposition to the Iraq war on "distortions of classic just war thinking" and on ideological biases "far more dependent on political and strategic intuitions of dubious merit than solid moral reasoning."[10]

According to these critics, the most significant distortion of the just war tradition is the notion that it begins with a presumption against war rather than with a presumption in favor of order.[11] They devote a great deal of attention to this battle of presumptions, even though the two do not necessarily conflict with each other; both classical and modern just war teaching allow for war, if necessary, to uphold order, even while preferring to avoid war, when possible, given the violence it unleashes. Weigel, however, believes the very idea of a presumption against war is an "intellectual toxin" designed to weaken military resolve.[12] He and his fellow critics see it as door through which pacifist principles are smuggled into the just war tradition.[13] James Turner Johnson argues that modern Catholic thinking on war tends to "magnify the evils to be expected from a resort to force" so much that a presumption against war "becomes a springboard to functional pacifism."[14] Eric Patterson complains about the tradition's "quasi-pacifism."[15] And Weigel has long blamed the failings of modern Catholic military teaching on its becoming infected by the "intellectual weakness" of pacifism, and he continues to condemn "the functional pacifism embedded in much of what has passed for just war thinking" in the church today.[16]

While charges of functional pacifism are overstated, Catholic doctrine has certainly become more skeptical of war and reluctant to sanction its use. This moves the tradition in exactly the wrong direction for its neoconservative critics, who are instead committed to more rather than less war. Speaking soon after the September 11 attacks, Weigel condemns those cautioning against a military overreaction, saying, "In fact, it seems to me that the real danger, right now, is that we are going to be satisfied with too little."[17] Schall writes, "Human, moral, and economic problems are greater today for the lack of adequate military force," which is why those who favor less rather than more military action "have unacknowledged blood on their hands."[18] Indeed, for all their alarm about forgetting the classical just war framework, neoconservative critics frequently support setting aside even its traditional restraints—prohibitions on preemptive war or last resort requirements, for example—as irrelevant in the modern world.[19] Weigel even praises the Bush administration's 2002 *National Security*

Strategy of the United States, with its policy of unilateral preemptive war to crush any challenges to American military dominance around the globe, as a "sober-minded" and "morally serious" path to world peace.[20] Equating world peace and American war-making power is a long-standing feature of Weigel's writing. In his first significant work on war, he accuses Catholic critics of U.S. Cold War policy—from the arms race with the Soviets to proxy wars in Central America—as being a primary obstacle to global peace and justice.[21] More recently he makes the remarkable claim that more frequent, aggressive, and overwhelming military force by the United States would have prevented or quickly ended the Second World War, the threat of Soviet communism, the Vietnam War, the Iranian Revolution, genocide in the Balkans, and both wars against Iraq.[22] In other words, more rather than less war (at least when launched by the United States) is what the world needs to achieve a peaceful order.

One of the largest obstacles to a more permissive war stance in contemporary Catholic teaching is its heightened concern with *jus in bello* principles, especially the death of noncombatants, which makes this concern a principal target for neoconservative critics. In his voluminous writings on war over the last several decades, it is stunning how little Weigel speaks to the actual conduct of war. In spite of his claims to moral realism, his treatment of war is remarkably abstract; the voices of those who experience it, especially the organized killing at its heart, are almost entirely absent from his accounts. His primary focus is on those *jus ad bellum* factors that justify going to war and the fecklessness of war opponents who fail to recognize them. When he and his fellow critics do mention *jus in bello*, it is almost always to criticize those who focus on it too much.[23] From Vietnam to the nuclear arms race to American interventions in Central America during the 1980s to the war on terrorism and invasion of Iraq, Weigel consistently condemns excessive concern with *jus in bello* as a distraction from the necessity of military force.[24] He complains about the "series of hurdles" to war that religious leaders set up by raising "*in bello* questions of proportionality and discrimination."[25] Similarly, Neuhaus condemns Catholic leaders for "badgering" government officials with "nervous hand-wringing" about civilian casualties in the Iraq war.[26] Schall dismisses the "growth industry" in worrying about the horrors of war among "those who do not choose to fight in them."[27] Elbridge Colby criticizes Catholic leaders for failing to recognize that military planners "cannot always afford to dedicate sufficient focus to avoiding noncombatant injury without sacrificing their legitimate objectives."[28] And Patterson complains that "the demands of *jus in bello* have become so constraining, especially that of non-combatant immunity, that it has become almost impossible to fight a war, even in self-defense, that meets these fortified criteria."[29] The outer edge of this dismissal of *jus in bello* principles even has Catholic neoconservatives, such as Marc Thiessen, justifying the torture of suspected terrorists when "necessary for public order" on explicitly Catholic grounds, even though the church expressly condemns such a conclusion.[30]

Catholic teaching's peacemaking agenda is another object of particular scorn for neoconservative critics. On their account, it foolishly puts too much faith in multilateral cooperation, international law and treaties, global institutions such as the United Nations, and efforts on behalf of economic justice. For Weigel, these priorities reflect a misguided "sentimental fondness for Third World perspectives."[31] He calls trying to construct a multilaterally organized and run international order based on "some form of international governance, in which multilateral and international bodies play the leading role," an "inexplicably stupid" idea and a recipe for "dithering, indecisiveness, feckless multilateralism, and lack of strategic vision."[32] Johnson criticizes "a utopian form of pacifism in which the right kind of international institution would mean the end to all war."[33] In the wake of the September 11 attacks, an editorial in the Neuhaus-edited journal *First Things* warns against the United States being "held hostage to the veto power of a coalition in which the most timorous member calls the plays."[34]

The United Nations is especially suspect here. Neuhaus laments that "some in the Curia seem bent on hitching the wagon of the Catholic Church to the dubiously constructed institution that is the U.N.," and Weigel argues that no "serious analyst of world politics" trusts the United Nations as a primary instrument for building a just political order.[35] Finally, its neoconservative critics routinely equate Catholic teaching's peacemaking agenda with the forces of secularism, moral relativism, and anti-Americanism.[36] The *First Things* editorial accuses religious leaders urging military restraint of "contempt for patriotism," and Neuhaus writes that Vatican officials critical of the Iraq war merely reflect the views of European countries that "have run out of steam and resent the vibrancy of America."[37] Weigel calls for "cultural nerve" to defeat the anti-Western, particularly anti-American, multiculturalism behind calls for international understanding and military restraint, one driven by a "coalition of Islamists and postmodern leftists."[38]

These criticisms reveal how deeply unrealistic neoconservative critics consider contemporary Catholic teaching on war and peace. Weigel contrasts his own "clear thought," "seeing things how they are," and "clarity of moral vision" with the "naiveté" and "crackpot idealism" and "utopianism" of those committed to international cooperation and nonviolent peace-building.[39] Indeed, whether criticizing its presumption against war, purported functional pacifism, excessive *in bello* concerns, or peacemaking agenda, certain words and phrases occur again and again in the neoconservative backlash against Catholic teaching: "myopia," "fecklessness," "appeasement," "utopianism," and "sentimentality" must always be met by "moral clarity," "moral seriousness," "Christian realism," and intellectual "rigor."[40] (Sometimes it seems Weigel just randomly runs these words together, as when he describes his defense of American military might as a simple matter of "morally serious political realism."[41]) Colby argues that Catholic teaching needs to tone down its "fervor" for arms control in favor of "sobriety and prudence" about the realities of a "fallen world."[42] According to the editors of *First Things*, "going on endlessly about how violence breeds violence and how we must address the root causes of resentment, etc., etc." flies in the face of the "common sense" of "ordinary Americans" who understand the "reality" that September 11 demands war as a response.[43] Patterson considers the "unswerving commitment" to the distinction between combatants and noncombatants in contemporary Catholic teaching "out of touch with contemporary realities" in the age of terrorism.[44] And claiming the mantle of Augustinian realism, Schall considers calls for the worldwide elimination of war "a sign of either utopianism or of madness," one "blind to living men," losing "any real contact with or understanding of human experience or history," and based on "a frivolous hope that nothing bad will happen no matter what we do or do not do."[45]

For neoconservative critics, contemporary Catholic doctrine's lack of realism when it comes to war is not only foolish but dangerous, threatening to cripple the ability of the United States to respond to its enemies. While this line of argument centered on communism during the Cold War, it has now shifted to dangers posed by Islamic terrorism.[46] For Weigel, the seductions of a peaceful and multilateral international order following the Cold War led the United States to "take a holiday from history," responding to the gathering threat of militant Islam with "fecklessness" and "appeasement."[47] He argues that forgetting the lessons of classical just war teaching is a threat to "the public moral hygiene of the Republic—and our national capacity to think with moral rigor about some very threatening realities of today's world."[48] He warns, for example, that excessive concern about *in bello* rules of war will tie the hands of the military, allowing terrorists to practice what he calls "lawfare" against the West.[49] Schall and Weigel both claim that expansion through violence is central to Islam and must be resisted aggressively, including through preemptive war.[50] Weigel maintains that while those suffering under politically correct "multiculturalist delusions" may not want to face this, the time has come for some hard truth telling about the Islamic threat, especially its "salami tactics" of forcing slice after slice of concessions until it takes over entire nations, and non-Muslims become second-class citizens in their own countries.[51] While Europe may choose the path of weak-kneed appeasement, Weigel praises the Bush administration's use of military power, including the invasion of Iraq, as part of a "Coalition of Those Who Understand" the need for a more realistic approach.[52]

War, then, is a continuing necessity in a dangerous world according to the neoconservative critics of Catholicism's contemporary understanding of war. In their account, this understanding is overly critical of war, too concerned with its effects, especially harm to noncombatants, and un-realistic in its vision for building international peace. It forgets a central reality of political life: at times force is necessary to uphold a just and peaceful order, something as true in international affairs as it is in the domestic realm. According to Thiessen, just as when a policeman sees a criminal who is about to kill an innocent person, he may use lethal force to stop him, when "a foreign enemy threatens your country, it is permissible to go to war."[53] For Schall, thinking international peace and security is possible without the possibility and the exercise, when rea-sonable, of just war is as foolish as thinking domestic law enforcement will work without using violence "to deal with those who are bound by no concept of legal order" in the domestic sphere.[54] And a full decade after the Iraq war, Weigel is still writing statements like this: "There are outlaws abroad; someone has to organize the posse to deal with them, and the only plausible candidate for sheriff is the United States."[55]

Notes

[1]Schall 2004, 62.

[2]See, for example, Weigel 1987, chaps. 3 and 5 compared to chaps. 6-10. As Stein-fels 1987 shows, even Weigel's attacks on proxies often depend on his systematically distorting their actual statements.

[3]Weigel 1987, 280; Weigel 2006, 35; and Weigel 2009b.

[4]Ford 1970; and Murray 1960, 265.

[5]O'Brien 1980, 126.

[6]For good overviews of this change, see Whitmore 2005; and Massaro and Shan-non 2003.

[7]For statements from these leaders condemning the war, see Brady 2008, 283-84; and Massaro and Shannon 2003, 118-19.

[8]Weigel 2003a, 21. See also Johnson 2005.

[9]Neuhaus 2003, 77 and 79.

[10]Weigel 2006, 35; and Weigel 2003a, 21.

[11]See, for example, Johnson 2005; Patterson 2007; Weigel 2003a, 22-23; Weigel 2003b; and Novak 2003.

[12]Weigel 2009a.
[13]Weigel 2004, 19.
[14]Johnson 2005, 21.
[15]Patterson 2007, 25.
[16]Weigel 1987, 246; and Weigel 2008, 5.
[17]Weigel 2001.
[18]Schall 2004, 59 and 63. See also Novak 2003.
[19]See, for example, Weigel 2001, 2003a, and 2006; Novak 2003; and Schall 2004.
[20]Weigel 2006, 40. See also Weigel 2007, 93.
[21]Weigel 1987, 387.
[22]Weigel 2010, 39. See also Weigel 2007, 154.
[23]See, for example, Weigel 2004 and 2006; O'Brien 1992; Schall 2004; Colby 2011; Neuhaus 2003; Patterson 2007; and Novak 2003.
[24]Weigel 1987, chaps. 7 and 9-10; Weigel 2001; Weigel 2003a, 22-23; Weigel 2003b, 8.
[25]Weigel 2003a, 23 (italics in original).
[26]Neuhaus 2003, 79.
[27]Schall 2004, 63.
[28]Colby 2011, 28.
[29]Patterson 2007, 28 (italics in original).
[30]Thiessen 2010, 186-92; Thiessen 2009; Elliott 2011; and *Catechism of the Catholic Church* 1994, no. 2297.
[31]Weigel 1987, 202 and part 2 generally.
[32]Weigel 2011b.
[33]Johnson 2005, 21.
[34]*First Things* 2001.
[35]Neuhaus 2003, 78; and Weigel 2013, 48. See also Weigel 2003a, 26-27; Weigel 1987, part 2; and Schall 2004, 68-69.
[36]See, for example, Weigel 1987, part 2; Weigel 2007; and Weigel 2004, 19.
[37]*First Things* 2001; and Neuhaus 2003, 79.
[38]Weigel 2007, 99, 149, and part 3 generally.
[39]Weigel 2010, 37-39.
[40]See, for example, Weigel 1987, 2003a, 2003b, 2004, 2006, 2007, 2009b, and 2010; Johnson 2005; Schall 2004; and Neuhaus 2003.
[41]Weigel 2013, 49.
[42]Colby 2011, 31.
[43]*First Things* 2001.
[44]Patterson 2007, 27.
[45]Schall 2004, 61-62 and 64-65.
[46]See, for example, Weigel 1987 on communism and Weigel 2007 on Islam.
[47]Weigel 2010, 34-37; Weigel 2007, 52-53; and Weigel 2003b, 9-10. See also *First Things* 2001.
[48]Weigel 2003a, 21.
[49]Weigel 2007, 145.
[50]Schall 2004; and Weigel 2003a and 2007.
[51]Weigel 2007, 72, 59, and 118.
[52]Weigel 2007, 143 and 78.
[53]Thiessen 2010, 184-85.
[54]Schall 2004, 70.
[55]Weigel 2013, 49.

SECTION II

THE IMMORALITY OF WAR

6

Killing the Innocent: Civilians

War is the large-scale slaughter of innocent human beings. This makes it, by its very nature, inherently immoral. There can be no such thing as a just war. Since war inescapably violates one of the core moral principles of Catholic doctrine—the prohibition on intentionally killing the innocent—it should repudiate war completely, rejecting it as always and everywhere morally impermissible.

According to the *Catechism*, deliberately killing an innocent person violates a universally valid moral law, one that "obliges each and everyone, always and everywhere." It is wrong "under any circumstances."[1] In *Evangelium Vitae*, John Paul II calls human life "sacred," having an "incomparable worth" and "inviolability." While using force, even to the point of death, may be sometimes necessary to protect against "criminals and unjust aggressors, the commandment 'You shall not kill' has absolute value when it refers to the innocent person." This absolute inviolability of innocent human life is a core doctrine of the church's magisterial teaching: "Therefore, by the authority which Christ conferred upon Peter and his Successors, and in communion with the Bishops of the Catholic Church, I confirm that the direct and voluntary killing of an innocent human being is always gravely immoral."[2]

The most obvious violation of this principle in war is the deliberate killing of civilians. This is why contemporary Catholic doctrine so strongly endorses the *jus in bello* principle of discrimination: the prohibition on intentionally targeting noncombatants. The idea of civilian immunity, however, has not always been part of Catholic just war theory.[3] Augustine's just war framework makes no distinction between combatants and noncombatants. A just war punishes wrongdoing, and all subjects of the country in the wrong share in its guilt. In this way, Augustine introduces the categories of innocence and guilt into just war theory, but for him everyone on the just side of the war, civilians and soldiers, are innocent and cannot legitimately be killed, while everyone on the unjust side, civilians and soldiers, are guilty and can legitimately be killed.[4] This view remained largely unchanged through the Middle Ages. Aquinas, while paying some attention to the conduct of war, leaves its punitive justification largely intact and does not include a significant principle of discrimination, though the medieval period did introduce the idea of clergy immunity and codes of chivalry emphasizing a fair fight among combatants, both of which are precursors to a more robust principle of civilian immunity.

The real shift comes in the sixteenth and seventeenth centuries when scholastics, such as Vitoria and Suárez, challenge, in the words of Colm McKeogh, the "convenient fiction that all in the population whose leadership had done wrong shared in the guilt" and introduce the principle of civilian immunity, essentially "narrowing down the enemy from the entire population of one's adversary to just its combatants." These thinkers still consider punishment of wrongdoing the justification for war and its killing, but they argue that noncombatants on both sides of the war must be presumed innocent and spared from attack whenever possible: "Their innovation was the claim that in war non-combatancy may be taken as prima facie evidence of innocence."[5] Vitoria and Suárez recognize the suffering and death that war often brings to civilians who have little or nothing to do with its causes and whose main concern is simply avoiding it. Their intent is to replace the guilt Augustine assumes for noncombatants, at least on the unjust side, with an assumption of innocence for noncombatants on both sides, preserving the necessity of killing in war but limiting its scope.

This is a crucial development in just war theory. It separates civilians from the wrongdoing that launched the war in the first place and justifies its killing. Doing so does require a broad presumption—that civilians as a group are not culpable for an unjust war. This is so, even though some of them may in fact be its enthusiastic supporters, or, more directly, may include media figures whipping up war frenzy, business leaders pushing war with an eye toward profit, or government officials deciding to launch an unjust attack itself. Nonetheless, the presumption of civilian innocence is sound. While some civilians may have various levels of culpability, in any given war most of them are clearly not responsible for launching it, and many want nothing to do with it. This is what Desiderius Erasmus means when he writes that "princes wage war unscathed and their generals thrive on it, while the main flood of misfortune sweeps over the peasants and humble citizens, who have no interest in war and gave no occasion for it."[6] Even in democracies there is no direct connection between the civilian population as a whole and military action by their elected government. And for those in the population of any country, democracy or not, who do support unjust wars, is death really the appropriate punishment? By any fair understanding of Catholic just war theory, for example, the preemptive U.S. invasion of Iraq in 2003 was unjust, but this doesn't mean the millions of Americans who supported it deserve to be killed. For those civilians, especially a country's leaders, who do bear direct responsibility for an unjust war, Vitoria, Suárez, and just war theorists since them do endorse individual criminal prosecution after hostilities cease, but they insist on the principle of civilian immunity during the war itself. The fact that a small number of civilians may bear culpability for an unjust war cannot justify the indiscriminate killing of civilians generally while that war is under way. Doing so will clearly kill massive numbers of innocent people who in no way deserve to die.

Protecting the innocent from lethal attack, then, is the basis for the principle of civilian immunity, a principle especially prominent in modern Catholic doctrine. Papal encyclicals and other Vatican documents routinely denounce the "indiscriminate" killing of "innocent people" in war.[7] The *Catechism* condemns "indiscriminate destruction" and the killing of "Non-combatants," while the *Compendium of the Social Doctrine of the Church* calls targeting civilians in war always unacceptable.[8] The U.S. Bishops also point to the vital importance of protecting "noncombatants and other innocent persons" in war, urging strict attention to the principle of discrimination in order to spare "innocent civilians" from death.[9]

* * *

Noncombatant immunity, however, is one of those principles noted mainly for its violation. Far from an exception, the indiscriminate killing of civilians is the norm in war, and has been from its very beginning.[10] Even before written history, the archaeological and anthropological evidence of warfare among prestate peoples organized into tribes and chiefdoms reveals routine killing of combatants and noncombatants alike. In their examination of war in its earliest forms, Steven LeBlanc and Katherine Register find that "the act of massacring civilians is as ancient as war itself," and it is not unusual to find that "the goal is annihilation" of the entire rival group.[11] With the rise of ancient civilizations, warfare became more complex, but the reality of indiscriminate killing remained. Putting entire cities to the sword was a regular practice in ancient war.[12] The An Lushan Revolt in eighth-century China resulted in so much indiscriminate killing that the empire's population dropped by two-thirds.[13] The chronic warfare of medieval and early modern Europe killed enormous numbers of noncombatants as war rolled across their farms and villages.[14] The Thirty Years War famously killed a third of Germany's civilian population.[15] And South America's War of the Triple Alliance killed over half the population of Paraguay in the 1860s.[16]

The twentieth century's war tally was an estimated sixty-two million dead civilians alongside forty-three million dead soldiers.[17] Even in the First World War, considered relatively safe for civilians, one in five deaths were of noncombatants.[18] The Spanish Civil War killed half a million, most of them civilians.[19] Most of the fifty million people killed in the Second World War were noncombatants.[20] The Korean War claimed over two million noncombatant lives, the Vietnam War one to two million, and most of the dead in the years following the U.S. invasion of Iraq, where estimates can vary from around 100,000 to close to a million, were civilians.[21] In 1971, the Pakistani army and its militia allies likely killed over a million civilians in Bangladesh, and the war following the Soviet invasion of Afghanistan had a similar civilian death toll.[22] The series of central African wars around the Democratic Republic of Congo starting in the mid-1990s killed several million people, the vast majority of them noncombatants.[23]

Civilian deaths are not some kind of minor side effect of war. Throughout history, war has killed at least as many noncombatants as combatants, a pattern that continues today.[24] In the 1990s alone, wars around the world killed two million children.[25] Indeed, killing noncombatants is so routine and widespread, and happens in such massive numbers, that even getting precise accounts of civilian deaths in war is extraordinarily difficult.[26] So many civilians die in war that it's hard to keep track of them all.

While the methods and reasons given may vary over time, indiscriminately killing civilians is a constant feature of war, both ancient and modern. Civilians have been massacred with rocks, clubs, swords, spears, arrows, starvation through sieges and ruined crops, fire, ropes, poisoned wells, rifles, bayonets, pistols, machine guns, disease spread through dead animals or infected blankets, trampling under horses, artillery shells, aerial bombing, intentional flooding, deadly gas, machetes, exposure in prison camps, and nuclear weapons. They have died because those killing them considered them weak, less than human, enemy sympathizers, racially or ethnically inferior, obstacles to victory, apostates or heretics, guilty of wrongdoing, threats to the social order, cursed by God, strategically inconvenient, occupiers of land not rightfully theirs, politically dangerous, responsible for atrocities committed by those similar to them, impure, economic parasites, or breeders of future enemies.[27] Sometimes they are considered disposable—their lives simply don't matter—and other times they are considered collectively guilty—they deserve to die as a group—but the result for civilians in war is the same across history: death.

It is important to remember that behind this larger pattern of non-combatant killing is the grim reality of countless individual persons and their killers. Consider some typical examples.

- A Hopi story tells of an entire village put to death when attackers trapped the people inside their underground kivas and set fire to the roofs: "There was crying, screaming, and coughing. After a while the roof beams caught fire. As they flamed up, they began to collapse, one after the other. Finally, the screams died down and it became still."[28]
- Similar accounts appear in the oral traditions of the Inuit when attackers "would have to try and eliminate everyone in the village one by one, going from house to house and killing them while they slept."[29]
- A captive of the Yanomamo, a prestate people of the Amazon rainforest, described an example of their ancient form of warfare:

  > Then the men began to kill the children: little ones, bigger ones, they killed many of them. They tried to run away, but they caught them, and threw them on the ground, and stuck them with arrows which went through their bodies and rooted them to the ground. Taking the smallest by the feet, they beat them against the trees and rocks.[30]

- Shalmaneser III, a ruler in ancient Assyria, boasted of his actions after defeating a rival: "In my mighty strength I trampled on his land like a wild bull, and his cities I reduced to ruins and consumed with fire."[31]
- An eyewitness to the Roman sack of Carthage in 146 B.C.E. described how soldiers slaughtered the population and filled pits with the dead and living alike: "Human beings filled up the gullies. Some were thrown in head down, and their legs protruding from the ground writhed for some little while. Some fell feet down and their heads were above the surface. Their faces and skulls were trampled by the galloping horses."[32] In the words of Robert Holmes, "The Romans annihilated the Carthaginians in the third Punic War as effectively as if they had dropped a nuclear bomb on them."[33]
- Thirteenth-century Mongol armies invading what is today the Middle East put entire cities to the sword, collecting ears in sacks to keep track of the body counts for each soldier. They likely killed well over a million people.[34]

- From an account of the Thirty Years War: "After the sack of Madgeburg in 1631, in which only the cathedral and 140 houses were left standing, some 30,000 men, women, and children had been slaughtered."[35]
- After his Puritan community exterminated the Pequot nation in 1638, minister and future Harvard president Increase Mather thanked God "that on this day we have sent six hundred heathen souls to Hell," and Oliver Cromwell expressed a similar sentiment after butchering every person in the Irish city of Drogheda, telling Parliament that it "has pleased God to bless our endeavor" of putting "to the sword the whole number."[36]
- In explaining his actions against civilians during the American Civil War, General Sherman said, "We are not only fighting hostile armies but a hostile people . . . and must make old and young, rich and poor, feel the hard hand of war."[37]
- Early twentieth-century British colonialism included herding thousands of civilians into camps during the Boer War (where we get the term "concentration camp"), in which over a third of them died, and using poison gas on civilian populations in Iraq and Afghanistan, prompting Winston Churchill to say, "I do not understand this squeamishness about the use of gas . . . I am strongly in favor of using poison gas against uncivilized tribes."[38]
- In June of 1916, French pilots intentionally bombed a circus tent in Germany, killing those inside, including 154 children enjoying the show.[39]
- In 1932, British Prime Minister Stanley Baldwin told the House of Commons that the age of aerial bombing meant that "you will have to kill more civilians, more women and children first, if you want to save yours from the enemy."[40]
- Commenting on the siege of Leningrad, which killed over 600,000 civilians, a German officer in the Second World War said, "Sentimentality would be out of place." Another German soldier wrote to his wife about killing Jews in Belarus:

  During my first try, my hand trembled a bit as I shot, but one gets used to it. By the tenth try, I aimed calmly and shot surely at the many women, children, and infants. I kept in mind that I have two infants at home, whom these hordes would treat just the same . . . Infants flew in great arcs through the air, and we shot them to pieces in flight, before their bodies fell into the pit and into the water.[41]
- The Second World War also witnessed saturation bombing of cities, called "terror bombing" at the time, designed to kill as many civilians as possible, up to 100,000 or more in one

night in some cases, in order to demoralize the enemy.[42] A teenage girl in Hamburg described fires so intense the asphalt on streets melted: "There were people on the roadway, some already dead, some still lying alive but stuck in the asphalt. They must have rushed onto the roadway without thinking. Their feet had got stuck and they had put out their hands to try and get out again. They were on their hands and knees screaming."[43] An American officer said, "There are no civilians in Japan," and General Curtis LeMay, who oversaw the bombing campaign in Japan, said he intended to "bomb and burn them until they quit."[44] In deciding to destroy Japanese cities with the atom bomb, President Truman regretted killing "all those kids," but he also thanked God for the bomb and prayed that God "may guide us to use it in his ways and for his purposes."[45] A Japanese woman saw its results up close: "People's clothes had been blown off and their bodies burned by the heat rays . . . their skins hung in tatters . . . I saw people whose intestines were hanging out of their bodies. Some had lost their eyes. Some had their backs torn open so you could see their backbones inside."[46]

- When American troops during the Korean War, following orders to prevent infiltrators by killing refugees indiscriminately, massacred around four hundred Koreans at No Gun Ri, one commander told his soldiers, "To hell with all those people. Let's get rid of all of them."[47]

- A father whose young children died during aerial bombing of northern cities and villages during the Vietnam War said, "My daughter died right here. She was feeding the pigs. She was so sweet. She is dead. The pigs are alive . . . Tell them she was only a schoolgirl."[48] A soldier who participated in the massacre of around five hundred Vietnamese villagers at My Lai said, "We were told to leave nothing standing. We did what we were told, regardless of whether they were civilians. They was the enemy. Period. Kill." Lieutenant Calley, the leader of the massacre, asked simply, "What the hell else is war but killing people?"[49]

- From a Nigerian government official blocking food from reaching civilians in the secessionist region of Biafra in 1968: "Starvation is a legitimate weapon of war, and we have every intention of using it."[50]

- After witnessing Israeli soldiers luring kids from a Palestinian refugee camp only to shoot them, the war correspondent Chris Hedges wrote,

> I had seen children shot in other conflicts I have cov-
> ered—death squads gunned them down in El Salvador
> and Guatemala, mothers with infants were lined up and
> massacred in Algeria, and Serb snipers put children in
> their sights and watched them crumple onto the pave-
> ment in Sarajevo—but I had never watched soldiers
> entice children like mice into a trap and murder them
> for sport.[51]

These examples—and similar ones could fill several books—help dis-
prove what Hugo Slim calls "the strange idea . . . that civilians only
really began to suffer massively in war during the last century" with
the advent of total war.[52] For most civilians across the centuries, war
has always been total. The technology of death may evolve, but the
reality of civilian massacre is a constant in the history of warfare. This
notion, one often reflected in contemporary Catholic teaching, that war
has become especially indiscriminate with the rise of modern weapons,
is largely based on taking a particular period of European history as
the norm rather than the exception. Between the Peace of Westphalia
in 1648 and the French Revolution in 1789, Europe did experience an
era of more restrained war, in which monarchs pursued limited military
goals, and combatants often met in formal set-piece battles away from
civilian areas. But this relatively short period in one region of the world
is not representative of war around the globe or in the centuries before
and since. Indeed, even in Europe during this period, war still killed
plenty of civilians, and countries routinely used irregular troops, with
what military historian John Keegan calls their "habits of loot, pillage,
rape, murder, kidnap, extortion, and systematic vandalism," in addition
to professional armies.[53] And, of course, this period also saw these same
European powers fight colonial wars of expansion in other parts of the
world that made no attempt to discriminate between combatants and
noncombatants.[54] Wars in which belligerents respect civilian immunity
are few and far between, not just in today's world but across the entire
history of armed conflict.

*   *   *

Given this reality, the just war tradition's attempt to develop and uphold
the principle of discrimination is a noble one. It suffers, however, from a
fatal inconsistency—it both rejects and accommodates killing civilians,
seeking to minimize their death, but not to the point that war becomes
impossible. The just war framework condemns unrestrained civilian
killing, but, recognizing that dead civilians are an inevitable feature of

war, it creates space for their permissible killing under certain conditions. Of course, those fighting wars often seize this space and expand it even more since, as Elizabeth Anscombe points out, the "principal wickedness which is a temptation to those engaged in warfare is the killing of the innocent."[55]

The most direct way accounts of the just war, including some offered by Catholic thinkers, accommodate killing noncombatants is through a fairly straightforward escape clause: killing innocent civilians is wrong unless absolutely necessary to win the war. Civilian immunity is a general rule, but it can be overridden in the name of military necessity.[56] Vitoria argues that killing the innocent is permitted when essential to victory since otherwise war would be impossible and the unjust side would triumph.[57] Michael Walzer's influential contemporary just war theory includes a "supreme emergency" provision that in extraordinary circumstances trumps his otherwise strong protections for noncombatants: "Can soldiers and statesmen override the rights of innocent people for the sake of their own political community? I am inclined to answer this question affirmatively, though not without hesitation and worry."[58]

He is right to worry. Military necessity is one of the most frequent justifications for killing innocent people in war.[59] During the First World War, Kaiser Wilhelm II said, "My soul is torn, but everything must be put to fire and sword; men, women, and children and old men must be slaughtered and not a tree or house be left standing. With these methods of terrorism, which are alone capable of affecting a people as degenerate as the French, the war will be over in two months."[60] A Spanish Civil War general defended his attacks on civilians more bluntly: "It is necessary to spread an atmosphere of terror."[61] And in her study of twentieth-century veterans from several countries, Joanna Bourke finds that military chaplains, including Catholic priests, routinely reassured soldiers upset about killing civilians that such killing was necessary for victory.[62]

This necessity escape clause is not surprising. In any theory of just war, the logic of *jus ad bellum* threatens to overwhelm the limits of *jus in bello*. If the cause is righteous enough to warrant going to war—if the moral stakes are that high and losing that threatening to justice—then whatever is required to win the war becomes acceptable, too. If the war is just enough, the step toward countenancing civilian killing when necessary is a short one.

An even more common method that proponents of just war theory use to accommodate killing civilians, one that often goes hand and hand with appeals to military necessity, is the principle of double effect, which is based on the fact that actions can have multiple outcomes. If firefighters put out a fire in your apartment (a good outcome), they might cause water damage to a friend's car parked out front with its windows down (a bad outcome). Even though they foresaw the possibility of damaging the car when they trained their hoses on your building, it was not their intent, but only an unfortunate side effect of the good that they did, and since this good outweighed the harm, their actions were not wrong. According to the principle of double effect, actions producing bad outcomes that are foreseen but not intended can be morally permissible, as long as the good achieved outweighs the bad, and the bad outcomes are truly side effects rather than the actual means by which the good comes about. Doctors rely on it when performing surgery they know might produce painful complications, parents when delivering news they know will hurt a child's feelings, and judges when sending criminals to prison knowing their families will be devastated.

Double effect is an especially important concept in Catholic formulations of the just war. Recall that it is always wrong *intentionally* to kill the innocent, and so the *deliberate* targeting of civilians is prohibited. But if a commander or individual soldier does not intend to kill civilians—they are not targeted directly—then their deaths, even if foreseen, can be a permissible side effect of otherwise legitimate military activity, as long as the military advantage achieved outweighs those deaths, and they are not themselves the means to that advantage. This is what the term "collateral damage" refers to: death or destruction in war that is an unintended parallel outcome to permissible actions in combat. This is why the U.S. Bishops can argue that "justifiable defense against aggression may result in the indirect or unintended loss of innocent human lives," something that is "tragic" but that "may conceivably be proportionate to the values defended."[63]

Double effect is a valid moral principle in many areas of life, but it cannot justify the civilian death that inevitably accompanies war. Start with its proportionality mechanism. Here is a typical statement defending a recent military action that killed a large number of civilians: "In such a case, a proportionality test has to be enacted, according to which the foreseeable collateral death of civilians will be proportionate to the military advantage that will be achieved by eliminating the target."[64] We are not dealing here with damage to a car, surgical complications, a child's hurt feelings, or a family member going to prison. This is about killing innocent people, as grave a moral evil as there is, and this concrete, immediate evil is justified by proportionate appeal to tactical military advantages that are speculative and uncertain at best.[65] The dead civilians are real, while the action that justifies their death is just another in a long series to gain military advantage in a war whose ultimate outcome is unknown. At the heart of double effect reasoning in war is the cold willingness to weigh innocent human lives against political goals deemed more important than those lives. And notice who gets to make this calculation: those doing the killing rather than those doing the dying, the powerful rather than the vulnerable. If those civilians killed in war, who in no way deserve to die and never consented to having their lives or those of their children sacrificed for what others considered proportionate ends, were to be given any say, it is likely they would reach different conclusions.[66]

The principle of double effect's treatment of intentionality is also famously subject to abuse. In their classic condemnations of aerial bombing in the Second World War, Anscombe and John Ford both criticize its double effect justifications—that the real intention was not to kill civilians but to destroy military targets in those cities, or to break the will of the enemy, or to save lives by ending the war sooner.[67] As Ford says, this is "merely playing with words."[68] A gravely immoral action, such as knowingly destroying a building full of innocent people, can't be magically transformed into a moral one by simply claiming something else as your real intention. When the Catholic neoconservative Marc Thiessen justifies the systematic torture of terror suspects because "the intent of the interrogator is not to cause harm to the detainee" but "to render the aggressor unable to cause harm to society," he is engaging in just this kind of perverse sophistry.[69] So too was Timothy McVeigh when he claimed, after his 1995 bombing of a federal building in Oklahoma, that his real intention was to make a political statement, and those killed in the bombing were just "collateral damage" similar to civilians killed in the first Gulf War, where he fought as an American soldier.[70] As the philosopher Judith Lichtenberg points out, our choices are "package deals" that do not allow us to duck responsibility for what we knowingly do by pretending that consequences flowing directly and inevitably from them are mere accidents.[71] The double effect is rendered meaningless when it can justify anything, and too often this is the case in war.

Nonetheless, even though the double effect principle can become a transparent loophole to explain away indiscriminate killing, sometimes those fighting wars do make sincere efforts to uphold it. Most modern, professional, and well-trained militaries prohibit targeting noncombatants deliberately, and most of their soldiers do not intentionally kill civilians. The reality of warfare, however, means that even these good-faith efforts fail.

Take the often obvious gap between formal rules and what actually happens in combat. Just as medieval codes of chivalry didn't prevent knights from frequently massacring civilians, researchers find that even among modern militaries with clear rules against noncombatant killing, atrocities still occur regularly.[72] The stress of combat, dehumanizing of the enemy, powerful in-group bonds among soldiers who see their comrades killed, and the simple opportunity war affords for indulging lethal impulses all produce at least some deliberate civilian reprisals and thrill killings. Sometimes commanders do not clearly communicate rules of engagement, or they create a culture in which soldiers receive mixed signals and are not held accountable for violations of the rules. In defending a general for failing to uphold formal rules of engagement in Vietnam, an army lawyer said, "It's a little like the Ten Commandments—they're there, but no one pays attention to them."[73]

Those fighting wars face pressure to demonstrate progress through body counts, to take the battle to the enemy, and to protect their own troops from attack. Particularly in wars where distinguishing combatants from noncombatants is difficult to begin with, these factors create an environment in which civilians are routinely killed during offensives, on patrols, at check points, or in attempts to suppress enemy fire.[74] The journalist Raffi Khatchadourian provides a chilling account of an American brigade in Iraq that tracked enemy deaths on a "Kill Board" and whose colonel instructed his soldiers to think of themselves as "the dominant predator on this street" and to shoot at any sign of danger since "the guy that is going to win on the far end is the one who gets violent the fastest." One brigade lieutenant, when told that fleeing cars he had ordered fired upon might have women and children inside, said, "F--k that, it's collateral damage."[75] In his report investigating a civilian massacre by Marines in Iraq, a U.S. general wrote,

> All levels of command tended to view civilian casualties, even in significant numbers, as routine and as the natural and intended result of insurgent tactics . . . Statements made by the chain of command during interviews for this investigation, taken as a whole, suggest that Iraqi civilian lives are not as important as U.S. lives, their deaths are just the cost of doing business, and that the Marines need to "get the job done" no matter what it takes.[76]

Perhaps the most significant moral fact about war is its extraordinary low threshold for killing. Even rules of engagement that prohibit intentionally killing noncombatants do allow soldiers to intentionally kill lots of people who turn out later to have been noncombatants. Rather than applying to individuals, these rules apply to types of people or behaviors—those acting in a manner that might be threatening or those suspected of being enemy combatants based on a particular "signature" such as age, gender, location, or sometimes vague intelligence reports.[77]

People who fall into these often ambiguous categories can be deliberately killed, even if they later prove to have been innocent civilians—the family with young children who don't understand directions to stop well short of a checkpoint, the wedding party gathering in a location suspected of hosting terrorist meetings, the farmers thought to be burying explosives, the news photographers taking pictures with telephoto lenses. In his study of killing in war, Dave Grossman points to the commonplace nature of "gray-area killings," those cases where soldiers, unsure of the status or threat of a target, are nevertheless permitted by the rules of engagement to deliberately fire. Sometimes they are proven correct, sometimes mistaken, and usually they will never know.[78] If this kind of killing doesn't deliberately target noncombatants, it does deliberately target people who may well be noncombatants without requiring much certainty either way. After killing a group of civilians at a checkpoint in Iraq, an American soldier said that "we didn't know what was in that bus . . . I'd rather see more of them dead than any of my friends."[79]

Add the regular use of highly lethal weapons to this environment of uncertainty and a low bar for launching attacks, and is it any surprise that innocent civilians frequently end up dead? Airstrikes, artillery, and even concentrated small weapons fire on enemy positions can wreak tremendous havoc on those in the vicinity. Even precision-guided missiles can miss their targets completely, especially if bad intelligence enters the wrong information, and when they do hit their targets, they still have enough explosive power to potentially kill lots of others as well. A December 2009 cruise missile attack on a terrorist target in Yemen did kill a suspected fourteen al Qaeda members, but forty-one civilians, including twenty-three children, died as well, and many others who survived did so only with terrible burns and lost limbs.[80] The successful bombing of a high-ranking government official at the start of the Iraq invasion also destroyed a house next door, where a fifty-year-old man spent all next day digging out his dead family members one by one. They were

As'ad 'Abd al-Hussain al-Tayyar, 30, son.
Qarar As'ad al-Tayyar, 12, grandson.
Haidar As'ad al-Tayyar, 9, grandson.
Saif As'ad al-Tayyar, 6, grandson.
Intisar 'Abd al-Hussain al-Tayyar, 30, daughter.
Khawla Ali al-Tayyar, 9, granddaughter.
Hind Ali al-Tayyar, 5, granddaughter.[81]

While casualty estimates for the U.S. program of remote-controlled drone strikes in Afghanistan, Pakistan, and elsewhere can vary widely, it appears that at least as many civilians are killed for each intended target, and even many of these intended targets are themselves selected on rather loose "signature" criteria.[82] Perhaps most overlooked are weapons that, while not originally intended to kill civilians, do so in huge numbers long after their initial use. The vast majority of deaths from landmines and cluster bombs are to civilians, a trail of killing that can last for decades. Over thirty years after the Vietnam War, Southeast Asian countries were still suffering hundreds of deaths a year from these weapons as well as diseases from chemical defoliants such as Agent Orange.[83] Finally, the growing practice, especially by the United States over the last two decades, of bombing infrastructure targets—transportation, communication, and power grids—does not kill as many civilians initially, but the subsequent impact on public health caused by impure drinking water, malnutrition, drug shortages, and similar effects kills tens of thousands in the months and years following.[84]

The actual conditions of war, then, continually defeat efforts to prohibit killing civilians. Warfare is an environment in which killing is the norm. Rules against killing civilians are often ignored. And even when upheld, these rules still allow considerable room to intentionally target people whose status is in fact unclear. They still sanction weapons that routinely hit the wrong targets or whose lethality spills over beyond those targets. All this is inevitably part of war, and it is why the double effect principle cannot justify killing civilians in the course of fighting one. The choice to fight a war is the choice to intentionally expose civilians to the risk of death, a risk that will surely get a significant number of them killed, as a means to success in that war. Going to war and the conduct of operations within it are deliberate decisions to impose lethal levels of peril on noncombatants, levels that are fundamentally connected to the prospects for military success. Since these decisions are both intentional and themselves means toward the war's objectives, they do not meet the double effect principle's requirements, and so war's killing of noncombatants remains wrong.

Those who fight wars know the reality of unavoidable civilian death. Responding to criticism about civilians killed during the Vietnam War, an official Pentagon statement pointed out that in war "it is impossible to avoid all damage to civilian areas."[85] During the American Civil War, General Sherman stated, "If the people raise a howl against my barbarity and cruelty, I will answer that war is war."[86] A Second World War veteran, reflecting on civilian deaths in bombing raids, perhaps put it best: "But in war the innocent suffer, don't they?"[87] Yes they do. When neoconservatives pushing back against contemporary Catholic teaching complain that excessive concern for civilian immunity makes it "almost impossible to fight a war," they are correct.[88] The grim reality of war is that it inevitably kills innocent noncombatants. Dead civilians are a feature, not a bug. Just war theory recognizes this, which is why it speaks in terms of *minimizing* rather than *eliminating* noncombatant deaths, why its principles accommodate as well as prohibit killing civilians.

This is the central contradiction in just war theory's view of civilians. It recognizes that killing the innocent is wrong, that civilians are innocent, and that war inevitably kills them. But rather than conclude that wars are therefore inherently immoral enterprises, it searches for ways to keep fighting them. The just war framework chooses to give up the prohibition on killing the innocent rather than give up war. This is morally backward. If it is impossible to fight wars without intentionally exposing large numbers of innocent people to war's death and destruction as a means toward winning those wars, then fighting wars is in and of itself immoral and the just war is a contradiction. The growing concern with war's civilian death toll in contemporary Catholic teaching is admirable, but it doesn't go far enough. Since what John Paul II calls the "absolute inviolability of innocent human life" is so central to Catholic teaching, that teaching should move from its current position of deep moral skepticism about war to one that entirely repudiates war itself as wrong under any circumstances.[89]

Notes

[1]*Catechism of the Catholic Church* 1994, nos. 2258 and 2261.

[2]John Paul II 1995a, nos. 2, 40, and 57.

[3]The best overview of the development of civilian immunity within the just war tradition is McKeogh 2002. See also Johnstone 1986; Hartigan 1965; Lammers 1990; Lichtenberg 1994; and Slim 2008, chap. 1.

[4]For Augustine, if soldiers on the just side do not fight in the right spirit—if they fight out of hatred or lust for battle—they are guilty of a different kind of sin, even if they remain innocent of the *jus ad bellum* cause that justified the war itself.

[5]McKeogh 2002, 65, 87, and 90.

[6]Erasmus 1990, 306.

[7]See, for example, Second Vatican Council 1965, no. 80; Paul VI 1975, no. 37; John Paul II 1991a, no. 52; and John Paul II 1996, no. 2.

[8]*Catechism of the Catholic Church* 1994, nos. 2313-14; and Pontifical Council for Justice and Peace 2004, no. 504.

[9]United States Conference of Catholic Bishops 1983, nos. 311-12.

[10]See, for example, Slim 2008; Dyer 2004; Keegan 1993; and Potts and Hayden 2008.

[11]LeBlanc and Register 2003, 199 and 155.

[12]Dyer 2004, chap. 5; and Keegan 1993, 265, and 322-23.

[13]Pinker 2011, 194.

[14]Goldstein 2011, 26-30.

[15]Dyer 2004, 217.

[16]Pinker 2011, 197.

[17]Hedges 2002, 13.

[18]Hallock 1999, 156.

[19]Sheehan 2008, 112.

[20]Sheehan 2008, 128-29.

[21]Tirman 2011, 92, 123, 229, and 240; and Groeger 2011.

[22]Pinker 2011, 340; and Wright 2006, 157.

[23]International Rescue Committee 2007.

[24]Goldstein 2011, chap. 10.

[25]Hallock 1999, 158.

[26]See Tirman 2011; and Goldstein 2011, chap. 9.

[27]On the variety of methods and justifications for civilian killing over time, see Slim 2008; and Tirman 2011.

[28]LeBlanc and Register 2003, 66.

[29]LeBlanc and Register 2003, 67.

[30]Dyer 2004, 76.

[31]Dyer 2004, 143.

[32]Dyer 2004, 172-73.

[33]Holmes 1989, 6.

[34]Pinker 2011, 196; and Goldstein 2011, 31-32.

[35]Potts and Hayden 2008, 245.

[36]Pinker 2011, 333-34.

[37]Dyer 2004, 248.

[38]Slim 2008, 78; and Sheehan 2008, 96.

[39]Sheehan 2008, 85.

[40]Sheehan 2008, 130.

[41]Sheehan 2008, 129; and Snyder 2010, 173, and 205-06.

[42]Tirman 2011, chap. 3; and Dyer 2004, chap. 7.

[43]Dyer 2004, 4.

[44]Sheehan 2008, 129; and Tirman 2011, 54.

[45]Hallock 1999, 112.

[46]Dyer 2004, 284.

[47]Tirman 2011, 107.

[48]Tirman 2011, 167.

[49]Tirman 2011, 295; and Bourke 1999, 159.

[50]Gourevitch 2010, 102.

[51]Hedges 2002, 94.

[52]Slim 2008, 71.

[53]Keegan 1993, 5.

[54]Dyer 2004, chap. 6.

[55]Anscombe 1970, 44.

[56]For more on this dynamic in just war theory, see McKeogh 2002; Slim 2008, chap. 4; Christopher 1999, chap. 10; and Lichtenberg 1994.

[57]McKeogh 2002, 86 and 89.

[58]Walzer 1992, 254.

[59]Slim 2008, chap. 1.

[60]Holmes 1989, 188.

[61]Slim 2008, 159.

[62]Bourke 1999, chap. 9.

[63]United States Conference of Catholic Bishops 1983, no. 286.

[64]Halbertal 2009, 23, examining an Israeli military operation in Gaza.

65Ford 1960; and McKeogh 2002, chap 8.

66Johnstone 1986, 319-22.

67Anscombe 1970; and Ford 1960 and 1970.

68Ford 1970, 28.

69Oppenheimer 2010.

70Potts and Hayden 2008, 256-57.

71Lichtenberg 1994. See also Holmes 1989, chap. 6; Hull 2000; Bica 1999; and McKeogh 2002, chap. 8.

72Slim 2008; Tirman 2011; Bourke 1999; Hallock 1999; and Grossman 2009.

73Bourke 1999, 195.

74See Tirman 2011, especially chap. 9. For specific recent examples, see Wright 2009; Finkel 2009; Oppel 2010; Chandrasekaran 2010; and Scahill 2008.

75Khatchadourian 2009.

76Tirman 2011, 304-05.

77Tirman 2011; and Khatchadourian 2009.

78Grossman 2009, 199-201.

79Tirman 2011, 251.

80Filkins 2011a, 47-48.

81Richardson 2009.

82Rosenbaum 2010; *America* 2011; Woods 2011; Mayer 2009b; and Filkins 2011b, 61.

83Winright 2011; and Tirman 2011, chap. 5.

84Tirman 2011; Shue 2010; and Lopez 2002.

85Tirman 2011, 163.

86Dyer 2004, 248-49.

87Bourke 1999, 301.

88Patterson 2007, 28.

89John Paul II 1995a, no. 57.

7

Killing the Innocent: Soldiers

Catholic teaching's absolute prohibition on intentionally killing innocent persons faces another problem in war: soldiers. This may sound strange, since the last chapter just argued that war wrongly kills noncombatants, a category of people defined precisely as not being soldiers. But recall why it is wrong to kill civilians: because most of them are clearly innocent of the wrongdoing that led to the war and ostensibly justified its killing in the first place. They are caught up in a conflict beyond their control, one they neither caused nor invited. Since almost all of them haven't done anything wrong, it is immoral to indiscriminately kill them. Here, then, is the problem when we turn to soldiers. They too are almost all innocent in the same way, something just war theory itself recognizes, even as it nonetheless endorses their deliberate slaughter.

If intentionally killing the innocent is wrong, then the most straightforward way to justify killing soldiers in war is to consider them guilty. This punitive approach is just war theory's original position, beginning with Augustine's claim that enemy soldiers, as well as civilians, share in their country's guilt for the wrongdoing that initially justified the war. Even as Vitoria and Suárez move to associate civilians with innocence, they retain the association of soldiers and guilt. And some modern formulations of the just war, including those of Catholic thinkers such as Elizabeth Anscombe and John Ford, continue to base the permissible killing of enemy soldiers on the guilt they bear for participating in an unjust aggression.[1]

This punitive justification is not sustainable.[2] Holding all ordinary soldiers responsible for the wrongdoing of their leaders is as unreasonable as holding all ordinary civilians responsible. The vast majority of soldiers on any side of a war have no influence in the larger political conflicts that bring it on. American and Iraqi soldiers didn't get a say in the 2003 standoff between their national leaders that would soon have them killing each other. As Noam Zohar writes, "The point is that, even if we suppose the enemy state guilty of aggression—which is, presumably, why our state is justified in its war effort—many (or even most) of the enemy soldiers as individuals cannot necessarily be saddled with the blame for that aggression."[3] Caught up in a conflict largely beyond their control, soldiers as a group simply can't be connected to the *jus ad bellum* reasons for the war that supposedly justify its killing.

Most soldiers who end up on the unjust side of a war are there because it was their bad luck to be born in a particular time and place. These who join the military voluntarily usually do so for a variety of reasons—civic duty, economic desperation, national pride, social or family expectations, the example of friends, an escape from their village or neighborhood—completely unconnected to the reasons a particular war gets fought. Many soldiers on whatever side act in good faith, doing their duty and sincerely believing their cause righteous, even when this belief may be wrong on one side, the other, or both. Of course, it is also the case that many soldiers throughout the history of warfare don't serve voluntarily. Methods such as slavery, kidnapping, the press gang, and the draft have filled military ranks since the advent of armed conflict.[4] Battles between conscripted armies, where soldiers on both sides have no choice in the matter but are forced to slaughter each other nonetheless, are routine in warfare, ancient and modern. And forced combat is not limited to adults; child soldiers have always been a feature of war, and they are fighting in the majority of wars around the globe today.[5] Indeed, given the frequency with which people are forced to serve in the world's armies and militias, the decision to fight a war to defeat an evil regime and save its victims from oppression usually means deliberately butchering large numbers of those very victims—a perverse exercise in intentionally killing the innocent in the name of saving the innocent.

The fact that most soldiers on either side of any given war are innocent of its larger causes, that they are caught in a common and often terrible experience not of their making, is the basis for a frequently noted experience in war: the recognition of moral equality among combatants. Michael Walzer describes it thus: "It is the sense that the enemy soldier, though his war may well be criminal, is nevertheless as blameless as oneself. Armed, he is an enemy; but he isn't my enemy in any specific sense; the war itself isn't a relation between persons but between political entities and their human instruments."[6] Soldiers on both sides are merely trying to survive, to protect themselves and their buddies, and make it home alive. Yes, they are trying to kill each other, but they often express the view that it isn't personal and that they view soldiers on the other side with a kind of grudging respect and recognition of their common fate.[7] A British paratrooper who lost a leg in combat during the war with Argentina over the Falkland Islands said, "I'm not angry at the Argentine soldiers; they were just doing their job, like we were," and another British veteran of the war, reflecting on a meeting years later with Argentine soldiers who had fought in the same battle, said, "I sat across the table from people who had killed friends of mine, and I'd killed friends of theirs. We felt no hatred for each other, only respect."[8]

Sometimes this sense of moral equality interferes with combat itself. In his study of when soldiers do and do not kill, Dave Grossman writes, "There is a constant danger on the battlefield that, in periods of extended close combat, the combatants will get to know one another as individuals and subsequently may refuse to kill each other."[9] There are accounts throughout the history of warfare of precisely this happening when soldiers come face to face and refuse to kill. A veteran of the First World War offered a typical example:

> I saw a young German coming towards me and at that moment I just could not murder him and lowered my gun, he saw me do so and he followed suit, shouting "What the h— do you want to kill me for, I don't want to kill you." He walked back with me and asked if I had anything to eat? At once the relief inside me was unspeakable, and I gave him my iron rations & my army biscuit.[10]

That same war saw a famous Christmas truce in 1914, when soldiers up and down the front line spontaneously left their trenches and began singing, eating, and playing sports together, panicking their commanders on either side who took several "days to get everybody back in their trenches and start the killing again."[11]

More awful is when soldiers recognize the moral equality of those they do kill, something that often haunts them for the rest of their lives.[12] A veteran of the Second World War tells of one such incident:

> Then one day I killed a soldier. He was Japanese. His wallet came out of his jacket, and I opened it up and I looked at it. And there was a picture of him, his wife, and his three children. And I said, "What the hell am I doing here?" There's a guy that's never done a thing to me, and yet I had to kill him because his boss said "go to war" and my boss said "go to war."[13]

The just war framework clearly recognizes the innocence and moral equality of ordinary soldiers on both sides of a war. One of its cornerstones is the separation of *jus ad bellum* from *jus in bello*. Regardless of the war's larger justification, combatants on both sides are subject to a common set of rules and protections.[14] While they can deliberately kill each other during the normal course of combat, they may not kill those who are wounded or surrendering. Prisoners may not be held beyond the end of hostilities or otherwise abused for merely being on the other side. Even soldiers fighting on the unjust side are permitted to kill soldiers on the just side without blame or punishment, either during the war if taken prisoner or after the war's conclusion. As we have seen, modern Catholic teaching on war strongly endorses these *jus in bello* principles. Even Vitoria, who nominally retains the punitive justification for killing soldiers, opposes punishing them for their actions in combat as long as they followed the rules of war, and contemporary Catholic versions of just war theory acknowledge that soldiers can "fight justly in an unjust cause."[15] This is why the head of the Vatican's Pontifical Council for Justice and Peace, when calling the U.S. invasion of Iraq an unjust war, nonetheless refused to criticize Catholic members of the U.S. military: "The responsibility is not theirs, it is of those who send them."[16]

Why is it wrong to kill soldiers who are wounded or surrendering? Why is it wrong to execute, imprison, or otherwise punish soldiers who fought on an unjust side of a war once it is over? It is wrong because they are innocent. They haven't done anything to deserve such measures. This is the central contradiction in just war theory's view of ordinary soldiers: since they are innocent, they may not be punished for merely fighting in a war, even on the unjust side, but those on both sides may nonetheless be legitimately slaughtered during the course of the war. So they don't deserve to die for anything they have done, but die they do, and in shocking numbers. How many of the 30,000 sailors and marines who drowned in one afternoon at the 1571 battle of Lepanto deserved to die? Or the 622,000 soldiers who died in the American Civil War? Or the one million French conscripts taken from their families never to return from Napoleon's imperial wars?[17] From famous battles—700,000 soldiers killed at Verdun in the First World War—to largely overlooked wars—40,000 mainly conscripted soldiers killed in the Ethiopia-Eritrea conflict of the late 1990s—how many of the dead were somehow guilty enough to warrant a penalty of death?[18]

War is the moral absurdity of innocent people lined up to butcher each other—from the "bloody shoving matches" of ancient phalanx warfare, to the orderly "firing squad" volleys of musket warfare where soldiers would stand to be shot by the enemy or bayonetted by their own officers if they turned to run, to the "lethal steel sleet" filling the air in modern war.[19] The scenes after battles across the centuries bear mute testimony to the horror war brings to the soldiers caught in it. Of one ancient Greek battle, Xenophon wrote,

And now that the battle had ceased, it was a sight to see where the encounter took place, the earth bedabbled with gore, the dead lying cheek by jowl, friend and foe together, and the great shields hacked and broken to pieces, and the spears snapped asunder, the daggers lying bare of sheaths, some on the ground, some buried in the bodies, some still clutched in the dead men's hands.[20]

After Ernie Pyle, the Second World War correspondent, was killed, a column found on his body spoke of being unable to forget "the unnatural sight of cold dead men scattered over hillsides and in the ditches along the high rows of hedge throughout the world."[21] The Gulf War in 1991 saw the famous "highway of death" attack on retreating Iraqi soldiers that produced a scene "akin only to a scrap yard containing not only hundreds of bombed-out vehicles, but also thousands of dead, burned, and putrefying Iraqi soldiers," as well as silent mounds of sand under which screaming Iraqi conscripts had been buried alive in their own trenches by bulldozers.[22]

For an especially powerful example of an innocent soldier serving in an unjust cause, the Catholic tradition need look no further than retired pope Benedict XVI himself. The Nazi regime was the paradigmatic unjust aggressor, launching a brutal war of expansion, destruction, and genocide that killed tens of millions, and a young Joseph Ratzinger served in its military.[23] As a boy Ratzinger was forced to join the Hitler Youth to keep his place in school. At sixteen, he was conscripted to serve in an antiaircraft unit targeting Allied planes to protect a variety of facilities, including a BMW plant making aircraft engines with slave labor from the Dachau concentration camp. Ratzinger survived at least one deadly attack on his unit. He was later drafted into the regular army, serving in a unit near the Hungarian border where he witnessed some of the over 600,000 Hungarian Jews killed by the regime being transported to death camps. Following Hitler's death, with the Germany military in collapse, he deserted his unit and headed for home. At one point, Ratzinger was stopped by German soldiers with orders to shoot deserters, but, in his words, "Thank God that they, too, had had their fill of war and did not want to become murderers."[24] Eventually captured by American forces, he spent just over a month as a prisoner of war before being released.

By all accounts, Ratzinger was a reluctant soldier. His family was strongly anti-Nazi. He only served under compulsion, never fired his rifle, and resisted pressure to join the SS. He hoped for a quick German defeat to end the war. Like many others in his position, Ratzinger was a young draftee caught in a terrible war he did not cause. Fortunate to be captured by American rather than Soviet troops, he was not shot or otherwise punished for being in the German army, but rather quickly released at the war's end. His military service to the Nazi regime did not disqualify him from becoming a Catholic priest, bishop, cardinal, and pope. On his elevation to the papacy, commentators such as George Weigel rightly defended him against those who objected to his service in the Second World War, arguing that he was innocent of anything that would render him unfit for the office.[25] Here, then, is the obvious problem. If Ratzinger was not guilty of anything that warranted punishment after the war, or that even rendered him unfit to lead the Catholic Church as Pope Benedict XVI, then what could justify actively seeking his death in wartime? During his boyhood military service, just war theory tells us that it would have been perfectly moral to shoot, bomb, burn, stab, asphyxiate, or otherwise kill Joseph Ratzinger, even when he was marching, eating, sleeping, or quietly reading his Bible. Though innocent, intentionally trying to kill him was perfectly legitimate. Fortunately, these efforts failed, and he went on to lead a rich and inspiring life, but how many more soldiers, innocent like him, never came home, not just from the Second World War but from all the wars across all the centuries?

* * *

Just war theory has long recognized the problem of killing innocent soldiers. It has not, however, embraced the obvious conclusion: anything that intentionally and systematically kills that many innocent people as part of its regular operation cannot be moral, no matter what the larger causes at stake. Instead, just war thinkers have found alternative grounds to justify killing soldiers in battle. The most important of these centers on the threat posed by soldiers, substituting a preventative justification for a punitive one. Soldiers may not bear guilt for the war itself, but their material participation in combat renders them a real danger within the war, making it permissible to kill them in self-defense. With origins in the work of Grotius, Emmerich de Vattel, and several centuries of international law, this is now the dominant view in contemporary just war theory.[26]

In chapter 3 we saw the importance of domestic parallels in just war arguments. This justification for killing soldiers, including the innocent among them, is especially dependent on what it considers the analogous case of individual self-defense outside of war. Several philosophers, most notably Judith Jarvis Thomson, argue that individuals have a right to use lethal force against attackers, even if those attackers are morally innocent.[27] In this "no-fault" account of self-defense, it is the threat someone poses to your life alone that justifies a lethal response.[28] As

Thomson says, "What I think is clear in any event is that if the aggressor will (certainly) take your life unless you kill him, then his being or not being at fault for his aggression is irrelevant to the question whether you may kill him."[29] For her, this applies to reluctant attackers (perhaps their families are being threatened), mentally unaware attackers (perhaps they are under the influence of mind-altering drugs), or even those who are not active agents at all (perhaps they have been thrown off a cliff and will crush you unless you deflect them away from your ledge and to their deaths). In each case, it is the threat the persons represent rather than their intention, fault, or agency that matters. This justifies your killing them if necessary, while prohibiting your killing those, such a bystanders, who are no threat to you.

It is clear why this kind of self-defense framework is attractive to just war theorists. It allows soldiers to kill each other in combat given the material threat they represent, but prohibits killing those out of combat—civilians, the wounded, prisoners—because they are not threats. For Grotius, the "right of self-defense" does not depend on the "injustice or crime of the aggressor," but applies "even if the assailant be blameless, as for instance a soldier acting in good faith, or one who mistakes me for someone else, or one who is rendered irresponsible by madness or by sleeplessness."[30] According to Robert Fullinwider, just as a person walking down the street suddenly attacked by a gunman may return fire in self-defense without determining the actual guilt of the attacker, soldiers may "intentionally kill combatants, even the morally innocent among them," given the danger they pose, while they may not intentionally kill civilians, even those who may in fact be "morally guilty" for causing the war.[31] For Thomas Nagel, since guilt and innocence don't line up with combatant and noncombatant status in war, its killing must instead depend on who represents a threat (soldiers) and who does not (civilians), producing "the consequence that in war we may often be justified in killing people who do not deserve to die, and unjustified in killing people who do deserve to die."[32]

There are Catholic versions of this self-defense justification for killing soldiers, including the innocent among them, but they come with a strange twist, one made necessary by how Catholic teaching justifies self-defensive violence. Remember that early Catholic thinkers such as Ambrose and Augustine condemned killing in private self-defense. Aquinas, however, does allow for it under certain circumstances. On his account, individuals may legitimately defend themselves against attackers but only with the minimum of force necessary to repel the assault. They may not intentionally kill attackers, though if in using a level of force necessary to stop them, the attackers die, this is permitted by the principle of double effect.[33] The *Catechism*, citing Aquinas's double effect justification, gives a similar account of individual self-defense.[34] So too does John Paul II, pointing to the same Aquinas passage. In *Evangelium Vitae*, he writes, "Unfortunately it happens that the need to render the aggressor incapable of causing harm sometimes involves taking his life. In this case, the fatal outcome is attributable to the aggressor whose action brought it about, even though he may not be morally responsible because of a lack of the use of reason." Notice that John Paul II suggests that killing an attacker, where the attacker's death is not intended but is a secondary result of the force necessary to stop the assault, is even justified in those rare cases where the attacker does not bear moral guilt for the assault due to mental impairment. Such an unintended secondary effect of legitimate self-defensive action against "criminals and unjust aggressors" does not violate the "absolute" prohibition on intentionally killing an "innocent person."[35]

The double effect principle's central place in Catholic doctrine's understanding of self-defense complicates the threat-based preventative justification for killing innocent soldiers during warfare. It means, essentially, that it is permissible to kill soldiers in war as long as their deaths are not intentional. For example, a Catholic ethics manual from the 1920s argues that since "I may kill a man who makes an unwarranted attack upon my life, whether the aggressor is innocent or guilty," and since killing in war is "of the nature of self-defense and not punishment," one in which the "distinction between innocent and guilty enemy-subjects does not arise," it is permissible to kill opposing soldiers only if such killing is not deliberate. Since "the natural law forbids the direct aiming at the death of the enemy," combatants must only use force with the intent of stopping or incapacitating enemy soldiers, meaning any deaths that result are actually unintentional.[36] Even prominent contemporary Catholic philosophers such as Germain Grisez and John Finnis endorse this odd-sounding claim about not deliberately killing soldiers in war.[37] Disputing the common "belief that war must involve *intending to kill*," Finnis points to Aquinas's self-defense formula and claims that when soldiers defend themselves from attack in war, the death of opposing soldiers may only be an unintended "side effect."[38] Grisez, admitting that "no one using military force can be confident that the enemy personnel he kills is guilty of anything," similarly applies Aquinas's account of self-defense to war, arguing that "each act of warfare that kills must in and of itself have a good effect which is alone intended." This intent must be to impede the enemy's force rather than to actually kill enemy soldiers. According to Grisez, "As in self-defense, a soldier on the battlefield can shoot straight at an enemy soldier, intending to lessen the enemy force by one gun, while not intending to kill. Similarly a military camp or factory producing military goods can be bombed."[39]

In spite of determined efforts by just war theorists, a parallel to domestic self-defense cannot justify killing soldiers in war.[40] One obvious reason is that a simple argument from analogy—that a country can defend itself from invasion by another just as individuals can defend themselves from intruders in the night—is not adequate. Not only does the analogy not fit most wars—civil wars, those marked by a blend of valid and invalid claims on both sides, those resulting from an escalating series of aggressive moves by all parties—it also obscures the nature of the action involved. In war, countries don't literally kill other countries. It is specific people doing the killing and the dying. Zohar writes that "it is morally obtuse to offer an answer to the question 'When may we fight the enemy state?' without also focusing explicitly on the question 'How can we kill all these (enemy) persons?' "[41] Justifications for killing particular persons must apply to them as persons. Even Grotius, who supports the preventative-based justification for killing soldiers, acknowledges that it must apply to them as individuals rather than by analogy to larger political entities, arguing that it is "not sufficient that by a sort of fiction the enemy may be conceived as forming a single body" that your country can kill in self-defense.[42]

But even taking soldiers as particular persons, it is clear that a parallel to domestic self-defense cannot justify their deaths. The paradigmatic case of individual self-defense, especially the kind Catholic thinkers from Aquinas to John Paul II have in mind, has certain features that simply cannot translate to the reality of killing in warfare. To see why, consider more closely when one can kill someone in self-defense. First, you may do so only in unusual circumstances of grave danger. You can't routinely kill people in response to any provocation or minor harm. Using lethal force is presumptively wrong unless you face a real and serious threat. Second, force is a last resort. If you can diffuse the situation nonviolently or are able to escape the attack—what the law often calls the "duty to retreat"—you must do so. Killing the attacker is only permitted if there is no other way to prevent the attack. Third, the threat must be immediate. You can't go around killing people who you believe may attack you at some point in the future. Fourth, as we have seen, Catholic doctrine includes the requirement that killing the attacker not be intentional. You may only use force sufficient to immobilize the attacker or give yourself the opportunity to escape. Deliberately killing him or her is wrong. Fifth, you must have done nothing to warrant the attack. You are, for example, asleep at home or peacefully walking down the street. You can't claim self-defense when someone you are trying to kill fights back, thereby endangering your life, too.

This last requirement is crucial. While thinkers, such as Thomson, favor a "no-fault" account, self-defense is actually meaningless without some kind of "moral asymmetry" between attacker and victim.[43] By its very nature, the case of justifiable self-defense describes a relationship of moral inequality in which only one side can legitimately use force. Smith is permitted to use lethal force and Jones is not, because Smith did nothing to warrant an attack initiated by Jones. The fact that one party launches an attack that the other party did nothing to deserve is what tips the balance in the conflict of life versus life. Without this element, self-defense becomes mere self-preservation, where one person substitutes his or her life for another's—Smith's grabbing a spot in a full lifeboat by pulling Jones, who by occupying the last spot threatens Smith's life, out and into the water. It also renders self-defense absurd, since based on threat alone all parties in a conflict may be permitted to kill each other in self-defense, whether it is street gangs in a gunfight over turf, hostage takers shooting back at police snipers, or murderers killing their victims in self-defense once the victims fight back. Notice how John Paul II's statement above, where he addresses an attacker not fully responsible for his or her actions, retains this crucial asymmetry between an innocent victim and an "aggressor," one "whose action brought it about" and to whom the "fatal outcome is attributable."

So why can't these factors that justify killing an attacker in individual self-defense also apply in war? Take them each in turn. First, the size, scope, and frequency of killing in war bear no resemblance to cases of domestic self-defense. It sweeps up enormous numbers of people in escalating and continuous cycles of killing. Rather than being presumptively wrong save for extraordinary circumstances, killing is the norm in warfare. As Joanna Bourke points out, killing human beings is the "characteristic act" of war, the very "heart of military strategy and practice."[44] Especially when it comes to *innocent* attackers, instances in domestic self-defense are so rare that philosophical justifications must resort to extraordinary scenarios involving cliffs, hallucinating truck drivers, or babies with guns. In war, by contrast, killing innocent soldiers is routine, an ongoing everyday occurrence.

Second, killing in battle is not a last resort. Soldiers don't have the responsibility to try nonviolence first. There is no "duty to retreat" when coming into contact with the enemy. Instead, there is a duty to advance toward enemy combatants, to actively find and kill them. Killing soldiers on the other side during combat is not merely a first resort; it is the goal of combat itself, the very thing a great deal of prior planning and training aims for.

Third, war kills soldiers when they are not actually engaged in aggressive actions. Like massacring civilians, killing wounded or surrendering soldiers is routine in the history of warfare.[45] A soldier in the First World War wrote, "At this point, I saw a Hun, fairly young, running down the trench, hands in air, looking terrified, yelling for mercy. I promptly shot him. It was a heavenly sight to see him fall forward."[46] During the American Civil War, the Confederate policy was to execute all black Union soldiers taken prisoner.[47] And in the Second World War, killing Japanese prisoners was an unspoken rule, encouraged by Allied commanders, something confirmed by Charles Lindbergh when he wrote at the time: "Our men think nothing of shooting a Japanese prisoner or soldier attempting to surrender."[48]

Even when observing strict rules of war, soldiers routinely kill enemy combatants who pose no immediate threat. Those sitting around the fire, sleeping, cooking meals, fixing trucks, crewing re-supply ships, or writing a brigade newsletter well behind the front lines are all legitimate targets in war. Even in combat, military researchers have found a remarkable number of soldiers refuse to kill and therefore do not pose an actual threat to those on the other side. They hang back, play dead, pretend to fire unloaded weapons, or intentionally fire well over the heads of the enemy.[49] Since such soldiers are impossible to distinguish from those who are genuine threats, both types are legitimate targets for killing in combat. Additionally, one of the oldest features of warfare is the fact that most deaths occur once one side has broken and is retreating in disarray, which is why military tactics have always emphasized maintaining contact with a defeated enemy as long as possible to maximize its destruction.[50] As Grossman says in his study of actual combat conditions, "The vast majority of killing in historical battles occurred during the pursuit when the enemy has turned his back."[51] Modern war sees this phenomenon, too. In the 1991 Gulf War, the United States killed approximately thirty thousand retreating Iraqi soldiers.[52]

The history of combat is really the centuries-long attempt to gain tactical advantage over the enemy, to kill as many of them as possible without them having the opportunity to do the same to you. Grossman points to the frequency of kills that "are ambushes and surprise attacks in which the enemy represents no immediate threat to the killer, but is killed anyway, without opportunity to surrender."[53] Modern militaries with technological advantages such as night-vision, satellite tracking, and precision-guided munitions slaughter entire enemy units unknowingly sitting miles away in their barracks or trenches.[54] Snipers tell of the strange feeling of seeing distant, unaware, and completely nonthreatening enemies through rifle scopes, then pulling gently on the trigger to end their lives.[55] A British veteran of the Falkland Islands war, recounting a planned night assault, said that "we hoped to be able to bayonet them in their sleeping bags before they even had a chance to grab a weapon."[56] Clearly, sailing thousands of miles to sneak up on and deliberately bayonet a complete stranger in his sleep is not something Aquinas, John Paul II, and others who justify killing in individual self-defense have in mind.

Fourth, despite the bizarre arguments about unintentionally killing enemy soldiers offered by Finnis, Grisez, and others, killing in war is clearly intentional. The history of innovations in weaponry is the story of methodically and deliberately figuring out how more effectively to kill the enemy. Killing is not a side effect but the very purpose—from the crossbow for better penetrating medieval armor, to grapeshot for scouring enemy decks during naval battles, to antipersonnel cluster bombs spraying lethal shards across troop formations, to bullets intentionally designed to fragment on impact and create "untreatable wounds."[57] Any honest examination of war's reality acknowledges that intentionally killing the enemy is the heart of the enterprise. Soldiers know it is their job, and preparing them to do so effectively is the explicit purpose of military training and tactics.[58] From Sennacherib, an ancient Assyrian king, bragging that he "cut their throats like sheep" and "filled the plain with the corpses of their warriors," to Mao Tse-Tung emphasizing almost three millennia later the need to "encircle the enemy forces completely, strive to wipe them out thoroughly and do not let any escape from the net," military commanders have always understood that deliberately killing enemy soldiers is what war is all about.[59] During the Second World War, General Patton told his officers,

> When we meet the enemy, we will kill him. We will show him no mercy. He has killed thousands of your comrades, and he must die . . . when you get within two hundred yards of him, and he wishes to surrender, oh no! That bastard will die! You must kill him. Stick him between the third and fourth ribs. Tell your men that. They must have the killer instinct.[60]

Ordinary soldiers understand this too. As a veteran of the British army said, "We were professional soldiers, and that's what professional soldiers do—kill people. You don't need to sit down and have a think about that too much. It stands to reason."[61] An American sniper in Iraq who killed over 150 people one by one described his role simply: "My job was killing."[62]

Fifth, while domestic self-defense depends upon a fundamental asymmetry between victim and attacker, one that justifies force by the former against the latter but not the other way around, this difference does not exist in warfare. As we have seen, the moral equality of soldiers is a key feature of war, one central to just war theory itself. The position of a person surprised by an intruder at home or attacked while walking home from work one evening is fundamentally unlike that of soldiers in war. In combat, soldiers on both sides actively seek the opportunity to kill each other. They both launch and repulse attacks. Unlike cases of domestic self-defense, both sides in the conflict are expected to kill each other and do so without blame. War, then, is the moral absurdity of large numbers of people systematically trying to kill each other, all of whom are acting in self-defense. Soldiers on both sides, in the words of Erasmus, "must either slay without mercy, or fall without pity!"[63] Roman gladiators fought each other to the death in self-defense, but far from justifying their deaths, this is precisely what made the spectacle itself inherently immoral.[64]

Clearly the conditions that justify killing an attacker in individual self-defense cannot apply in war. If soldiers were to conform to these conditions—killing only as a last resort, favoring nonviolence and retreat whenever possible, targeting only those engaged in attacks actually under way, never initiating a lethal attack themselves, never intentionally killing an enemy soldier—it would render them no longer soldiers engaged in warfare. Indeed, rather than justifying war's killing, the very limiting conditions that can make domestic self-defense legitimate also make the conduct of war morally impossible. This is why it is entirely consistent for pacifists to oppose all war as morally wrong, even while endorsing the use of lethal force against individual attackers under certain circumstances.[65]

* * *

Recall how when faced with the inevitable killing of civilians in warfare, just war theory finds ways to accommodate it rather than repudiate war as always immoral. It makes a similar choice for soldiers. Even when its justifications for killing them prove untenable, proponents of just war theory still can't bring themselves to repudiate war. One strategy is to take refuge in outlandish claims, such as soldiers are not intentionally killed in warfare, essentially choosing to wall off moral theories about war from its reality. A more common approach in contemporary just war theory is basically to give up, accepting that war's killing of soldiers cannot be justified in normal moral terms but endorsing the possibility of a just war anyway if the cause is important enough. In these accounts, it is permissible to kill soldiers in war because that's simply the way war works. The license to kill soldiers is a convention unique to war, one based either on a customary arrangement among countries or on a separate moral logic internal to war itself. While killing them as persons may be wrong, their having a separate status as combatants makes them legitimate targets. In short, you can kill soldiers because they are soldiers, and war would be impossible if you couldn't. [66]

This line of argument offers no real justification for killing soldiers other than mere description; combatant status alone becomes its own justification. But simply classifying a group of people as combatants does not change the moral reality of their deaths. If it is always wrong to intentionally kill innocent people, a convention based on some kind of custom or alternative morality can't make it right. Instead, the prohibition on killing the innocent renders the convention itself wrong. Far from justifying their killing, war's taking large numbers of human beings, most of them innocent of any wrongdoing, and putting them into a category that permits them to kill and be killed with impunity is precisely what renders it an immoral enterprise.

Appeals to convention or combatant status that place war outside the bounds of ordinary morality only highlight war's unjust treatment of soldiers. War exempts an entire category of people from the usual morality of killing: "They need not be guilty in order to be killed, and they do not incur guilt by killing."[67] This essentially negates their status as moral agents, transforming them from human beings into military instruments. Simone Weil famously identifies this transformation in the imagery of the *Iliad*, one of our oldest accounts of armed conflict, where warriors become either impersonal forces doing violence or the helpless objects of that violence.[68] According to Colm McKeogh, the war convention "accepts that, in the special circumstances of war, some people can have their human status suspended." They "may be treated as non-persons, instruments, as means to military or political objectives." When "in the role of combatant, it is accepted that a person's life can be treated as of instrumental value, both to his commanders and to the enemy."[69] Military leaders certainly understand this. Over the centuries the causes of particular wars have come and gone, but the reality of countless soldiers being continuously fed into battle to kill and die remains constant. Napoleon said, "Troops are made to get killed."[70] And an officer in the Second World War wrote of soldiers under his command:

> This is one of the most painful things, having to withhold sometimes your affection for them, because you know you are going to have to destroy them on occasion. And you do. You use them up: they're material. And part of being a good officer is knowing how much of them you can use up and still get the job done.[71]

Most of the ordinary soldiers "used up" in humanity's long history of war have been innocent. Like the young Joseph Ratzinger, they did not deserve to die for being caught up in a conflict beyond their control, something we have seen just war theory itself recognizes. Yet die they have, and die they continue to do. That war is the intentional slaughter of innocent soldiers is undeniable. The question is what moral conclusion to draw from this reality. While just war accounts, including Catholic versions, continue to endorse the possibility of morally permissible warfare, this is not consistent with Catholicism's own moral principles. If Catholic doctrine really deems intentionally killing innocent persons "always gravely immoral," something deeply wrong "always and everywhere" and "under any circumstances," then it must completely reject the conduct of war as inherently wrong, even while continuing to sanction legitimate uses of force in certain circumstances of individual self-defense.[72]

Notes

[1] For an overview of the punitive justification over time, see McKeogh 2002. For examples of contemporary Catholic versions of it, see Ford 1960; Anscombe 1970; and Shaw 2005. For a secular version of it, see Rodin 2002.

[2] On the failure of a punitive justification given the innocence of soldiers in war, see Lichtenberg 1994; Kahn 2002; Zohar 1993; Teichman 1986, chap. 7; Grisez 1970; McKeogh 2002; Norman 1988; Christopher 1999, chap. 10; McMahan 1994; Nagel 1974; Mapel 1996; Fullinwider 1975; and Cochran 1996.

[3] Zohar 1993, 607.

[4] Keegan 1993; Dyer 2004; and Slim 2008, chap. 3.

[5] Slim 2008, chap. 3; and Kassimeris 2006, 6.

[6] Walzer 1992, 36.

[7] See Walzer 1992, 35-37 and 138-43; Grossman 2009, 116-19; Christopher 1999, chap. 8; and many of the personal accounts of soldiers in Bourke 1999; and Hallock 1999.

[8] Hallock 1999, 307-08.

[9] Grossman 2009, 158.

[10] Bourke 1999, 136.

[11] Dyer 2004, 250-51.

[12] Grossman 2009; Bourke 1999; and Hallock 1999 all have examples throughout.

[13] Hallock 1999, 97.

[14] For overviews, see Walzer 1992, chap. 3; Christopher 1999; Kahn 2002; and McKeogh 2002, chap. 6.

[15] Lammers 1990, 65; and Thomas 2007, 510.

[16] Allen 2003.

[17] Dyer 2004, 186, 244, and 231.

[18] Sheehan 2008, 75; and Slim 2008, 88.

[19] Dyer 2004, 178, 220-21, and 250.

[20] Xenophon 1998, 11.

[21] Hedges 2002, 176.

[22]Hallock 1999, 198; and Zahn 1993, 205.

[23]For details on Ratzinger's Second World War military service, see Ratzinger 1998, 14-38; Allen 2000, 15-23; Bernstein and Landler 2005; Rising and Surman 2005; and Sparks, Follain, and Morgan 2005.

[24]Ratzinger 1998, 36.

[25]Weigel 2005, 135-38 and 153-63.

[26]For historical development, see Rodin 2002; and McKeogh 2002, chaps. 6 and 8. For modern examples, see Kahn 2002; Christopher 1999, chap. 10; Nagel 1974; and Fullinwider 1975.

[27]Thomson 1991.

[28]Miller 1993, 330.

[29]Thomson 1991, 286.

[30]Grotius 2005, book 2, chap. 1, sec. 3.

[31]Fullinwider 1975, 92-97.

[32]Nagel 1974, 19-20.

[33]Aquinas 1947, 2-2.64.7.

[34]*Catechism of the Catholic Church* 1994, nos. 2263-64.

[35]John Paul II 1995a, nos. 55 and 57. See also McCarthy 1994; Anscombe 1970, 45-46; Prümmer 1957, 127; and Cronin 1922, 97-103.

[36]Cronin 1922, 664-73 with quotations on 668-69.

[37]Grisez 1970; Grisez and Shaw 1980; Finnis, Boyle, and Grisez 1987; and Finnis 1996.

[38]Finnis 1996, 33-34 (italics in original).

[39]Grisez 1970, 71 and 91.

[40]On the failure of self-defense-based arguments for killing combatants, see Rodin 2002; Lichtenberg 1994; Ryan 1983; Reitan 1994; Zohar 1993; McMahan 1994; Mapel 1996; Duffey 1995; and Cochran 1996.

[41]Zohar 1993, 606.

[42]Grotius 2005, book 3, chap. 11, sec. 16.

[43]McMahan 1994; Rodin 2002; Zohar 1993; Miller 1993; and Cochran 1996.

[44]Bourke 1999, xiii-iv.

[45]Keegan 1993; Dyer 2004; Bourke 1999, especially chap. 6; and Ferguson 2006.

[46]Ferguson 2006, 134.

[47]Davis 2006, 301.

[48]Ferguson 2006, 150-51.

[49]Grossman 2009 has an excellent overview of this line of research.

[50]LeBlanc and Register 2003, 67; Dyer 2004, chaps. 4-5; and Grossman 2009, 70 and 127-29.

[51]Grossman 2009, 70.

[52]Boggs 2005, 181.

[53]Grossman 2009, 198.

[54]Tirman 2011, 202, and 227.

[55]See, for example, Bourke 1999, 55; and Grossman 2009, 198.

[56]Hallock 1999, 60.

[57]Scahill 2008, 142-43.

[58]Grossman 2009; Bourke 1999; and Khatchadourian 2009.

[59]Dyer 2004, 161 and 398.

[60]Bourke 1999, 171-72.

[61]Hallock 1999, 66.

[62]Kyle 2012, 253.

[63]Erasmus 1972, 23.

[64]Rodin 2002, 172-73.

[65]See, for example, Cochran 1996.

[66]For arguments along these lines, see Mavrodes 1975; Lichtenberg 1994; Mapel 1996; Zohar 1993, 618-19; Kahn 2002, 4; Walzer 1992, 144-45; Phillips 1990, 184-86; Woodruff 1982, 173-76; and Teichman 1986, 66.

[67]McKeogh 2002, 12.

[68]Weil 1977.

[69]McKeogh 2002, 12.

[70]Dyer 2004, 231.

[71]Dyer 2004, 17-18.

[72]John Paul II 1995a, no. 57; and *Catechism of the Catholic Church* 1994, nos. 2261 and 2258.

8

Policing, War, and Force

The last two chapters considered the nature of killing in war. What is remarkable about this killing is how different it makes warfare from policing. As we saw in chapter 3, a parallel between the two runs through the history of just war theory, from its origins in Ambrose and Augustine to its advocates today. But the parallel is false.[1] Rather than helping justify war, a closer look at policing actually throws war's immoral killing into sharper relief.

Policing isn't always just. Depending on the time, place, and regime, it can be corrupt, ineffective, brutal, or a tool of political repression. But it doesn't have to be this way. Unlike war, policing can be morally legitimate. When done right, policing is how society upholds the rule of law and maintains public order. By providing security, protecting basic rights, and ensuring justice, it creates a space in which people can live their lives in safety and dignity. And it can do so, even when resorting to force, without inevitably crossing into the kinds of killing that render warfare morally impermissible.

Policing power is an extension of government authority. It derives its legitimacy from being part of a legitimate political order. Law enforcement officers are part of the same community and subject to the same rule of law as those they police. In the words of Tobias Winright, "Police and the citizens share a stake in the common good and welfare of their community."[2] This relationship is very different than that between opposing soldiers in warfare, where a common governing authority is precisely what is lacking.

In policing their communities, officers certainly intervene to stop crimes in progress, and arrest those suspected of previous lawbreaking, but they also perform a variety of other functions: crowd control, responding to accidents, visiting schools, resolving minor disputes, giving medical assistance, finding lost children, and so on. Actually using physical force on people is infrequent in policing, even when taking lawbreakers into custody, and deadly force is extremely rare. Most police officers go entire careers without firing their guns. This is qualitatively different than the reality of wartime combat, where the primary job of soldiers is to identify and kill each other, where lethal violence is the norm rather than the rare exception. Indeed, the rise of modern law enforcement, beginning in London with Sir Robert Peel, is based precisely on the idea that normal military measures are far too brutal and indiscriminate for policing.[3] As Gerald Schlabach points out, effective military strategy "tends toward greater and greater firepower," while effective policing "inherently narrows the use of violence."[4]

In policing, officers only target persons based on factors unique to them as individuals—something they have done in the past or are currently doing. In war, however, people are targeted not "because of what they have done" but "because of who they are."[5] As we have seen, war distinguishes not among individuals but among categories of people. Targets include broad classes of people who count, often ambiguously, as combatants and who can be killed with impunity.

Since policing targets persons as individuals based on specific wrongdoing, any instance of force between an officer and a suspect is one of moral asymmetry. When police officers take someone into custody, the suspect has no right to use violence against them in self-defense. Criminals can't legitimately fight back; if they do, they will rightly face additional charges of resisting arrest or assaulting a police officer. In war, however, such moral asymmetry does not exist. Soldiers on both sides have the right to kill each other without being punished for it, rendering the mutual self-defense grounds for their use of deadly force against each other morally absurd in a way that is not true of policing.

Mistakes are possible in law enforcement. This is why police cannot arrest people without probable cause, usually supported by a warrant, and why those who are placed under arrest are considered innocent until proven guilty. Determining such guilt requires a trial, overseen by yet another party (a judge rather than the arresting officers themselves), that affords the accused a full range of due process rights: an attorney, protections against double jeopardy and self-incrimination, the right to confront witnesses, and so on. Only after their guilt is established beyond a reasonable doubt may such persons be punished for their wrongdoings. Warfare has no such procedural protections, even as its much greater scale of violence makes the probability of wrongly harming people exponentially greater. Its shockingly low threshold for killing represents the mirror image of policing's judicial safeguards, guaranteeing that masses of people who haven't done anything wrong will receive sudden and arbitrary death sentences. As Erasmus writes, "He who is convicted judicially, suffers the punishment which the laws impose; but in war, each side treats the other as guilty, and proceeds to inflict punishment, regardless of law, judge, or jury."[6] Force in war is arbitrary and capricious in ways that legitimate law enforcement procedures explicitly reject.

The goal in policing is to apprehend suspects with as little force as possible, to "detain and restrain" using the "least restrictive alternative."[7] On those rare occasions when police do legitimately use deadly force, it is permissible precisely because it conforms to the conditions justifying self-defensive killing outlined in the previous chapter. It is not a preplanned, intentional action, but only a last resort to prevent an immediate and grave threat to innocent life—a crime victim, a bystander, the officers themselves. Such force targets only the specific person responsible for the threat, only at the actual time of the threat, and only with the intent to incapacitate the attacker (in the United States, for example, police may not use deadly force to stop a fleeing suspect). These strict limits are why police departments thoroughly investigate cases where officers use, or even come close to using, deadly force. Such cases, even when legitimate, represent a kind of failure. They violate the norm of restraint and the goal of diffusing violent situations without deadly force at the core of good police practice.[8]

This understanding of deadly force obviously differs dramatically from warfare, in which killing enemy soldiers is a normal and deliberate activity carefully planned in advance. As we have seen, such killing is a first resort, permits attacking enemy combatants at times when they are not themselves engaged in combat, and, because of the tactical advantages of surprise or long-range strikes, usually gives the enemy no chance to surrender. While the goal of effective policing is not having to fire your gun, the goal of effective warfare is to fire first. Indeed, while police departments consider the discharge of weapons a problem worthy of investigation, the military invests considerable effort in addressing the problem of soldiers who don't fire their weapons.[9]

Finally, while war considers civilian deaths an unfortunate but regular and acceptable byproduct of war, there is no equivalent position in policing. As Paul Kahn writes of law enforcement, "We can no longer speak of acceptable collateral damage; we need to obtain a strict correspondence between injury and guilt."[10] Police officers take exceptional measures to prevent deaths to innocent bystanders, even if doing so makes them less effective in stopping criminals. The types of weapons and tactics they rely upon, and those they reject, clearly reveal this. Measures that are standard in warfare—airstrikes, artillery barrages, concentrated small-arms fire, bombing locations where targets may be hiding, free-fire zones, shooting-to-kill based on mere suspicion of being an enemy combatant, "signature" strikes, and so on—are all unacceptable in policing. The national shock and outrage following the 1985 decision by Philadelphia police to drop a bomb on a house at the center of an armed standoff, a decision that resulted in dozens of burned homes and five dead children, illustrates the different understandings of force embodied by policing and war.[11] The kind of action that is routine in warfare is precisely the kind of action that renders policing in such cases morally wrong. Indeed, when police operations do engage in unjust killing, their defenders usually resort to war parallels to excuse it. Defending a 2010 police raid on a poor Jamaican neighborhood to arrest a drug kingpin that killed scores of innocent people, one government spokesperson said, "There was warfare." Another said, "The community has to take some responsibility. I'm sure the entirety of Germany wasn't guilty of the crimes of the Second World War, but an entire generation of Germans had to suffer the consequences of Allied bombing."[12]

*   *   *

If attempts to justify war through a parallel to policing fail because of their differences, it is also important to recognize that attempts to blend the two in practice cannot make war just. It is common for soldiers to perform both policing and war-fighting functions, especially when occupying a disputed territory, but this doesn't make the war side of their operation morally permissible, any more than steamed vegetables on one side of my plate makes the General Tso's Chicken on the other side healthy. While it is difficult for an outside force to police a territory justly, it can be done, especially with local cooperation and legitimacy. This is why, as we will see in chapter 21, some humanitarian and peacekeeping operations under the authority of international law can be morally legitimate. But to remain permissible, such policing efforts must limit themselves to the understanding of force embodied by policing itself. They cannot be combined with warfare and remain a just enterprise given the nature of war's killing.

Take the example of recent U.S. military policy in Afghanistan and Iraq. Both involved traditional combat actions, especially in their early phases, as well as later counterinsurgency strategies that included policing activities such as civilian protection and local dispute resolution. Such blending, however, did not render the war-fighting dimensions of the operations any more just given the kinds of killing they entailed. The initial phases of both wars saw mass killing of enemy troops and militia members, many of whom were conscripts caught unawares sitting in their barracks and trenches, and almost all of whom never posed any threat to the United States themselves. Even with later shifts to counterinsurgency tactics, the low thresholds for killing as a first resort and without due process inherent in war remained.

Soldiers patrolling Baghdad in 2008 were told by their commander that "if you see someone with a weapon, f--king drop him. Don't even ask questions."[13] A year earlier, soldiers in a helicopter opened fire on a group of men walking down the street because one of them, who was actually a reporter with a camera, appeared to have a gun and then destroyed a van, which turned out to have children inside, that stopped to help one of the wounded. The military deemed the action consistent with the rules of engagement.[14] John Tirman reports that "permission to kill all military-age men was a standing order in places like Anbar."[15] Commenting on civilians killed by American and NATO troops from convoys and at checkpoints in Afghanistan, one general said, "We have shot an amazing number of people, but to my knowledge, none has ever proven to be a threat."[16] Reporting on conversations with U.S. government officials about drone strikes in Afghanistan and Pakistan, Dexter Filkins concludes that they "are not directed at specific individuals" and that the military "doesn't know the identities of the people it is firing at," only the types of people who are likely to be in such locations.[17] And in a typical week in early 2011, four children were killed in four separate incidents in Afghanistan—two while sleeping when soldiers raided their homes, one at a protest, and one while she was gathering firewood too close to a suspected insurgent position.[18] What is remarkable about all of these examples is, first, how routine and unexceptional they are in warfare and, two, how shocking and outrageous they would be in domestic policing. If police officers doing such things in Dallas would be morally wrong, then soldiers doing them in cities and towns elsewhere in the world are, too.

Why is the fundamental difference between policing and war important for the Catholic tradition? It means rejecting war as inherently immoral does not push Catholicism toward a rejection of ordinary state power. Rather than a sectarian withdrawal from the world, a hallmark of the Catholic tradition is engaging the world as it is, and this includes endorsing the necessity of government institutions, at times backed by force, to protect the common good and preserve public order. This is precisely what legitimate policing does. Catholicism, then, can embrace pacifism given how war inevitably violates its prohibition on intentionally killing the innocent, while at the same time endorsing the morally appropriate role policing plays in enforcing the law, protecting rights, and upholding justice. While policing cannot furnish a viable moral parallel to war, it can, as we will explore in this book's final section, furnish a viable moral alternative to it.

Notes

[1]For good overviews of the differences between the two, see Schlabach 2007a and 2007b; Winright 1995, 1999, and 2007; Luban 2002; Malloy 1982; Kleinig 1996; and Paskins and Dockrill 1979, part 3.

[2]Winright 2007, 141.

[3]Winright 2007, 140-41; and Winright 1999, 88-89.

[4]Schlabach 2007a, 75.

[5]Kahn 2002, 4.

[6]Erasmus 1972, 33.

[7]Kleinig 1996, 99-102.

[8]Kleinig 1996, chap. 6; and Malloy 1982, chap. 1.

[9]Grossman 2009.

[10]Kahn 2002, 4.

[11]Winright 1999, 85.

[12]Schwartz 2011, 68.

[13]Finkel 2009, 247.

[14]Finkel 2009, 96-105; and Khatchadourian 2010.

[15]Tirman 2011, 314.

[16]Oppel 2010.

[17]Filkins 2011b, 61.

[18]Davidson 2011.

9

Lawlessness, Disorder,
and Dehumanization

Policing is necessary to uphold a just and lawful order. Recall, however, that just war advocates make the same claim for war. From Augustine's "tranquility of order" to John Courtney Murray's "justice, law, and order," this claim has always been central to just war theory.[1] Indeed, "forgetting" this presumption in favor of order is a chief charge made against contemporary Catholic doctrine by its neoconservative critics. George Weigel even takes Augustine's "tranquility of order" phrase for the title of his first book on war, *Tranquillitas Ordinis*.[2]

Church teaching since the Second Vatican Council, however, is right to see warfare as more threatening to a just order than its guarantor. Part of what makes warfare a uniquely unjust enterprise is how so many of its features directly violate the very principle its advocates claim it protects. While legitimate policing protects a just order—which Catholic teaching associates with social trust, mutual aid, the rule of law, security, rights, and human dignity—the reality of war amounts to its systematic negation.

One of war's most frequently noted features is the way it turns ordinary morality on its head. In the third century, St. Cyprian observed that "murder, which in the case of an individual is admitted to be a crime, is called a virtue when it is committed wholesale."[3] Centuries later, an Irish veteran of the First World War said, "You do such things and get praise for them, such as smashing a fellow's skull, or putting a bullet through him, which if you were to do at home you'd soon be on the run, with a hue and cry and all the police of the country at your heels."[4] War's literal meaning is discord or strife. It unleashes, even celebrates, the very violence, cruelty, destruction, and chaos that conventional moral life condemns and resists.

In the Catholic tradition, war's most eloquent critic on this score is

Erasmus, who argues that "from war proceeds at once every kind of evil which disturbs and destroys the happiness of human life." Obliterating order and civility, war releases "a torrent of thieves, robbers, sacrilegists, and murderers," pulling society into a "whirlpool of mischief and confusion." While God created us to live in love, friendship, and peace, war brings murder, theft, and rape; produces widows, orphans, and childless parents; and leaves behind a landscape of burned homes, ruined fields, and defiled churches. Far from ensuring security, war creates a "constant state of fear and alarm." Rather than a peaceful order where "laws retain their vigor," where "the discipline of police prevails," and where "justice bears sway," war creates violent disorder where "laws are compelled to silence" and "justice has no dwelling place." While learning, laughter, and the arts are signs of human flourishing, war "overwhelms, extinguishes, abolishes, whatever is cheerful, whatever is happy and beautiful."[5] For Erasmus, both natural law and the clear teachings of Jesus condemn war, its violence, and its "encircling ocean of all the evils in the world." War is the "greatest immediate destroyer of all piety and religion," and it inevitably corrupts both "individual morals and public discipline."[6] On his account, "There is nothing more unnaturally wicked, more productive of misery, more extensively destructive, more obstinate in mischief, more unworthy of man as formed by nature, much more of man professing Christianity."[7]

Erasmus is correct in his diagnosis. War is often called development in reverse. The wealth devoted to it rather than building up communities amounts to, in the words of Paul VI, "an act of theft" that feeds conflicts even if it means starving the poor to death, and war's conduct leaves, in the words of John Paul II, "families and countries destroyed, an ocean of refugees, misery, hunger, disease, underdevelopment and the loss of immense resources."[8] Laying waste to enemy lands is as old war itself. The ancient Mesoamerican glyph for war is a burning building.[9] War's terrible physical, environmental, and economic destruction creates perfect conditions for the spikes in poverty, famine, and disease that come in its wake.[10] These scourges, closely linked to war across its history, account for a greater number of its victims than combat itself.[11] War also produces streams of refugees fleeing its violence and social collapse, people especially vulnerable to abuse, illness, hunger, and hopelessness, many of whom will never see their homes and loved ones again. The Second World War created sixty million such refugees, including a full third of the Japanese population. Afghanistan saw the same percentage of its population flee the country following the Soviet invasion, and the war following the U.S. invasion of Iraq produced one of the largest refugee flows in more than half a century.[12]

War corrodes the ordinary virtues necessary for a lawful and humane social order. This is what John Paul II means when he speaks of war "eating away at the very fabric of the social environment," threatening the "disintegration of human relations," and unleashing division that "weakens the moral foundations of society."[13] In place of neighborliness, trust, and mutual aid, war breeds suspicion, desperation, and isolation. In the words of Chris Hedges, war zones open up a "vast moral void" that is "ruled by fear." By his account,

> War breaks down long-established prohibitions against violence, destruction, and murder. And with this often comes the crumbling of sexual, social, and political norms as the domination and brutality of the battlefield is carried into personal life. Rape, mutilation, abuse, and theft are the natural outcome of a world in which force rules, in which human beings are objects. The infection is pervasive. Society in wartime becomes atomized. It rewards personal survival skills and very often leaves those with decency and compassion trampled under the rush.[14]

This is why areas ravaged by war are marked by extreme levels of lawlessness and disorder. War zones see surges in murder, theft, assault, drug abuse, corruption, kidnapping, gang violence, looting, and extortion. Warlords and mafia organizations flourish as the rule of law breaks down and lucrative opportunities emerge for war profiteering, smuggling, human trafficking, and racketeering.[15]

Armies have long considered local populations subject to the kinds of assault and plunder that would be criminal offenses outside of war. Genghis Khan said, "Happiness lies in conquering your enemies, in driving them in front of you, in taking their property, in savouring their despair, in raping their wives and daughters."[16] Even better disciplined modern armies have not eliminated abuse of civilian persons and property. A South Korean Catholic priest during the Korean War told American soldiers that his people were "sick of war and ruin," of "the bombs and the burning and the raping behind the battle line," concluding that the soldiers "appear to despise us."[17] While American armed forces today do not engage in the wholesale sacking of civilian areas that is common in the history of warfare, and that still happens among some armies and militias, there are still plenty of cases in which individual soldiers and military contractors, usually protected from local prosecution by status of force agreements, commit crimes with relative impunity.[18]

Sex crimes have a particularly long and close relationship with war. Hugo Slim writes that "almost every army ever raised has organized or patronized a network of brothels for the sexual gratification of its troops." Many of the women in such establishments are trafficked and held against their will, the most infamous example of which is the over 100,000 "comfort women," mainly Korean, forced into sexual slavery by the Japanese military in the Second World War.[19] A U.S. law against sex trafficking in war zones such as Iraq and Afghanistan has gone largely unenforced over the years in spite of considerable evidence that such trafficking is common.[20]

Augustine acknowledged rape as an ancient custom of war, and he was right.[21] Rape is so common in warfare, including every kind of conflict in every part of the world, from its prestate origins to today, that it is difficult not to see it as one of war's inevitable features.[22] In prestate war, it was routine for men in one village to attack another "for the express purpose of kidnapping women, whom they would gang-rape and distribute as wives."[23] In the closing stages of the Second World War, Soviet troops moved into Germany and systematically raped German women in community after community: "Young and old, rich and poor, healthy and sick, Nazi sympathizers and resisters—hundreds of thousands were raped, often many times and over prolonged periods; thousands were killed by their assailants or died as a result of their ordeals."[24] While not on the same scale, Iraq too saw a sharp increase in the number of rapes in the years following the U.S. invasion, some by occupying troops, but many more by those taking advantage of the atmosphere of lawlessness and social collapse the war created.[25] And, of course, soldiers themselves can be victimized by their own comrades. Women in the U.S. armed forces are twice as likely to be raped as civilian women, and an estimated one in three are victims of sexual assault while in the military, even as perpetrators of such assaults are almost never held accountable.[26]

As routine sexual assault and other crimes demonstrate, human rights are precarious in wartime.[27] In addition to sex trafficking, other forms of involuntary labor are closely associated with war. The most obvious is conscription, which has thrown countless people into combat against their will. As Robert Holmes points out, "Even convicted felons are not made to engage in compulsory killing."[28] In addition to soldiers, however, armies have long forced people into such jobs as road builders, porters, munitions workers, food producers, sappers, and human shields. Even modern professional militaries rely on a shadow workforce of foreign laborers to keep their bases running. Tens of thousands of such workers serve U.S. military personnel in combat zones, many of them trafficked and held against their will by corrupt subcontractors, cheated of pay, living in often brutal conditions (they are frequently housed in shipping containers), and suffering casualty rates similar to soldiers.[29] Freedom of movement is another victim of warfare. Curfews, checkpoints, communities divided by walls or minefields, forced relocation, and detention camps are all common features of war. So too are violations of basic civil liberties. War zones regularly see restrictions on speech and the press, property arbitrarily confiscated, religious freedom suppressed, and martial law substituted for due process in judicial proceedings. Commenting on the use of torture against terror suspects following the September 11 attacks, one U.S. official said, "If you don't violate someone's human rights some of the time, you probably aren't doing your job."[30] And, of course, the most fundamental human right of all is worth little in war. Whether it is a surge in infanticide/abortion rates in war zones, the slaughter of soldiers, routine civilian massacres, greater likelihood of disease and famine, or genocide, which almost never happens outside of an area not already experiencing armed conflict, warfare represents a massive and comprehensive assault on the right to life.[31]

In his 1994 annual peace message, John Paul II argues that while the family is a crucial institution for sustaining an enduring peaceful order, the violence and hatred of war "weaken and destroy family structures," thereby undermining such an order.[32] He is right to point to war's particularly harsh impact on families and damage to the social order that results. War tears families apart. It destroys homes and livelihoods. It brings pervasive fear and creates deep and lasting scars of loss, guilt, and humiliation. It leaves children orphaned, parents childless, and spouses widowed. Hundreds of thousands of child soldiers are serving in armies and militias around the world, some of them forced to kill their own family members to cement their abductors' hold over them and plied with drugs and alcohol before being sent into battle.[33] The First World War left ten million orphans and three million widows. A woman who lost her fiancé, brother, and several close friends in that war wrote that she would "live to the end of my days without confidence and security" in a world where "love would seem perpetually threatened by death."[34] During the Second World War's siege of Leningrad, one young girl awoke in the night to fight off her mother, who was trying to kill her own child to end her suffering from hunger, and another left a heartbreaking diary listing each family member who slowly died over the course of several months.[35] An Iraqi parent caught in the cycle of violence following the U.S. invasion of his country wrote, "I cannot imagine a father or mother hating their children. But in our miserable existence, we come very close to that." The constant anxiety about his children's safety created "a dull pain of helplessness and fury in the heart," which "eats you alive." He concluded, "You then realize that it is your love for them that is killing you. You begin to hate that love."[36] A letter left at the Vietnam Veterans Memorial in Washington, DC, reads, "I have dreamed of the day you'll come home and finally be my dad."[37]

While we saw in chapter 7 that war sometimes produces feelings of mutual respect among combatants across enemy lines, at other times it instead creates a surge of hatred, revenge, and dehumanization, suppressing any trace of love, forgiveness, and respect for the common humanity of the enemy combatants, and civilians alike. In the words of one Vietnam veteran, "When you live in an environment of hate and anger, you become hate and anger."[38] After seeing his friends die, another said of enemy soldiers, "For every one that I killed I felt better."[39] This tendency to see people as part of a large group deserving collective punishment, rather than as individual persons deserving respect, is a powerful dynamic in war. A Polish commander leading reprisals against ethnic Germans at the end of the Second World War ordered his troops to "treat them as they treated us."[40] Indeed, war often negates the very personhood of others, associating them with images of racial inferiority, animals, or insects, all of which makes violence against them easier to justify. In 1641, an English commander explained his order to kill Irish Catholics by the thousands: "Kill the nits and you will have no lice."[41] Justifying a massacre in Vietnam, a soldier said that "it wasn't like they were humans" but instead "a gook or a Communist and it was okay."[42]

War tends to drive out ordinary kindness and mercy, replacing them with a callousness and casual acceptance of suffering and death that would shock our sense of moral order in other areas of life. A soldier in the First World War wrote to his wife about killing Germans: "I have no compunction, no sympathy . . . I can't be bothered to waste tears."[43] A terrorist leader planning attacks on Israeli civilians nonchalantly stated, "This is war, and innocent people get hurt."[44] When told by an advisor, "People are going to die" in a military response to the September 11 attacks, President Bush's response was a simple "That's war." Similarly, "We are at war" was his CIA director's reaction to the use of torture on detainees as part of that response.[45] And his secretary of defense famously responded to the violent chaos unleashed in Iraq by the U.S. invasion with "stuff happens."[46]

While this cold acceptance of war's destruction and disregard for its victims is troubling enough, even more so is the actual reveling in violence that warfare can also bring. While civic order depends on controlling violent impulses, war's bloody disorder frequently unleashes them. Many soldiers describe the rush of joy and power that comes with killing, often comparing the experience to the pleasure of hunting or sex.[47] A First World War mortar officer remembered: "I secured a direct hit on an enemy encampment, saw bodies or parts of bodies go up in the air, and heard the desperate yelling of the wounded . . . I had to confess to myself that it was one of the happiest moments of my life."[48] A Vietnam veteran said, "I enjoyed the shooting and the killing. I was literally turned on when I saw a gook get shot."[49] A helicopter crew member in the same war remembered, "I had enjoyed killing the three Vietcong who ran from the tree line near the village. Feeling like a glorious bird of prey swooping down, I watched the mini-gun rounds splash through the paddy toward the running men, then ripping and tearing their bodies to lifelessness."[50] An American general, describing battles in Iraq and Afghanistan, said simply, "It is fun to shoot some people."[51]

War is at its most chilling when it takes on a "carnivalesque spirit," when a contagious violence upends the moral order embedded in human civilization.[52] As Slim writes, "The uninhibited fun of the rampage has been a thrill in wars ancient and modern."[53] Going beyond mere lawlessness, war zones regularly descend into an anarchy of senseless destruction and killing, where breaking taboos becomes an end in itself. Women are raped in front of husbands and children, families are burned alive in their homes, people are tortured for amusement, and religious objects are defiled.[54] Coming into an enemy camp while its men were away, an Inuit raiding party killed every woman there, then "cut off their vulvas, strung them on a line, and headed quickly toward home."[55] The 1937 Japanese attack on the Chinese city of Nanking saw tens of thousands of men "mowed down by machine guns, used for bayonet practice, or soaked with gasoline and burned alive," while tens of thousands of women "were raped—and many soldiers went beyond rape to disembowel women, slice off their breasts, nail them alive to walls."[56] When in 1998 the Taliban took Mazar-e-Sharif, an Afghan city held by a rival militia, they launched a two-day frenzy of violence against the population—slitting throats, raping women, slowly suffocating people in shipping containers, and mutilating the genitals of the dead.[57]

In fact, desecrating dead bodies, especially in sexualized ways, is a practice as old as war itself. From Achilles dragging Hector's body around Troy to Somali militias dragging the body of a dead soldier around Mogadishu, human bodies that would be treated with respect in times of peace are defiled in times of war.[58] A Vietnam veteran remembered,

We used to cut their ears off. We had a trophy. If a guy would have a necklace of ears, he was a good killer, a good trooper. It was encouraged to cut ears off, to cut the nose off, to cut the guy's penis off. A female, you cut her breasts off. It was encouraged to do these things. The officers expected you to do it or something was wrong with you.[59] Outside of war, of course, it is *doing* such things rather than *not doing* them that indicates "something is wrong with you." Most people would be distressed to receive a human skull in the mail, but in 1944 *Life* magazine published the photo of a young woman posing proudly with the skull of a Japanese soldier that her boyfriend fighting in the Pacific had sent her. He autographed the skull and described it as "a good Jap—a dead one."[60]

*   *   *

In war's death, mayhem, and depravity, soldiers occupy an ambiguous place. They are its primary instruments but also its victims. Among the charges John Paul II lays against war is that it "teaches how to kill" and "throws into upheaval even the lives of those who do the killing."[61] Reflecting on his experiences in the Second World War, one veteran wrote, "You think about it and you know you're going to have to kill but you don't understand the implications of that, because in the society in which you've lived murder is the most heinous of crimes . . . and you are in a situation in which it's turned the other way round."[62]

For soldiers, going through the experience of war means enduring a deeply dehumanizing process. This begins with military training.[63] Armies and militias have long relied on often brutal techniques to turn ordinary people into effective soldiers. According to Dave Grossman's influential work on military training, its purpose is to overcome a person's natural resistance to killing and "throw off the moral inhibitions of a lifetime."[64] Doing so means silencing the voice of conscience, suppressing individual thought, and quashing feelings of empathy and mercy, cultivating instead the harshness, obedience, and reflexive violence soldiers will need on the battlefield. One veteran remembered: "But what was most devastating was the psychological manipulation aimed at making me what I was not and did not want to be—a killer . . . Anger, frustration and hatred built up inside of me; tenderness and compassion were destroyed, and we became beasts, killing machines."[65] As Grossman details, this process of "battle proofing," of desensitizing people to violence and its effects, also includes extensive techniques to dehumanize the enemy, making it easier for soldiers to kill when they can "deny the humanity of the victim."[66]

Such training is so important because combat can be so brutal. Its violence, deprivation, fear, filth, confusion, and exhaustion stretch human endurance to its limits and frequently beyond, which is why desertion, suicide, and psychological breakdowns have always been a routine feature of warfare.[67] As one solider said of trench warfare in the First World War, "It was no place for a human being to be, really."[68] The experience of killing enemy soldiers and of seeing one's comrades killed themselves can be especially devastating, sparking intense guilt, anger, and despair. As one American sergeant said during the Iraq war, "How can anybody kill and function normally afterward? Or see someone get killed and function normally afterward? It's not the human response."[69] Not surprisingly, many soldiers who survive wars carry both physical and psychological wounds that last a lifetime. Disabilities and chronic health problems, unemployment and homelessness, shame and anger, depression and posttraumatic stress disorder, drug and alcohol abuse—these are all part of war's legacy, touching not only many veterans themselves but sending a chain reaction through their families, too.[70]

Whether assessing its impact on soldiers or civilians, on individuals, families, communities, or entire societies, it is clear that endorsing war as the protector of a just social order has things backward. Unlike legitimate policing, war inevitably subverts such an order, bringing instead death, ruin, abuse, lawlessness, disintegration, and dehumanization. To use Augustine's phrase, which neoconservative critics such as Weigel are so fond of using, war produces neither tranquility nor order. This is why contemporary Catholic teaching, in shifting its emphasis on a just order from endorsing war to more frequently condemning it, has moved in the right direction, and yet another reason it should take that last step and repudiate war entirely.

Notes

[1]Augustine 1950, book 19, chap. 13; and Murray 1959, 10.
[2]Weigel 1987.
[3]Cyprian 1903, 277.
[4]Bourke 1999, 355.
[5]Erasmus 1972, 12-22.
[6]Erasmus 1990, 289 and 311.
[7]Erasmus 1972, 11.
[8]Paul VI 1977, 243-44; and John Paul II 2000, no. 3.
[9]LeBlanc and Register 2003, 62.
[10]See, for example, Collingham 2012 on famine and the Second World War.
[11]Slim 2008, especially chap. 3.
[12]Sheehan 2008, 141; Dyer 2004, 281; Wright 2006, 157; and Tirman 2011, 246.
[13]John Paul II 1993a, no. 4; and John Paul II 1999, no. 11.
[14]Hedges 2002, 168 and 103-04.
[15]For examples, see Hallock 1999, chap. 6; Tirman 2011, chap. 7; Slim 2008, chap. 3; Sheehan 2008, chaps. 3-6; Glenny 2008; Scahill 2008; Hedges 2002; and Spierenburg 2008, 198-200.
[16]Dyer 2004, 154.
[17]Tirman 2011, 105.
[18]Johnson 2004; and Scahill 2008.

[19]Slim 2008, 67-68.

[20]Schwellenbach and Leonnig 2010.

[21]Slim 2008, 60-61.

[22]See Bourke 1999, chap. 6; Grossman 2009, sec. 5; Potts and Hayden 2008; Slim 2008, chap. 2; Diamond, J. 2008; and Anderson 2011.

[23]Pinker 2011, 46.

[24]Sheehan 2008, 130.

[25]Tirman 2011, 252-54.

[26]Erdely 2013.

[27]For details on the range of human rights violations found in war zones, see Slim 2008, chap. 3.

[28]Holmes 1989, 46.

[29]Stillman 2011.

[30]Scahill 2008, 340.

[31]On infanticide/abortion, see Spierenburg 2008, 151; and Meehan 2012. On genocide, see Slim 2008, chap. 3.

[32]John Paul II 1994, nos. 4-5.

[33]Slim 2008, 88-89 and chap. 6.

[34]Sheehan 2008, 101.

[35]Snyder 2010, 174-75.

[36]Tirman 2011, 247-48.

[37]Hallock 1999, 340.

[38]Hallock 1999, 313.

[39]Bourke 1999, 215.

[40]Snyder 2010, 326.

[41]Pinker 2011, 326.

[42]Bourke 1999, 193.

[43]Bourke 1999, 354.

[44]Hassan 2001, 39.

[45]Mayer 2009a, 31 and 132.

[46]Tirman 2011, 228.

[47]See, for example, Grossman 2009, sec. 3; Bourke 1999, chaps. 2 and 5; Hedges 2002, chaps. 4 and 7; and Potts and Hayden 2008.

[48]Bourke 1999, 19.

[49]Bourke 1999, 20.

[50]Hallock 1999, 50.

[51]Scahill 2008, 157.

[52]Bourke 1999, 25.

[53]Slim 2008, 238.

[54]See accounts throughout Slim 2008; Bourke 1999; Hallock 1999; Hedges 2002; Dyer 2004; Snyder 2010; Potts and Hayden 2008; and Sheehan 2008, parts 1 and 2.

[55]Pinker 2011, 45.

[56]Hallock 1999, 233.

[57]Wright 2006, 304.

[58]Hedges 2002, 89.

[59]Bourke 1999, 30.

[60]Ferguson 2006, 152.

[61]John Paul II 1991a, no. 52.

[62]Dyer 2004, 30.

[63]See Grossman 2009; Bourke 1999, chap. 3; Hallock 1999, chap. 3; Dyer 2004,

chap. 2; and Slim 2008, chap. 6.

[64]Grossman 2009, 87.

[65]Hallock 1999, 98.

[66]Grossman 2009, 178 and 128.

[67]Grossman 2009, especially sec. 2; Bourke 1999, chaps. 7-8; Dyer 2004, chap. 1; and Finkel 2009.

[68]Dyer 2004, 255.

[69]Finkel 2009, 117.

[70]See Hallock 1999; Mujica 2011; Grossman 2009; Sherman 2012; and Hedges 2002, chap. 7.

10

Lies and Illusions

As we saw earlier, those who argue for war's necessity claim the mantle of realism, of seeing things as they really are. Contemporary Catholic teaching's neoconservative critics in particular describe their view as rooted in moral and intellectual clarity, in cutting through sentimental delusions by telling hard truths. But, of course, war is a notoriously hazardous environment for truth. John Paul II writes in *Centesimus Annus* that "violence always needs to justify itself through deceit."[1] Few enterprises are as subject to lying about, distorting, or denying reality as war. And its proponents are susceptible to their own particularly potent form of naïve utopianism, continually embracing a false faith in war's power and efficacy.

War unleashes a powerful set of social dynamics that create what Chris Hedges calls a "warped version of reality."[2] Nationalism and militarism drive people into opposing groups where the only way to ensure the unity and security of one's own is to destroy the other. Hermann Goering famously said it is easy to create war frenzy in a population: "All you have to do is tell them they are being attacked and denounce the pacifists for lack of patriotism and exposing the country to danger."[3] Here critical thought and moral complexity give way to stark dichotomies: our collective innocence and virtue against their collective guilt and depravity, our suffering against their atrocities. This is why in addition to terrible violence against persons, war zones around the world see continual streams of propaganda, sweeping proclamations of ethnic or religious superiority, farfetched conspiracy theories, dueling narratives of group victimization, history books hastily rewritten, and evidence of a rival group's very existence destroyed.[4]

Among war's lies, one of the most frequent is what its participants are fighting for. Some leaders do enter wars for genuinely righteous reasons—opposing tyranny or protecting the innocent, for example—even if such reasons cannot make war morally legitimate given its nature, especially the kinds of killing even well-intentioned ones entail. Across human history, however, such wars are the exception. Much more frequent are the ordinary motives of dynastic ambition, territorial expansion, national glory, economic self-interest, balance-of-power maneuvering, or sheer conquest and plunder. Even just war supporters such as Elizabeth Anscombe readily acknowledge that "wars have mostly been mere wickedness on both sides."[5] While such motives usually drive war, the purported cause is almost always more noble: defending justice, upholding freedom, doing God's will, and so on. Pretexts and righteous sounding fictions routinely clothe war's real purposes. Unfortunately, a war's supporters often draft the just war tradition into service to rubber-stamp its moral legitimacy whatever its real motivation. Indeed, one of the oldest criticisms of just war theory is its frequent manipulation by those already intent on war. Erasmus, for example, condemns using the rhetoric of justice, especially implying God's approval, to "second the views of this or that earthly potentate" and provide "the varnish with which they endeavor to disguise their mischievous iniquity."[6]

Myths of the just and noble cause, as well as images of battle's adventure and glory, have long pulled people, especially the young, to war. One of the oldest themes in writing about war by those surviving it is how its horror, suffering, and senseless slaughter expose these notions as tragic illusions. When asked what he would say to a young person considering going to war, one retired U.S. admiral said that "I'd disabuse him of the notion that the military makes anything better" or that "we're going to be a force for uplifting people and the quality of life in the world," since war "exists to kill and destroy," and "everybody is the loser, humanity is the loser."[7] War's leaders always tell the families of those killed that their loved ones did not die in vain, even though there is little other realistic way to view all those human beings chewed up by war's butchery. Over the centuries and all around the globe, the righteous causes proclaimed by war's leaders come and go, while what remains constant is the reality of its mass killing, of death for countless persons with little individual connection to its larger purposes or ultimate impact on its outcomes. Especially tragic is the tendency of leaders to succumb to a "sunk-cost fallacy." Like gamblers afraid to go home with massive losses who bet even more to try to get back ahead, those fighting a senseless war often refuse to stop since doing so will reveal how its victims suffered and died for a folly.[8] Instead, they continue the folly, producing even more pointless victims. Writing about the stalemated First World War, the historian James Sheehan reflects on how national leaders on all sides "were willing to ask their peoples to bear ever greater burdens rather than admit that the burdens they had thus far carried were in vain."[9]

Falsehoods exist not only for war's larger causes. From fabricating body counts to issuing false progress reports to concealing civilian massacres, lies are woven into war's actual conduct as well. During the First World War, the Turkish government referred to its deportation of ethnic Armenians, one element of its genocide against them, as the "restoration of order in the war zone by military measures."[10] After crushing an ethnic Tamil insurgency in a 2009 campaign that included widespread rape, torture, and indiscriminate civilian killing, the Sri Lankan government erected a monument honoring the "humanitarian operation" to "restore the noble peace," and a government official said, "I can assure you that no Sri Lankan soldier deliberately killed a civilian."[11] On March 16, 1968, the U.S. military issued a routine daily press briefing that included this item: "In an action today, Americal Division forces killed 128 enemy near Quang Ngai City." This was the official account of what the world would come to know a year later as the My Lai massacre, in which hundreds of civilians, most of them women, children, and old men, were systematically butchered, some being raped and otherwise tortured first.[12]

As these blatant lies and cover-ups illustrate, war's dishonesty is particularly entrenched around the nature of its killing. If killing is war's central act, there exists a powerful tendency to overlook, minimize, obscure, and deny it.[13] Part of this is evident in how focusing on a war's moral cause, or the danger posed by the enemy, or its larger strategic considerations all deflect attention from the actual business of killing people at its heart. What John Kavanaugh calls the "fatal rationalizing that makes persons expendable for the sake of a supposedly higher goal" effectively removes them from the moral picture.[14] It is also obvious in war's dehumanization of the enemy, which provides a soldier with what Dave Grossman labels a set of "prepackaged denial defense mechanisms" that allow him to deny that he is actually killing another person, but instead that he has just "'engaged' another target." For Grossman, war's euphemisms are telling: "The language of war helps us to deny what war is really about, and in doing so it makes war more palatable." Battles become actions, killing becomes engaging or rendering harmless, and the enemy becomes a target, a threat, a cockroach, a weed, a gook, or a raghead.[15]

War reveals the remarkable ability people have to simply ignore deaths on the enemy side, especially civilian ones. Hedges describes the attitude as "Our dead matter, theirs do not."[16] In his study of civilian casualties in American wars from Korea to Afghanistan, John Tirman finds shockingly little public concern for noncombatant fatalities, including a resistance to even hearing about them. Public opinion data show that even in unpopular conflicts, such as Vietnam, public opposition centers almost entirely on U.S. casualties and a lack of progress in winning. He concludes that war has a certain "epistemology," which contains a remarkable "capacity to forget the carnage" to civilians in other countries, one that is not evident, for example, when it comes to overseas humanitarian disasters such as famine, earthquakes, or tsunamis.[17] Even the enormously popular genre of video games depicting war, which prides itself on its realism, almost never features the civilian killing that represents around half the fatalities in actual wars.[18]

Beyond its outright lies and its silences, war distorts thinking. It creates a false sense of power and safety, pulling its believers into unrealistic visions of what it can accomplish. This is why war's supporters repeatedly overestimate its ability to provide security and a peaceful order. It is why, as John Stoessinger demonstrates in his comparative work on war's origins, leaders continually misjudge their own military might, leading them time and time again into disastrous wars.[19] It is why war planners frequently pursue strategies whose costs clearly outweigh any real military advantage, as was the case, for example, in the cycle of long-range population bombing in Europe during the Second World War.[20] And it is why so many countries divert resources from development, which provides real peace and security for their people, to instead pursue grandiose military ambitions. A prime minister of Pakistan once boasted that his country would equal India's nuclear weapons power even if it meant his people would have to "eat grass."[21]

Exaggerated notions of war's capabilities often slip into a kind of utopianism, the false idea, in John Paul II's words in *Centesimus Annus*, that "the effort to destroy the enemy, confrontation and war itself are factors of progress and historical advancement."[22] From medieval crusaders to today's Islamic jihadists, religious belief in the power of violence to usher in a new age of peace, piety, and unity is an old one. There have long been secular versions of this impulse as well, embodied in the idea, most famously articulated by Woodrow Wilson, that fighting just one more war will, by finally defeating evil, end war itself and give birth to a new world of peace, democracy, and justice.[23] John Howard Yoder writes, "There is no more utopian institution than an idealistic war."[24] This merging of war with naïve idealism even influences those who create its very tools. Developers of new and deadlier weapons—attack submarines, TNT, the machine gun, nuclear arms—routinely cling to the belief that their inventions will be so terrible as to render all future war unthinkable.[25]

It is not that wars are never effective. While John Paul II does say that war "is always a defeat for humanity," some do achieve their narrower aims, be they good or evil.[26] China did successfully annex Tibet in 1951, while the United States did successfully prevent Iraq from annexing Kuwait in 1991. It is important, however, to recognize the limits of war's efficacy as a political tool. Many wars, perhaps even most, end with lots of death and destruction but none of the parties achieving their aims in any significant way, and even in cases where some parties do get what they want from a war, other parties obviously do not. Add up these possible outcomes, and we can see that parties experiencing failure in war far outnumber those experiencing success. War's success rate is fairly low. And a large, powerful military does not necessarily improve the odds either. It actually increases the likelihood of getting into more, rather than fewer, wars, and sheer military might has no impact on the chances of success in war, as the globe's two Cold War superpowers learned in Vietnam and Afghanistan.[27] Costa Rica abolished its military over a half-century ago and has since enjoyed more peace, prosperity, and democratic stability than its more militarized neighbors.[28]

Looking at its long-term impact, war's effectiveness is even more doubtful. Unintended consequences, military blowback, and new grievances are regular features of even seemingly successful wars. The wounds of the First World War led directly to the Second, not just in the harsh reparations imposed on Germany, but in how the war weakened law and order, undermined democracy, and replaced common decency and civic virtue with a culture of violence, division, and resentment that paved the way for new militarized regimes. Of course, the resulting Second World War immediately set up the Cold War, which included a U.S.-supported insurgency war against the Soviets in Afghanistan, which, in turn, gave birth to the Taliban, Osama bin Laden, and new invasions justified by a war on terror.[29] Many of today's civil wars from Africa to the Middle East to Asia are a direct result of colonial wars that welded a variety of regions and cultural groups into new artificial states. Such links run throughout the history of warfare all around the world. Taken by itself, each individual war is horrible enough, but viewed through a larger lens, we can see how wars become linked in persistent cycles of violence, the cumulative effect of which is an even more widespread and continuing assault on peace, security, and order. This is why the cycle of conflict is such a recurring theme in Catholic teaching about war, from Paul VI's rejecting "the force of arms" because "violence always provokes violence and irresistibly engenders new forms of oppression and enslavement," to John Paul II's accurately predicting at the start of the first U.S. war against Iraq in 1991 that "a peace obtained by arms could only prepare new acts of violence."[30]

The narrative is depressingly familiar. War's supporters accuse its opponents, those who urge alternatives to war, of being unrealistic. The

values at stake—peace, order, security, freedom, God's will—can only be
defended by force of arms. Now is not the time for half-measures. War
is the only effective option; any alternatives are doomed to fail. But the
comparison here is rigged. It demands certainty of success from war's
alternatives, while ignoring its own poor record. This is so, even though,
as we will see in the book's final section, the alternatives themselves
usually have better success rates than war. Those who reject war are
the true realists. Like every pope in the last half-century, they recognize
war's myopia, its distorted view of reality. They see its fabrications and
denials, its false certainties of success, and the long-range harm its cycle
of violence does to the very values it wrongly claims to protect.

$$* \quad * \quad *$$

Modern American militarism provides a good illustration of war's lies
and illusions in action.[31] In the decades since the Second World War,
the U.S. military has grown to become the dominant force in American
foreign policy. Accounting for half of the globe's total military spending,
it has troops permanently based in the majority of countries around the
world. It enjoys undisputed superiority in the air and on the high seas. It
is the largest supplier of weapons and military training to other nations
(of the nine countries involved in the bloody central African wars that began in 1998, eight were recipients of American military weapons and/or
training).[32] It controls an enormous international infrastructure of bases,
equipment, supply lines, and communications, as well as supporting a
vast network of private weapons manufacturers, security contractors,
and civilian workers. The Pentagon is the world's largest office building.

According to Andrew Bacevich, as "global military supremacy" has
"become central to our national identity," we as Americans have become
"beguiled" by the myth of our military's righteous power in the world.[33]
Whether in political rhetoric, movies, video games, sporting events, or
television advertising, celebrating a fusion of nationalism and military
might is ubiquitous. Indeed, in public life, patriotism is almost never
mentioned without some connection to the military. Public opinion
research finds Americans are far more supportive of war as a way to
solve international problems than Europeans, and among Americans,
the more people identify with their own racial or ethnic group, and
hold stereotypes about nongroup members, the more likely they are to
support warfare abroad and the less likely they are to express concern
about civilian casualties in such wars.[34]

Bound up with this celebration of war-making prowess are powerful
images of the nation's fundamental innocence and goodness in the world.

Our military defends freedom and justice. Our motives are honorable. We only go to war when our hand is forced. Of course, some American leaders are motived by such noble causes, but more often they are rhetorical cover for less lofty motives. Like many other countries through history, the United States uses armed force or its threat to increase its national power, check potential adversaries, guarantee favorable access to resources, and serve influential economic interests. For Bacevich, militarism offers Americans a sentimentalized story to obscure the reality of a military policy "having less to do with national defense than with imperial policing." It allows the country to believe its soldiers are "bringing peace and light to troubled corners of the earth rather than pushing ever outward the perimeter of an American empire."[35] Myths of American military innocence also allow the public to ignore or diminish the ugly effects of overseas wars, especially civilian casualties and human rights abuses by American forces or their proxies.[36]

The language of protecting the country's security and ideals against looming danger is central to another of militarism's deceptions. Rather than a way to defend against existing threats, maintaining such a large and powerful war-making capacity means continually finding threats sufficient to justify its existence. Military might becomes an end in itself. Like any large bureaucracy with influential political and corporate allies, the military has a long tradition of capturing greater power and resources.[37] Patriotic appeals to support the troops, pumping up external threats, inaccurate or outright false intelligence data, and covering up cost overruns or poor performance by new weapons systems are all routine in this process. The end of the Cold War was an especially creative time for American militarism, as its proponents tried out various rationales for maintaining global military dominance, finally settling on terrorism in the wake of the September 11 attacks, even though it presents a very different kind of adversary from the Soviet Union.[38]

The war against Iraq is an excellent example of American militarism's falsehoods at work. The Bush administration and its supporters offered an array of justifications, usually shifting as each become untenable, but the false assertions and insinuations about Iraqi weapons of mass destruction and ties to terror networks involved in the September 11 attacks were the centerpiece. Some of these claims were substantiated by fabrications secured under torture, itself a policy based on fanciful legal reasoning, secret memos, outright lies, and insidious euphemisms such as "enhanced interrogation."[39] Powerful images of imminent danger, protecting American ideals, and vengeance for September 11 drove support for the war. The war's critics faced demands to trust the government, which was said to have secret information it couldn't release due to national security, as well as the usual charges of being naïve or unpatriotic. A parade of former generals appearing in the media as independent analysts were, unknown to viewers, actually employed by defense contractors and fed talking points by the war's planners.[40] Private firms that were engaged in war profiteering and mercenary work used the rhetoric of patriotism and protecting freedom to cover their misdeeds, including atrocities against civilians, and they euphemistically named their lobbying arm the "International Peace Operations Association."[41] The military refused to collect data on civilian casualties and discredited attempts by independent groups to do so. A survey of the American public four years into the war, when hundreds of thousands of Iraqis had already died, revealed most people estimated Iraqi deaths at fewer than ten thousand.[42] And the war's pretexts, especially that it was somehow fought to defend American freedom, continued to shape public views about those fighting in it. One unit received a football from back home with the words "You're my hero" and "Kill some towel heads" written on it, a wounded soldier received a photo of an entire youth football team yelling "Freedom!," and a top Pentagon official told soldiers who had lost limbs that they had given them "as gifts to your nation. That we might live in freedom."[43]

A hallmark of American militarism is its undue faith in war's power and effectiveness. Its proponents often blandly dismiss resources spent on alternatives to war as a waste, even while demanding massive investments in the armed forces, including on weapons systems that prove to be enormously expensive boondoggles.[44] In the wake of the September 11 attacks, the Bush administration quickly concluded that its cause was America's being too soft, of projecting weakness, and the answer must be an overwhelming military response. In President Bush's words, "We will build our defenses beyond challenge, lest weakness invite challenge."[45] Dismissing international law, diplomacy, multilateral peacemaking efforts, and traditional policing as feeble and amounting to appeasement, U.S. policy was to use the only language the administration believed the Muslim world understood: decisive armed force.[46] This response, a form of what Bacevich calls "military activism" and the belief in war as an "all-purpose tool" for decisively solving international problems, is a clear example of militarism's utopianism.[47] President Bush stated his goal in responding to September 11 was to "rid the world of evil," and he described his choice of confrontation over negotiation with countries such as North Korea as an exercise in moral clarity, while Vice President Cheney said, "We don't negotiate with evil, we defeat it."[48]

An almost magical belief in war's ability to defeat evil, create democracy, and ensure security drove the country's response to the September

11 attacks. Its methods were, in the words of Fred Kaplan, "based not on a grasp of technology, history, or foreign cultures but rather on fantasy, faith, and a willful indifference toward those affected by their consequences."[49] In fact, methods such as war, military occupation, and torture are far less effective in defeating terrorism and ushering in democracy abroad than their alternatives.[50] A fixation on overwhelming military force, one that considers its alternatives tantamount to appeasement, has long led nations into wars much longer, more destructive, and less effective than they anticipated.[51] The invasion of Iraq in particular reveals how an unrealistic belief in war's power, in its ability to achieve a quick and easy transformation of another country, or in the outcome that its citizens would welcome American troops as liberators, left war planners appallingly unprepared for the chaos, disorder, and violence that engulfed the country in the invasion's wake. Even less well-known actions confirm this pattern. In 2006, a U.S.-encouraged and supported invasion of Somalia by Ethiopian troops in the name of fighting terrorism only managed to plunge the country into even deeper turmoil and violence.[52] Decades of heavy-handed military intervention in the Middle East, only accelerated after September 11, has had disastrous blowback effects—creating intense hostility to the United States, feeding terrorism, and sparking ongoing cycles of armed conflict.[53] Osama bin Laden and Saddam Hussein were only the most famous former military allies of the United States. One Afghan warlord, Gulbuddin Hekmatyar, who American troops are fighting in the country's ongoing insurgency, was a key American ally during the 1980s, one notorious for slowly skinning alive captured Soviet soldiers and who shelled civilian neighborhoods in Kabul with U.S.-supplied weapons after the Soviet pullout.[54] The Taliban itself arose as a movement of young orphans, amputees, and victims of theft, beatings, and rapes in the chaos unleashed by the Afghan civil war.[55]

If American militarism represents a deeply dishonest and distorted view of war, it is thanks in large part to its intellectual champions, the scholars, military strategists, and political activists who have worked hard to develop its arguments and rationales over the last several decades.[56] Among these are many of the neoconservative critics of Catholic doctrine on war, thinkers long dedicated to giving the veneer of religious sanction and just war legitimacy to the country's military adventures. As we saw in chapter 5, they emphasize the power of a globally dominant U.S. military, used frequently and aggressively, to champion freedom, peace, and justice in the world. The world's problems are caused by too little rather than too much American military action. They believe weakness invites attack, and defeating evil, from the Soviets during the Cold War to jihadism today, requires military resolve rather than the appeasement and anti-Americanism represented by those supporting multilateral cooperation, international law, and global institutions such as the United Nations. They write a great deal about war, but almost never about its actual killing, except to warn against badgering national leaders with hand wringing about civilian casualties.

George Weigel, for example, made his name as a steadfast supporter of military action against communism in places such as Latin America, continually ignoring the actual devastating impact American proxy wars had on social order, human rights, and civilian lives in that region.[57] The end of the Cold War found him worrying about how to maintain unilateral military assertiveness around the globe.[58] And the September 11 attacks led him quickly to advocate a comprehensive and aggressive military answer.[59] Catholic teaching's neoconservative critics were among the staunchest defenders of the Bush administration's strategic response to September 11, including its falsehoods and distorted thinking. Mark Thiessen defended torturing suspects, duly repeating the preferred euphemisms and arguing that the intent of torturers was not to hurt the suspects but to "safely help the terrorist do his duty to Allah, so he then feels liberated to speak freely."[60] Weigel's defense of the Iraq invasion continually conflated Saddam Hussein, weapons of mass destruction, and terrorist networks responsible for the September 11 attacks.[61] He argued that the invasion was necessary to ensure peace around the world and that it would bring the Iraqi people specifically the "peace of order, justice and freedom."[62] Richard John Neuhaus saw the war as the vehicle for "changing the politics and culture of the Middle East."[63]

And when this faith in the power of war met the reality of postinvasion Iraq? The response of the war's enthusiasts was largely silence.[64] To the extent that Weigel has reflected on the war's failures in the years following, it has been to minimize the postinvasion chaos and violence and to blame any problems that did occur on the war's not killing enough potential opponents in its initial phase, on underestimating the lack of respect for human life among Muslims, on poor intelligence, and on countries that opposed the war refusing to help fight it.[65] On his account, the real problem was that the United States lost the public relations game, allowing anti-American media to spread disinformation about the war's aftermath. For example, he mentions the notorious torture at Abu Ghraib prison but only to condemn a Turkish film for using it as anti-Semitic propaganda.[66] Weigel also continues to portray the war's critics as feckless and morally confused, and to defend it as necessary given the threat posed by the Iraqi regime, weapons of mass destruction, and terrorism. In 2006, he wrote that "no serious person" can doubt the ties between Iraq and "al-Qaeda terrorists."[67]

Neoconservative critics of Catholic doctrine on war pride themselves on their moral realism, even as they buy into war's lies and illusions of power. But it is the target of their critique, today's Catholic teaching, that has become more realistic. As it has moved to condemn war more forcefully, it has seen through war's deceptions and false promises more clearly. The U.S. Bishops call John Paul II's powerful denunciations of war an example of his "cold realism" about its true nature.[68] In recognizing war's terrible suffering and destruction, how it undermines rather than protects order, peace, and security, Catholic teaching has done much to unmask it. It only remains for this development in Catholic doctrine to close even the small space for morally legitimate war it still recognizes, matching its calls for war's abolition with a consistent rejection of all war as always and everywhere unjust.

Notes

[1] John Paul II 1991a, no. 23.
[2] Hedges 2002, 63.
[3] Gilbert 1947, 279.
[4] See, for example, Hedges 2002, especially chaps. 1-3; and Sheehan 2008, chaps. 3-6.
[5] Anscombe 1970, 44.
[6] Erasmus 1972, 18-19.
[7] Hallock 1999, 86.
[8] Pinker 2011, 219; and Hauerwas 2011, chap. 5.
[9] Sheehan 2008, 70.
[10] Bourke 2006, 29.
[11] Anderson 2011, 50 and 53.
[12] Kaplan 2011, 9.
[13] Grossman 2009.
[14] Kavanaugh 2001, 116.
[15] Grossman 2009, 257, 91-92. See also Bourke 2006, 27-32.
[16] Hedges 2002, 14.
[17] Tirman 2011, 121. See also Slim 2008, 248-50; and Bourke 1999, chap. 6.
[18] Thomsen 2011.
[19] Stoessinger 2005.
[20] Potts and Hayden 2008, 222-29.
[21] Dyer 2004, 426.
[22] John Paul II 1991a, no. 18.
[23] Howard 2008.
[24] Yoder 1992a, 76.
[25] Potts and Hayden 2008, 221.
[26] John Paul II 2003b.
[27] Biddle 2004; Ringsmose 2008; and Dyer 2004, 290.
[28] Fry 2007, 18-20.
[29] See, for example, Sheehan 2008, especially chaps. 3-6; and Wright 2006.
[30] Paul VI 1975, no. 37; and John Paul II 1991b.
[31] For overviews of contemporary American militarism, see Bacevich 2005; Johnson 2004; Boggs 2005; and Kaplan 2008.

[32]Kolbert 2011, 78.

[33]Bacevich 2005, 1 and 53.

[34]Kinder and Kam 2009, chap. 4; Potts and Hayden 2008, 352-53; and Sheehan 2008, xv-xvi.

[35]Bacevich 2005, 97-98.

[36]Boggs 2005, chap. 5; and Tirman 2011.

[37]See, for example, Dyer 2004, chaps. 8-9; Kaplan 2008, chap. 3; and Johnson 2004, chap. 3.

[38]Johnson 2004 and Bacevich 2005 are especially good here. See also Mueller 2006.

[39]Mayer 2009a, especially 135-38.

[40]Barstow 2008.

[41]Scahill 2008, 406.

[42]Tirman 2011, 255. See also Osborn 2011.

[43]Finkel 2009, 268, 213, and 202.

[44]Bacevich 2005, 216-17.

[45]Johnson 2004, 63.

[46]Mayer 2009a; and Geltzer 2009.

[47]Bacevich 2005, 166 and 19. See also Kaplan 2008.

[48]Pinker 2011, 360; and Kaplan 2008, 64-65 and 171.

[49]Kaplan 2008, 191.

[50]See, for example, Stephan and Chenoweth 2008; Chenoweth and Stephan 2011; Jones and Libicki 2008; Pape and Feldman 2010; and Mayer 2009a. We will explore the effectiveness of alternatives to war more fully in section IV.

[51]Morgan 2006, chap. 4. See also Yoder 1992a, 45-48.

[52]Anderson 2009.

[53]See, for example, Bacevich 2005, chap. 7; Wright 2006; and Tirman 2011.

[54]Crowley 2010.

[55]Wright 2006, 255-57 and 302-03.

[56]Kaplan 2008; and Bacevich 2005.

[57]Weigel 1987; Pfeil 2007; and Tirman 2011, chap. 6.

[58]Bacevich 2005, 81.

[59]Weigel 2001.

[60]Thiessen 2009. See also Thiessen 2010, chap. 6.

[61]See, for example, Weigel 2003a and how the three are consistently linked, explicitly and implicitly, throughout the essay.

[62]Weigel 2003a, 24; and Weigel 2003b, 10.

[63]Neuhaus 2003, 79.

[64]Dula 2004.

[65]Weigel 2007, 82-84, 87, and 91.

[66]Weigel 2006, 41-42; and Weigel 2007, 49-50.

[67]Weigel 2006, 37-39.

[68]United States Conference of Catholic Bishops 1983, no. 255. See also Hehir 1992, 249-50.

SECTION III

ABOLISHING INSTITUTIONALIZED VIOLENCE

11

War as an Institution

Why are war's lies so effective, its false claims to ensure peace, order, and security so convincing? Because they exist in a culture shaped by habitual acceptance of war itself. War is a form of what the Catholic tradition calls "structures of sin."[1] Sin is always rooted in the actions of individuals, but these can be shaped by "the social circumstances in which they live and are immersed from their birth."[2] How individual persons think and behave can, in the words of John Paul II, be "conditioned, incited and influenced by numerous and powerful external factors," what the *Catechism* calls "social situations and institutions."[3] Usually associated in Catholic doctrine with systemic poverty and political oppression, structural sin also includes those beliefs and practices that drive nations into violent conflict and help create a "culture of death," one that leads individuals to unquestioningly accept killing the innocent in the name of some good deemed more important.[4]

Structural sin operates through the power of social institutions to mold individual thought and action. In her groundbreaking work on such institutions, Mary Douglas demonstrates the extent to which they influence "the individual's most elementary cognitive process."[5] They shape how we categorize and make sense of the world around us—what we remember and forget, what we accept as important and discard as irrelevant, what behaviors we consider normal, acceptable, or reasonable. In furnishing established patterns of knowledge and ways of acting, institutions influence what individuals in different times and places, from scientists to moralists to ordinary people, consider self-evidently real, or right, or plain common sense, even if to outsiders such beliefs seem absurd. The ability of institutions to create a just-the-way-things-are impression is rooted in their use of "self-validating truth," their appeal to the fixed nature of the universe or God or the human condition.[6] Douglas shows how entrenched social institutions ground their legitimacy in reason and in nature, how when challenged they respond by claiming their view of reality is confirmed by "the nature of the universe" or the way humans just "naturally behave."[7]

War is a social institution of this kind. It rests on a powerful set of understandings, roles, and actions accepted as reasonable and natural by large numbers of people. It is a cultural default position. That war is sometimes necessary, morally legitimate, and the only effective way to protect what we value is taken for granted. To deny such common-sense statements is unrealistic, foolish, and utopian.[8] War's power as a social institution is revealed by how little the inconsistency between the values it claims to uphold its actual consequences undermines its legitimacy. Commenting on the tendency of human beings to kill in the name of protecting life, destroy in the name of protecting security, and plunder in the name of protecting order, Erasmus writes, "Who could believe that creatures so engaged were men, if the frequency of the sight had not blunted its effect on our feelings, and prevented surprise?"[9] It is a hallmark of powerful social institutions that from the inside their absurdities and contradictions have little impact on their legitimacy. As we will see in the next several chapters, it is only after such institutions decline or end entirely that most people look back and ask how such ideas and behavior could ever have been accepted.

Like most unjust social institutions, war claims that it is a natural and unavoidable consequence of the human condition. Civil War general William Sherman claimed that objecting to war made as much sense as an "appeal against the thunderstorm" since they are both "inevitable."[10] In his Nobel Peace Prize speech, President Obama said, "War, in one form or another, appeared with the first man."[11] Echoing this view, Khalid Sheikh Mohammed, the primary planner of the September 11 attacks, once said in his broken English, "War start from Adam when Cain he killed Abel until now. It's never gonna stop killing of people."[12] This is false. Humanity is not doomed to war by original sin, biology, evolution, a psychological death instinct, or any other inexorable force.[13] War is, as Margaret Mead famously put it, an invention. Like writing or burying the dead or jury trials, it hasn't always been part of human existence. For war to happen, the idea of it must be present, an idea that for Mead "is as essential to really carrying on war as an alphabet or a syllabary is to writing."[14] Wars cannot just spontaneously break out, any more than formal duels or owning slaves can. Each of these requires a cultural context in which it is accepted—a system of rules or laws, recognized roles, mental concepts, and patterns of behavior in which it makes sense, one that facilitates the complex planning and coordination it requires to carry out. Indeed, as John Keegan observes, social organization and discipline are so important to war precisely because it is intentionally marching toward the enemy and fighting to the death in massed groups that "defies nature."[15] For war to work, it needs to be institutionalized, and institutions don't happen spontaneously. They are invented, shaped, and sustained over time.

None of this is to say that war is not firmly rooted in human history. It is an invented social institution, but one that has been very common for a long time. For most of our existence, well over 95 percent in fact, human beings lived in small and relatively egalitarian hunter-gather bands. While firm conclusions about life during this period are obviously difficult to draw, and opinions among anthropologists and archaeologists vary, it is likely that some level of interpersonal violence was common, even as a range of nonlethal dispute resolution techniques helped control it. Such groups, however, lacked the level of social organization necessary for warfare as such. War began to emerge about 10000 to 12000 A.C.E. with growing social complexity. Larger tribes and chiefdoms developed patterns of prestate warfare—raiding parties, small-scale but frequent pitched battles, kin-based militias—that characterized many isolated prestate peoples even up into the contemporary period. Evidence indicates that this form of warfare, on a per capita basis, has likely been more lethal than even more modern forms. War evolved further with the earliest agriculture-based states—developing fortifications, professional armies, and phalanx-infantry tactics—as well as among nomadic pastoralists—developing the compound bow, long-range campaigning, and cavalry tactics.[16]

Like other social inventions—cooking meat, growing crops, fashioning certain tools—war spread to other groups. Not only did adopting it hold out the promise of more territory or mates or food in times of scarcity, but not adopting it left a group vulnerable to others nearby that had. Security dilemmas and arms races go back a long way. Even with this pressure to adopt warfare, however, there are plenty of groups, ancient and modern, who have either never engaged in it or who have given up their former warlike ways, even when surrounded by neighbors not so inclined.[17] From the !Kung to the Jains to the Swiss, there are communities that survive without engaging in war.

While war's development through human history has been driven largely by utility—technology and tactics designed to gain military advantages—as an institution it also retains what Keegan calls its "ritualism and ceremonialism."[18] Customs about how wars are fought have varied widely from culture to culture, and merely defeating the enemy is often not the only goal. Other objectives include demonstrating group pride, capturing prisoners for later religious sacrifice, proving one's valor in single combat, or initiating young males into manhood. Sometimes technology promising a military advantage is even rejected as inconsistent with customary notions of proper behavior in war, as when

Japanese combatants refused to use firearms for several centuries after they became available.[19] And, as we have seen, war frequently takes on an institutional momentum all its own, as groups or nations fight wars as if by habit, even though what they are actually contesting is unclear, or the costs to both will far outweigh any gains.[20]

Human beings are capable of war because we are capable of violence, but the latter does not make the former inevitable. Our capacity for violence, like our capacity for nonviolence, and a host of other capacities for that matter, are flexible and adaptable enough to be shaped in critical ways by our environments.[21] Social institutions are what transform the variety of things we are capable of into accepted and coordinated cultural practices, and such institutions are subject to change. Even the most powerful are not set in stone; they can be adjusted, radically transformed, or completely eliminated, leaving behind new institutionalized ways of thinking and behaving. This is why, as Douglas writes, "Rules that now seem to us moderns as monstrously unjust did not strike our forebears as wrong."[22] It is also why the Catholic tradition's concept of structural sin holds open the possibility of improvement—not by hoping to abolish all sin, but by diminishing or eliminating certain structural manifestations of it, by acting, in the words of John Paul II, to "destroy such structures and replace them with more authentic forms of living in community."[23] Abolishing war does not mean abolishing all violence, only war's particular way of institutionalizing it. This doesn't make it easy by any means, but it does make it possible. And recognizing the possibility is a crucial first step. The anthropologist Douglas Fry writes, "Widespread beliefs that war is natural and acceptable hinder the search for alternatives—and thus the inevitability of war becomes a self-fulfilling prophecy."[24]

Fortunately, we have examples of other forms of long-established and deeply entrenched institutionalized violence that humanity has dismantled. Like war, many of these were once considered an inevitable result of human nature, especially human sinfulness. Like war, they were once deemed necessary to ensure security, protect the innocent, and uphold a just and peaceful social order. Like war, their critics were dismissed as unrealistic, foolish, utopian, and dangerous. That today most people consider them so clearly wrong, and arguments on their behalf so clearly ridiculous, should give us hope that war too will someday join them.

Notes

[1]See John Paul II 1987, nos. 16, 36-37, and 39; John Paul II 1984, no. 16; Paul VI 1975, nos. 29 and 36; *Catechism of the Catholic Church* 1994, no. 1869; John Paul II 1991a, no. 38; Brady 2008, chap. 8; Dorr 1983, 202-03; and Gumbleton 1991.

[2]Second Vatican Council 1965, no. 25.

[3]John Paul II 1984, no. 16; and *Catechism of the Catholic Church* 1994, no. 1869.

[4]John Paul II 1987, no. 37; and John Paul II 1995a, no. 12.

[5]Douglas 1986, 45.

[6]Douglas 1986, 48.

[7]Douglas 1986, 45-47.

[8]Cady 1989, preface and chap. 1.

[9]Erasmus 1972, 16-17.

[10]Slim 2008, 25.

[11]Obama 2009.

[12]McDermott 2010, 38.

[13]Horgan 2012.

[14]Mead 2006, 219.

[15]Keegan 1993, 251 and 266.

[16]Fry 2007; LeBlanc and Register 2003; Horgan 2012; Potts and Hayden 2008; Keegan 1993; and Dyer 2004.

[17]Fry 2007, especially chap. 2 and appendix 2; and LeBlanc and Register 2003, chap. 8.

[18]Keegan 1993, 175. See also Dyer 2004, chap. 5.

[19]Keegan 1993, 40-46.

[20]LeBlanc and Register 2003, 209; and Dyer 2004, 350-55.

[21]Fry 2007; Malinowski 2006; and LeBlanc and Register 2003, chap. 8.

[22]Douglas 1986, 114.

[23]John Paul II 1991a, no. 38. See also Second Vatican Council 1965, nos. 53-55 and 73; Paul VI 1975, no. 36; and Benedict XVI 2009a, no. 78.

[24]Fry 2007, 201.

12

Trial by Ordeal and Combat

For centuries in medieval and early modern Europe, judicial proceedings regularly revolved around rituals that today seem absurd. In ordeals, accused people protesting their innocence would plunge their arms in boiling water, be thrown into lakes or rivers, wrap their hands around molten iron, or walk barefoot across red-hot ploughshares. In judicial combat, parties to a dispute would fight it out, often to the death, under the watchful eyes of governing officials and community members.[1]

The ordeal spread through Europe alongside Christianity, becoming widely adopted by the ninth century. Its heyday lasted through the thirteenth century, though witchcraft trials continued to use some forms of it for several centuries more. While not as universal, trial by combat developed in many parts of Europe as early as the sixth century and lasted well into the sixteenth, an impressive thousand-year run. Both were around for as long or longer than many judicial procedures we take for granted today, such as jury trials.

The ordeal and judicial combat were parts of a formal institutional structure overseen by both secular and religious authorities. Trials also included testimony from witnesses, elaborate sworn oaths, and, in later years, written evidence. Both rituals responded to the universal problem in judicial proceedings of not always knowing who is telling the truth, seeking to overcome this problem by calling on the omniscient judgment of God. In 501 C.E., the king of the Burgundians instituted trial by combat in his realm, claiming "it being just that every man should be ready to defend with his sword the truth which he attests, and to submit himself to the judgment of heaven."[2] Ordeals used water and fire, both Christian symbols of purification and punishing evil, especially water's association with the Great Flood and fire's association with Hell. Before ordeals and combats began, priests recited solemn prayers asking God to intervene and thereby reveal the guilt or innocence of the parties. A typical one read,

O God, the just judge, who are the author of peace and give fair judgement, we humbly pray you to deign to bless and sanctify this fiery iron, which is used in the just examination of doubtful issues. If this man is innocent of the charge from which he seeks to clear himself, he will take this fiery iron in his hand and appear unharmed; if he is guilty, let your most just power declare that truth in him, so that wickedness may not conquer justice but falsehood always be overcome by the truth. Through Christ.[3]

Determining God's verdict was fairly straightforward in judicial combat: the winning party had obviously enjoyed God's protection in the fight and was thereby vindicated. Ordeals could be more complicated. In boiling water or hot iron versions, sometimes an immediate absence of obvious pain or physical damage was enough to indicate God's favor, but usually the accused's burns would have to be inspected some days later, often three, to see if they were healing well, signifying innocence, or had become worse or infected, meaning guilt. In versions where the accused were thrown into bodies of water, floating indicated guilt since the water's purity would not receive them, while sinking meant innocence (every effort was made to pull them out before drowning). What counted as floating or sinking could be tricky, however, and this gave those watching more latitude to interpret exactly what God was saying.

All social classes participated in trials by ordeal or combat, though combat usually involved only members of roughly equal social status. Detailed legal codes specified their use for a full range of crimes and disputes, including murder, theft, heresy, witchcraft, treason, property ownership, paternity, adultery, and fraud. A Norwegian law stated that "if a man is charged with having carnal dealings with cattle of any sort, which is forbidden to all Christians, the bailiff shall bring action against him with witnesses to the fact of common rumour; and let him carry the hot iron or go into outlawry."[4] Some statutes allowed parties, especially women or nobility, to appoint champions—usually relatives, retainers, or servants—to participate on their behalf. The Thuringian region of Germany, for example, specified that if "a woman is accused of killing her husband by poison," then "let the woman's nearest relative prove her innocence in battle, or, if she has no champion, let her be sent to trial by the nine red-hot ploughshares."[5]

There were also detailed regulations as to how ordeals and judicial combat would be carried out—for example, the number of steps the accused had to carry hot iron; the number of days before inspecting wounds; the types of weapons used in combat; and provisions for participants who were blind, lame, or elderly. Much attention was devoted to making sure participants did not cheat through enchantment or mur-

muring magic incantations. In order to equal the playing field in judicial combat, a rule in Denmark specified that when a man faced a woman, the man would stand waist deep in a pit and use a club, while the woman had freedom of movement and used a stone bound in a leather sling.[6] Sometimes officials had to get creative. In a famous French case, when a dog, the only eyewitness to a murder, accused a man on the street by wildly barking and attacking him, the king decided to settle the matter through trial by combat between the man, armed with a lance, and the dog. The dog won.[7]

* * *

Like war, recourse to trial by ordeal or combat was ideally a last resort. Given the suffering involved, they were necessary only when other methods had failed. One twelfth-century English statute held that "the ordeal of hot iron is not to be permitted except where the naked truth cannot otherwise be explored."[8] A century later in Catalonia, trial by combat procedure specified that "if the accuser can prove his charge through authentic charters or through trustworthy witness, then that proof should be admitted and the battle should not be adjudged . . . men have recourse to the judgment of God only when human proof fails."[9]

The accused themselves frequently saw trial by ordeal or combat as the best way to clear their names. A priest charged with treason in 991 C.E. stated his case for innocence and said that "if any of you doubt this and think I am not worthy of belief, then believe the fire, the boiling water, the glowing iron."[10] As with war, these methods were considered necessary for protecting the innocent and providing the only effective means of self-defense under certain circumstances.

Also like war, the legitimacy of the ordeal and judicial combat rested on the view that they were essential to a peaceful and secure order. At the level of commoners, ordeals were most often used to test the truthfulness of strangers, serfs, and social outcasts. An English law referred to its being most appropriate for "the foreigner or friendless man."[11] Those distrusted the most, seen as most threatening to the established social order, experienced it most often. At the noble level, ordeals and trials by combat were most often used to settle questions of treason, broken truces, and the paternity of royal heirs—all matters with grave national security implications. Both were tools of state to protect the realm from its enemies, foreign and domestic.

In a world where sinful human beings will inevitably lie and break faith for their own advantage, people widely accepted the ordeal and judicial combat as strong deterrents needed by authorities to keep the peace. They were necessary to protect against those, in the words of Otto I, "who do not fear God and are not afraid to perjure themselves, make acquisitions by their oaths with the appearance of legality."[12] This consideration was especially important in efforts to limit the chronic violence of medieval Europe. In spreading the "Peace of God," rules designed to protect clergy and other noncombatants, and the "Truce of God," rules restricting the days on which battles among enemies could take place, religious leaders elicited sworn promises from nobles and their followers to uphold these rules. But given the reality of sin, such oaths were widely considered unreliable without the credible enforcement mechanisms provided by ordeals and judicial combat. According to Robert Bartlett's historical work on trials by ordeal and combat, they were considered indispensable to "meet the apparent danger of a breakdown of law and order" in the period.[13] And not just among nobles. Both were also seen as crucial to keeping all classes honest and law abiding. Some areas even saw a kind of early plea-bargain system emerge in which criminals would escape punishment by agreeing to challenge and fight in judicial combat other criminals and disreputable characters, used as a way to thin the ranks of those most threatening to security and order. As one commentator at the time said approvingly, it "is licit for such accusers to accuse and convict the wicked," to "clean up the land," and "win peace for the faithful."[14]

Criticisms of trial by ordeal and combat were present from their very beginning, often, as Bartlett writes, "echoing virtually all the arguments of later centuries."[15] In 713 c.e., Luitbrand, the King of Lombard, said, "We are not convinced of the justice of what is called the judgment of God, since we have found that many innocent persons have perished in defending a good cause."[16] From quite early, some church leaders, including popes, issued occasional condemnations of both ordeals and judicial combat, centering especially on the hubris of trying to "tempt God" into revealing information. The ninth-century archbishop of Lyon said, "The people should not believe that almighty God wishes to reveal men's secrets in the present life through hot water or iron."[17] Common people too had reasons to doubt. Some ordeals appeared fixed or the judges biased. At times judicial combat seemed to hinge more on the strength and ability of the fighters, including what would eventually become a highly paid class of mercenary champions fighting for those of noble birth, than innocence or guilt. Sometimes known witches would sink while upstanding citizens, volunteering to test the validity of the ordeal, would float.[18]

According to Bartlett, what is remarkable is how little effect such criticisms and doubts had through much of the history of ordeals and judicial combat.[19] Some rulers used them anyway, pointing to their importance to social stability or long-standing tradition. The skeptical Luitbrand, noted above, nonetheless said that "this custom is of such antiquity among the Lombards that we cannot abolish it, notwithstanding its impiety."[20] While some religious authorities had their doubts, most accepted both practices, and a still decentralized church meant even a pope's opposition made little difference. Like early just war theory, complex theological and philosophical investigations produced sophisticated justifications. Proponents pointed to David and Goliath and other biblical passages for support. Attacks on trial by ordeal or combat were widely understood as attacks on religious orthodoxy itself, as well as threats to a crucial guarantor of peace, security, and good order. Clerics were particularly vigilant in defense of the ordeal, in which they played an even more prominent and socially authoritative part than judicial combat.

Echoing the way war's injustices rarely shake popular faith in the righteousness of war itself, most people—common and noble, lay and clergy—did not question the validity of trial by ordeal or combat itself, even when they had misgivings about particular instances. As Bartlett writes of ordeals, "But for the most part, people found ways of retaining belief in the value of the ordeal as an institution even when they doubted its verdict in a given case." Frequently this required strange twists of logic, such as God's actually willing the guilty to pass the test for other reasons, or the innocent person who failed must have been guilty of something else.[21] It is a testament to the power of social institutions to shape thought and behavior that ordeals and judicial combat could be such accepted parts of European life for so many centuries, even as their flaws and contradictions were apparent from their very beginnings.

* * *

So what finally brought down these powerful and long-standing institutions? Why don't we still use ordeals and judicial combat to find the truth in our own judicial procedures, ones that also date back to older European models? Several interconnected factors came together by the thirteenth century to weaken and eventually eliminate both practices. In the religious sphere, the growth of lay confession and penance gave priests a new basis for social influence separate from secular courts. The church was also becoming more centralized, unified, and doctrinally rigorous. This reinforced a growing sense among church authorities that trials by ordeal and combat were sacramentally irregular and a misguided attempt to force God's hand, while at the same time allowing them to exercise more control over their far-flung clergy. While there was some sentiment for reforming these rituals and perhaps limiting the role of clergy in their application, echoing just war arguments to minimize and control armed conflict rather than eliminate it, abolitionists ultimately triumphed in the church. The ordeal, for example, was officially condemned at the Lateran Council of 1215.

The church also worked with secular authorities to suppress trial by ordeal and combat. These authorities were themselves consolidating power around the same time, including exercising greater social control through judicial proceedings. This meant more authority and discretion for judges and less unpredictable participation by litigants or the accused. As standardized courts became more powerful, local norms and traditions became less so. The idea of law was becoming more complex, formal, and specialized. Part of this process was separating it from what was considered the more irrational and superstitious realm of custom, which political and intellectual elites, especially those in the growing towns, increasingly associated with trials by ordeal and combat. Relying on new tools to ascertain truthfulness, the adversarial system, with its lawyers and juries, and the inquisitorial system, with its direct investigation and questioning by judges, both began to take shape at this time. Courts made greater use of written documents and attached more importance to confessions, including those secured under torture, a practice that grew as trial by ordeal and combat shrank.

The ordeal collapsed first and more quickly. From a routine and widely accepted procedure in 1200, it was extremely rare by 1300, used only in the occasional witchcraft trial thereafter before fading away completely. It was especially vulnerable given how dependent it was on religious imagery and participation by clergy. Trial by combat was able to survive somewhat longer without as much clergy participation, especially given how convenient some secular rulers found it to simply let parties to a dispute fight it out. The nobility also resisted its loss more forcefully, seeing judicial combat as a protector of aristocratic freedom and privilege against the centralizing power of monarchs. Even so, trial by combat eventually faded away under similar pressures as the ordeal and was gone by 1600, replaced in some respects by the rise of the duel, which existed outside the formal judicial structure.

So trial by ordeal and combat, forms of institutionalized violence at the heart of European practice for centuries, ones widely accepted as morally legitimate and necessary for self-defense, protecting the innocent, and insuring a peaceful and secure order, were eventually abolished, remembered now mainly as odd features of medieval life ripe for satire. Their abolition was possible because of interconnected changes in both cultural ideas, what people thought reasonable and morally appropriate, and political action, what authorities used their power to enforce. Both kinds of changes came embedded in shifting institutional structures—lay confession, a centralizing church, secular rulers consolidating power, new judicial arrangements and legal doctrines—that shaped how people thought and behaved in different ways. And some of these emerging ways of thinking and acting, such as judicial torture and the duel, were themselves new forms of institutionalized violence.

Notes

[1] This chapter relies primarily on Bartlett 1986; Holland 2003, chap. 1; Kiernan 1988, chap. 3; and Tewksbury 2002.

[2] Holland 2003, 9.

[3] Bartlett 1986, 1.

[4] Bartlett 1986, 19.

[5] Bartlett 1986, 10.

[6] Holland 2003, 10-11.

[7] Holland 2003, 11.

[8] Bartlett 1986, 26.

[9] Bartlett 1986, 109.

[10] Bartlett 1986, 14.

[11] Bartlett 1986, 32.

[12] Bartlett 1986, 105-06.

[13] Bartlett 1986, 51.

[14] Bartlett 1986, 113.

[15] Bartlett 1986, 75.

[16] Holland 2003, 10.

[17] Bartlett 1986, 72.

[18] Tewksbury 2002, 387.

[19] Bartlett 1986, 70.

[20] Holland 2003, 10.

[21] Bartlett 1986, 77-78.

The Duel

In 1765, Lord Byron, the famous poet's great-uncle, had dinner with a neighbor, argued with him about who had more rabbits on his estate, challenged him to a duel, and killed him.[1] Such a shocking method of resolution was anything but at the time; for a span of four hundred years in Europe and elsewhere, such actions were both common and widely accepted as legitimate, even obligatory, under certain conditions.[2]

While many cultures across human history have developed ritualized versions of one-on-one fighting, the modern duel arose in Italy in the sixteenth century, quickly spread across Europe, moved to other parts of the world with colonialism, and lasted into the early twentieth century. It grew partly out of earlier trials by ordeal and tournaments pitting knights against each other in single combat, but the duel also had deep roots in medieval understandings of when it was acceptable to kill another person.

Europe during the middle ages and early modern period was marked by high levels of interpersonal violence, much of it driven by an honor ethic demanding that males react to insults with a physical response, especially those touching on their strength, courage, and honesty, or on the sexual virtue of women under their protection. Honor and the willingness to defend it with physical violence were one and the same. As the historian Pieter Spierenburg details, there existed a widely understood distinction between such "honorable" killing, which was publicly visible, and "infamous" killing, which was secret and usually related to some other crime such as theft. This is why even when cases of killing for honor came to trial, acquittal was common, as, for example, when "jurors accorded self-defense to men who had stabbed to death an unarmed opponent for insulting them or grabbing them by the beard."[3]

The primary bridge between this understanding of legitimate killing and the rise of the duel was the vendetta. Ongoing feuds between families, neighborhood factions, and other social groups were common, at times endemic, in medieval and early modern Europe. They are what produced so many of the forts and towers still visible in towns and cities across the continent today. Vendettas might start over petty insults, land disputes, or broken marriage arrangements, but they could last for generations after the initial cause, taking on a momentum of their own where revenge for previous killings become the justification for future ones. It was not unusual to put off vengeance until a victim's young son grew to manhood and could even the score by killing the now much older offender himself or a member of his family. A key feature of vendettas was that their killing was open and public, designed to send a message that one's side had satisfied the demands of revenge and restored honor. Killing members of a rival family or faction on the steps of church Sunday morning or during a religious procession was especially popular. And, unlike the later duel, fair play was not expected. Surprising targets with overwhelming numbers and butchering them without mercy was common.

Vendettas pulled in not just extended families but friends, allies, servants, and retainers. They had, according to Spierenburg, "a broad social base."[4] They were widely believed to be inevitable and necessary to defend the honor and security of one's person, family, and social group. In order to limit their extent and destructiveness, elaborate social rituals, usually organized by women on both sides and featuring feasting, drinking, and oaths, were designed to reconcile participants and make peace. Like war, many conflicts went through cycles of active fighting, truces, mediation, broken agreements, and renewed fighting. For most of the vendetta's heyday, authorities did little to stop it. They were often involved in ongoing feuds themselves, and judicial institutions were too weak and undeveloped to do much anyway.

The vendetta eventually succumbed to the same forces that doomed trial by ordeal and combat. Religious leaders became more outspoken in opposition, and secular authorities gained more effective control over their territories. At first, courts worked alongside existing reconciliation rituals to encourage and enforce private agreements to end feuding, and, echoing just war doctrine, authorities tried to limit vendettas rather than end them, passing regulations on how long they could last or who could participate. In 1448, for example, a law in Zurich required that only close relatives could take part in a vendetta.[5] At the same time, social attitudes were changing. While the need to defend one's honor, with force if necessary, remained, the spectacle of bloody brawls in the streets and one-sided surprise attacks became less acceptable. The importance attached to manners, self-restraint, and fair play was growing. A cycle of greater government suppression and declining social support gradually weakened the vendetta, eliminating it from most parts of Europe by the end of the sixteenth century, though it continued off and on for some time longer in more remote regions that still lacked effective state control.

* * *

As a replacement for the vendetta, the duel still offered a socially approved way to defend against threats to honor with violence, but it avoided the vendetta's more chaotic fighting and dynamic of escalation over time. Its rules varied widely across its history, but the duel's central feature was one-on-one combat between two opponents, armed with the same weapons, and under the supervision of others, either a crowd of onlookers, formal seconds, or both. They were initiated when one party issued a challenge to the other, naming a specific grievance and demanding satisfaction. Sometimes mediators could intervene to head off the duel and satisfy honor with an apology and other ways of making amends, but often fighting was considered the only option.

While males at all levels of society participated in duels, its rules were tied closely to class. They could only be fought among people of roughly equal social standing. So, for example, if a nobleman was insulted by a commoner, the proper response was to have him beaten by retainers rather than fighting a duel. Weapons varied by class, too. Initially, the aristocracy used swords, the middle class swords or staffs, and the lower class knives. Later, pistols became more common among upper- and middle-class duelists. Lower-class duels were more immediate and less elaborate, but they still conformed to certain social conventions. Challenges were usually verbal—the practice of "house scorning," for example, was when a man would stand outside another's house and call him out to fight—and combat only began when both parties were armed and ready. In 1545, for instance, a Dutch man was killed after giving his extra knife to an unarmed man he had just challenged.[6] Middle- and upper-class duels were more elaborate, often with exchanges of written letters and negotiations over weapons and rules conducted by seconds. For one 1843 duel, a participant insisted on using pistols, producing a note from his doctor explaining why an elbow injury made his using a sword impossible.[7]

The norms of dueling drew heavily on military imagery. It was celebrated in military ranks around the world and especially widespread among officers. In addition to honor, it emphasized virtues such as duty, bravery, and dedication to principle. Consciously echoing just war theory, it emphasized the legitimacy of violence in self-defense but also the need to limit and control it within certain rules of engagement. In a duel, keeping one's composure, respecting one's opponent, and avoiding unnecessary cruelty were all important ideals. As in just war theory, dueling was considered a regrettable necessity, not something to be reveled in. One dueling manual advised that a participant "should step up quietly and firmly, as though he were going to shake hands with an old friend, instead of shoot one."[8] Combatants who had just tried to kill or injure each other would routinely express mutual respect and forgiveness afterward, even as one or both lay dying.

Lethality varied across time and place. In some phases, most duels ended once first blood was drawn or the first set of shots exchanged, but in others they were fought to the death. In France between 1589 and 1610, an estimated ten thousand people died in duels.[9] A duel's rules could increase or decrease the likelihood of death. For example, variations that had participants firing from only a few feet apart, or that tied them together by the left hand with knives in their right, or that locked them in a dark basement with swords until one emerged alive, tended to boost lethality. In 1808, two men and their seconds ascended over Paris in twin hot-air balloons, firing at each other's balloons upon reaching an altitude of a half mile. The loser's collapsed, plunging him and his second to their inevitable death, while the winner drifted to a peaceful landing twenty-one miles away in the French countryside.[10]

Duels arose from all kinds of disputes: political differences, romantic rivalries, business or property conflicts, professional disagreements, social slights, gossip, quarreling pets, a bump in the street, and so on. Accusing someone of dishonesty or physically striking him made a duel almost inevitable. Given how many situations could lead to disputes or harsh words and actions, the historian John Norris writes that "any man could find himself involved in a duel if he was unfortunate enough to be in the wrong place at the wrong time."[11] Those in political life, from journalists to politicians, were particularly at risk given the importance they attached to public reputation. A commentator in nineteenth-century France noted that "the journalist must make up his mind to a duel as one of the incidents of his profession."[12] Duels fought by political leaders, such as Aaron Burr and Alexander Hamilton, or by Lord Wellington, while serving as the British prime minister, are only the most famous cases of what was a routine political practice. In 1852, James Denver, the California secretary of state for whom Denver, Colorado, would later be named, killed a newspaper editor and former congressman over a dispute about how best to rescue the stranded Donner party, and eight years later the former chief justice of the California Supreme Court killed his erstwhile close friend and the state's sitting U.S. senator over their political disagreements.[13]

One of the things so striking today about dueling is how often people fought, maimed, and killed each other over trivial or absurd arguments. One Italian fought fourteen duels defending his view that Dante was the country's greatest poet, only to admit at the end of his life that he had never actually read Dante.[14] The great Danish astronomer, Tycho Brahe, wore an artificial metal nose most of his life after, as a young student, he had most of his own cut away by a classmate during a duel over who was the better mathematician.[15] Handel fought a duel with another composer over whose turn it was on the harpsichord during a 1704 opera performance.[16] And Francis Scott Key's twenty-year-old son was killed by a friend after they argued about the speed of a steamboat they were watching.[17]

Deadly combat over ridiculous arguments was not the only consequence of dueling's being a routine and legitimate social institution. As in war, the ideal of a just cause often met the reality of human greed and manipulation. It was common for people to manufacture duels, especially as a way to increase their own social standing. Ambitious young men, in particular, often actively looked for dueling opportunities. Some royal courts, for example, saw the absurd spectacle of numerous courtiers spoiling for a fight with each other, all purportedly in the name of self-defense. At the turn of the seventeenth century in the French court of Henri IV, Chevalier d'Andrieux killed seventy-two people in duels before he turned thirty.[18] Duels could also be a useful way to remove professional or romantic rivals, either by challenging a person oneself, or, better yet, by tricking him into a duel with someone else using deceit or a well-placed rumor. Like ordinary soldiers in war, it was not unusual for people to fight duels not fully knowing what their conflict was about and who was ultimately behind it.[19] As Kwame Anthony Appiah writes, "Dueling was one way of literally getting away with murder."[20]

As with trial by ordeal and combat, dueling had its critics from the beginning. An English commentator in 1617 called it a "corrupt custom" that made men kill each other to preserve their social status.[21] Similarly, Rousseau claimed duels were a license for deadly bullying, lamenting that they could transform scoundrels into upstanding citizens.[22] Many observers pointed to the irrationality of settling disputes in which the injured party was as likely to be killed as vindicated. That a man could be insulted by a boorish companion one evening and, as a result, shot dead by that same person the next morning seemed absurd. Critics also noted the way it encouraged an aggrandized sense of honor and led men to fight over trivial matters. Benjamin Franklin asked, "How can such miserable worms, as we are, entertain so much pride as the conceit that every offense against our imagined honour merits death?"[23] And Francis Bacon lamented its waste, saying that "it is to be deplored when so much gentle blood shall be spilt upon such follies."[24]

These critics included some religious leaders and secular authorities. In 1536, the Council of Trent banned dueling under threat of excommunication, and it was technically illegal in most places during most of its history. Religious and legal prohibitions, however, had little real impact. Clergy rarely challenged the duel publicly, and when they did, they were usually simply ignored. Decrees against it by kings were disregarded by their own courtiers. Laws banning it were seldom enforced, and on those rare occasions when someone was actually charged, judges and juries often acquitted or imposed only symbolic sentences. In an 1822 Scottish trial of a man who killed another in a duel, the judge explained his decision to acquit by pointing out the accused had not broken any of dueling's rules and, considering the insult he had endured, "the necessity, according to the existing law of society, of acting as he did."[25]

The reason opposition to dueling was so ineffective was the broad social acceptance and support the institution enjoyed. Among men and women, young and old, rich and poor, dueling was admired across society. Many found duels exciting, even if they didn't fight them personally. They were celebrated in songs, stories, plays, and novels. The most prominent were reported in the newspapers like sports scores today. An entire industry of published manuals, fencing and shooting schools, and specialized weapons grew up around the practice. As late as the early twentieth century, German university students formed dueling clubs where they hacked away at each other with sabers, bearing the scars on their faces with pride. In the early U.S. Navy, the official handbook for midshipmen included a printed dueling code.[26] The duel was simply part of the fabric of social life, especially for the nobility and those who aspired to it. One nineteenth-century Irish dueling enthusiast said,

> A duel was indeed considered a necessary part of a young man's education, but by no means a ground for future animosity with his opponent. When men had a glowing ambition to excel in all manner of feats and exercises they naturally conceived that manslaughter, in an *honest* way (that is, not knowing *which* would be slaughtered), was the most chivalrous and gentlemanly of all their accomplishments. No young fellow could finish his education till he had exchanged shots with some of his acquaintances. The two first questions always asked as to a young man's respectability and qualifications, particularly when he proposed for a lady wife, were "what family is he of?" and "Did he ever blaze?"[27]

The cost of refusing to duel, of either turning down a challenge or not offering one when insulted, was extraordinarily high. It meant humiliation and ostracism, a devastating loss of social position and respect. Such people would be "posted," publicly scorned as cowardly and dishonorable. One American wrote that "the opinion of mankind, which is as forceful as a law, calls upon a man to resent an affront, and fixes the contempt of a coward upon him if he refuses."[28] In his study of dueling culture, V. G. Kiernan calls it "an extreme form of social compulsion."[29] Refusing to participate would define a man for the rest of his life. It would also dishonor his family, which is why parents routinely pushed sons into duels that would ultimately kill them. For public officials, declining a duel was to risk political suicide, and military officers faced troops that would not follow them and, in many cases, being court-martialed or summarily cashiered out of service. An army report for the German state of Saxony in 1848 stated that "an officer who refuses to fight may expect automatic dismissal."[30] Forty years later, the Russian army required its officers to fight duels not only when they felt their honor had been questioned, but when anyone else had as well. A special "Court of Honor" was set up to collect reports of rumors and insults overheard second-hand in order to facilitate duels.[31]

The enormous social pressure to duel under certain circumstances produced countless reluctant combatants. Like wars in which soldiers on both sides do not want to fight, many duels were morally absurd exercises in which two parties tried to kill each other in self-defense, even though neither actually wanted to fight. Others featured men who realized they had unintentionally insulted someone and genuinely wished to apologize, but who couldn't once a challenge had been issued for fear of being branded cowards.[32] Just before he was killed in a duel in 1827, one American wrote, "It is needless for me to say I heartily protest and despise this absurd mode of settling disputes. But what can a poor devil do except bow to the supremacy of custom?"[33] A Canadian participant wrote before his duel, "I suppose that the usages of society require this sort of thing, but I think it is a most absurd way of settling a difficulty."[34] Just before dying in his famous duel with Aaron Burr, on the same ground and with the same pistols that had claimed the life of his own son in an earlier duel, Alexander Hamilton wrote that he opposed dueling on religious grounds but believed he needed to participate to preserve his honor and protect the good he could do in public life.[35] Like war, opposition to dueling faced a serious unilateral problem—it was a hard institution to reject if those around you didn't do so, too.

* * *

For most of its history, critics of the duel were dismissed as naïve, unrealistic, and faint-hearted. As with war, its defenders argued that since the dawn of time men have always settled certain disputes through combat.[36] They considered dueling an inevitable and necessary defense against attack. One particularly passionate nineteenth-century defender claimed that the duel "makes every one of us a strong and independent power," that it is necessary for "punishing what no code can chastise," that it "is to dueling alone that we owe the remnants of our civilization," and that critics "who have opposed dueling are either fools or cowards."[37]

Dueling's advocates often considered it a regrettable necessity, something that, like war or killing an intruder, may be unpleasant but was dangerously unrealistic to try and avoid. After killing his opponent, an American duelist said he was "sorry for the Necessity" but had only done what he was compelled to do.[38] Sometimes defending individual, family, or regimental honor left a man no other option. Samuel Johnson said of the duel that "it is never unlawful to fight in self-defense," and so "a man may shoot the man who invades his character, as he may shoot him who attempts to break into his house."[39] In a dueling manual published in 1838, John Lyde Wilson, the governor of South Carolina, argued that while dueling should only be a last resort, it was sometimes necessary, just like the American Revolution: "If an oppressed nation has the right to appeal to arms in defense of its liberty and the happiness of its people, there can be no argument used in support of such appeal which will not apply with equal force to individuals." He continued that when a man has no other recourse, "the first law of nature, self-preservation, points out the only remedy for his wrongs," and the duel would be with us "as long as manly independence and a lofty personal pride in all that dignifies and ennobles the human character shall continue to exist."[40]

Especially crucial to such arguments was the widely held view that the law provided inadequate protection for assaults on honor and reputation. As one seventeenth-century defender claimed, at such times there was no "other measure of justice left upon the earth but arms."[41] As in just war theory, where the lack of common legal authority able to restrain wrongdoing sometimes makes armed force necessary, dueling's proponents considered it essential given the limits of regular law enforcement and courts. Napoleon's state council rejected an antidueling bill, saying,

> There is a multitude of offenses which legal justice does not punish, and amongst these offenses there are some so indefinable, or concerned with matters so delicate, that the injured party would blush to bring them out into broad daylight in order to demand public justice. In these circumstances it is impossible for a man to vindicate himself otherwise than by a duel.[42]

More bluntly, Andrew Jackson's own mother taught him to settle matters of honor in person rather than in court, since "the law affords no remedy for such an outrage that can satisfy a gentleman. Fight." On her account, only the naïve thought the courts could protect them. The future president took her advice to heart, killing up to eighteen people in duels, depending on reports.[43]

While arguments in favor of dueling most directly emphasized its necessity in defense of honor, they also pointed to its broader social benefits. Sometimes this took on a national security focus, arguing that dueling's ability to keep up the country's martial spirit during peacetime, especially among its officer class, was crucial to success in times of war.[44] More common was a focus on its contributions to maintaining peace and order within the life of the country. The duel, it was said, served as a powerful deterrent to lying, adultery, cheating in business, and other vices that might get a person challenged. In a version of war's peace-through-strength formula, it was widely believed to improve manners, since the threat of a duel gave people more incentive to be restrained, respectful, and gentle in their dealings with each other. As with just war theory, the duel drew much of its public legitimacy from what Kiernan calls "the stock argument that the code limited bloodshed." Support-ers even produced comparative historical studies purporting to show how societies with dueling were more polite, respectful, and civilized than those without.[45] They also pointed with pride to how the more restrained duel prevented the uncontrolled violence of the vendetta and made society as a whole less violent. The historian Barbara Holland describes the conventional view at the time: "Blood was inevitable, but the duel would at least confine it to a couple of men and their seconds, constrained by regulations."[46] Like critics of Catholic doctrine on war who argue that world disorder results from too little rather than too much American war making, the duel's supporters argued that more dueling equaled more social peace.

For aristocratic proponents and participants in particular, the duel was closely connected to maintaining a stable society and their role in it. As Kiernan details, the period in which the duel flourished in Europe included severe challenges to aristocratic privilege from centralizing monarchs above and democratic forces below, as well as fluid notions of who counted as nobility, with newly wealthy families trying to break in and older ones with declining fortunes at risk of falling out. In this environment of threat and uncertainty, the duel became a marker of class solidarity and identity for the nobility, one linked to their image as the natural leaders of society. The causes of individual duels were not so much the point as the ritual itself, one best understood "as an institu-tion" designed to reinforce a particular "social order."[47] Dueling sent a two-part signal to the rest of society: that the aristocracy was willing to use violence to protect its social standing, which is perhaps why dueling was most popular among nobility in places where it felt most vulnerable, like Ireland, and that it had the virtues of honor, discipline, courage, and self-control necessary to fulfill its traditional leadership role. One aristocrat on trial for killing another after their dogs fought in Hyde Park argued to the jury that "the proper feelings of a gentleman" about his honor and its defense may be hard to put into words, but "their existence has supported this country for many ages, and she might perish if they were lost."[48] The jury did the patriotic thing and acquitted him.

* * *

So why don't two corporate managers today, after accusing each other of dishonesty in a deal gone bad, retire to the parking lot, pace off a set distance, and start firing guns at each other? How did such behavior go from being routine and legitimate to being absurd? Like trial by ordeal and combat, the duel, once thought inevitable and necessary for self-defense and social order, was abolished by a mutually reinforcing cycle of changing social norms and government action, both of which led to new institutional arrangements for handling disputes.

Always a practice that ebbed and flowed across time and from place to place, dueling began to disappear in many areas by the early to mid-nineteenth century, lasting toward the end of the century in places such as Ireland and the American South and West, and up to the First World War in places such as Germany. Everywhere its end was marked by declining social acceptance. Antidueling societies proliferated. Prominent citizens, clergy, and military figures spoke out against it more forcefully. Commoners began to see it as a symbol of aristocratic corruption and legal impunity. A growing middle class emphasized values such as meritocracy, lawfulness, business success, and respectable behavior. Rather than physical violence, honor was increasingly associated with dignity, self-restraint, inner virtue, and spiritual strength. In this changing moral environment, dueling gradually became associated with lawlessness and disorder rather than their opposite. The duel became the subject of ridicule instead of esteem. Social censure shifted from those avoiding duels to those fighting them. By the mid-nineteenth century, London duelists were being described as "juvenile," "venial," and "ridiculous."[49] At the same time, public officials and courts began to seriously prosecute dueling. Judges and juries became more willing to convict duelists for murder. Perhaps most significant, militaries began to court-martial and cashier officers who dueled rather than those who refused to. Dueling could now end a military career rather than make it.

As the duel declined, people increasingly turned to alternatives. Laws against libel and slander became more developed and widely used. Taking someone to court and winning monetary damages was now preferred to physical combat; it was both safer and more reliable.

Many personal disputes that formerly led to duels now became wars of words. The rich and famous fought their battles in the growing world of newspapers rather than on dueling grounds. The rest of society relied on gossip, social and professional rebukes, and, at times, fist fights. For men looking to prove their physical prowess, the rise of amateur sports offered boxing, rugby, football, and other outlets less lethal than dueling.

Most histories of dueling point to the First World War as the final nail in the institution's coffin. Whatever traces of glamorized honor-through-combat that remained, especially among Europe's fading nobility, died in the senseless slaughter of that war's trenches. The same conflict that did so much to de-romanticize war itself also locked in place today's image of the duel as an absurd anachronism.

Notes

[1]Holland 2003, 34-35.

[2]This chapter relies primarily on Spierenburg 2008; Holland 2003; Norris 2009; Kiernan 1988; Appiah 2010; and Roth 2009.

[3]Spierenburg 2008, 38 and 53.

[4]Spierenburg 2008, 32.

[5]Spierenburg 2008, 28-29.

[6]Spierenburg 2008, 69 and 81.

[7]Norris 2009, 77.

[8]Holland 2003, 56.

[9]Holland 2003, 22.

[10]Norris 2009, 125.

[11]Norris 2009, 93.

[12]Kiernan 1988, 266.

[13]Holland 2003, 176; and Kiernan 1988, 310.

[14]Norris 2009, 24.

[15]Holland 2003, 75.

[16]Kiernan 1988, 122.

[17]Holland 2003, 147.

[18]Holland 2003, 22.

[19]Norris 2009, 28.

[20]Appiah 2010, 22

[21]Kiernan 1988, 81.

[22]Norris 2009, 13.

[23]Norris 2009, 13.

[24]Appiah 2010, 29.

[25]Kiernan 1988, 208.

[26]Holland 2003, 142.

[27]Holland 2003, 94-95 (italics in original).

[28]Roth 2009, 160.

[29]Kiernan 1988, 156.

[30]Kiernan 1988, 273.

[31]Holland 2003, 32.

[32]Holland 2003, chap. 7; and Appiah 2010, 25.

[33]Norris 2009, 94.
[34]Kiernan 1988, 304.
[35]Holland 2003, 83, 115, and 118.
[36]Kiernan 1988, 213.
[37]Holland 2003, 5-6.
[38]Holland 2003, 104.
[39]Kiernan 1988, 179-80.
[40]Holland 2003, 150.
[41]Kiernan 1988, 11-12.
[42]Norris 2009, 35.
[43]Holland 2003, 51.
[44]See, for example, Kiernan 1988, 69.
[45]Kiernan 1988, 272 and 136-37.
[46]Holland 2003, 24.
[47]Kiernan 1988, 159.
[48]Holland 2003, 93.
[49]Appiah 2010, 41.

14

Slavery

Perhaps no form of institutionalized violence more closely paralleled war in its historical duration, widespread use, degree of human misery, and misguided moral justifications than slavery.[1] Indeed, the two were intertwined from their very origins. Like war, slavery required a level of social organization complex enough to make it possible, and the two arose around the same time among more sophisticated chiefdoms and the earliest states. The Code of Hammurabi included laws governing both slavery and military service, and, as John Keegan points out, ancient armies were often themselves "a military slave system."[2]

Since its invention, slavery also rivaled war in its prevalence across both time and culture. The historian Orlando Patterson writes, "It has existed in some form in every region of the world, at all levels of sociopolitical development, and among all major ethnic groups."[3] Across this long history, slavery took a variety of forms. It made slaves out of defeated enemies in war, unwanted children, debtors, religious nonbelievers, and members of different racial or ethnic groups. Some occupied higher-status jobs, though more often they performed their society's most difficult and degrading work. Slaves were field hands, miners, wet nurses, gladiators, skilled artisans, prostitutes, cooks, maids, tutors, soldiers, government administrators, industrial laborers, and objects of religious sacrifice.

Amid this diversity of forms, however, slavery had important commonalities. Cultures with slaves usually viewed them as incapable of independent thought, interested only in bodily functions such as eating or sex, superstitious, lazy unless forced to work, and prone to theft and petty lies. As the term "chattel slavery" shows, a dehumanizing parallel to animal behavior and control is a constant theme in the institution's history. In Patterson's influential formulation, slaves were marked by a powerful kind of "social death" that stripped away any autonomous social existence. Ownership by another person erased all honor, human worth, and meaning connected to their own independent existence or family lineage and offspring. Slaves' very lives were owned by their masters, their sustenance, security, and bodily integrity subject to that master's whim. Like war, slavery was an extreme form of systematic dehumanization: "The slave was the ultimate human tool, as imprintable and as disposable as the master wished."[4]

David Brion Davis, the most accomplished historian of global slavery and its abolition, argues throughout his writings that all slave societies embodied a fundamental moral contradiction. On the one hand, they treated slaves as things, denying their basic humanity and seeing them instead as mere objects to be exploited and discarded. On the other hand, however, slaves were obviously human beings, something recognized by laws holding them responsible for their behavior, by attempts to evangelize them, by the occasional practice of freeing them, or by sexual, even loving, relationships between slaves and nonslaves. Sustaining slavery always meant obscuring, denying, or simply refusing to recognize this basic contradiction.[5]

Like war, then, slavery depended on lies for its legitimacy, lies that were deeply woven into its social justification and practice, so deeply that most people, particularly those not slaves themselves, reflexively believed them to be true. Slavery could deny the reality of a slave's basic humanity because, like war, it was institutionalized. It was just part of how society operated, something taken for granted. This institutionalization was also necessary for the high level of social control slavery required to keep so many people in bondage as a normal part of daily life across generations. Slavery didn't just happen spontaneously when one person decided to own another. It could not work without an infrastructure of widely accepted roles, ideas, and behaviors. It required detailed legal codes that governed selling, owning, and inheriting slaves. It needed public officials to help control large slave populations. It depended on slavery being an ordinary part of everyday social and commercial interaction. As an institution, then, slavery shaped not only the lives of slaves, but of all members of slave societies, including owners. An escaped slave in the United States said of his former owners, "Talk not about kind and Christian masters. They are not masters of the system. The system is master of them."[6]

At the heart of this system, as in war, was violence and brutality. Physical supervision, domination, and coercion were what made any slave system run. In addition to being routinely worked to death, slaves were always vulnerable to beatings, torture, rape, and death at the hands of those placed over them. Sometimes these forms of violence were sudden and spontaneous, made possible by the lack of power and legal protection afforded slaves. Other times violence was formally prescribed by the laws governing slavery, laws that considered terrible physical punishments, often centering on whipping and bodily mutilation, necessary to maintain it. On sugar plantations in the Caribbean and Brazil, slaves not working hard enough or caught breaking rules were burned and branded, had noses cut off, or were executed, with their heads mounted on poles as a warning to others.[7] A 1723 Virginia law specified that slaves caught lying "have one ear nailed to the pillory, and there to stand for the space of one hour, and then the said ear to be cut off; and thereafter, the other ear nailed in like manner, and cut off, at the expiration of one other hour," all to be followed by "thirty-nine lashes, well laid on, on his or her bare back."[8] Perhaps most heartbreaking were the countless slave families pulled apart by force never to see each other again. One American slave in 1852 left a letter for her husband telling him that she and their two children were about to be split up and sold to separate traders, ending with the words "I am and will ever be your kind wife," while another, remembering when he was eleven and his father was sold away, said that owners "thought no more of selling a man away from his wife, or a mother away from her children, than of sending a cow or a horse out of state."[9]

Slavery across the long centuries was not just marked by common dynamics, but by actual historical connections among slave societies. Just as wars flow into each other in a cycle of violence, slave systems were linked by a history of brutal continuity. Slavery in the ancient world never disappeared but adapted as older civilizations gave way to new ones. After inheriting the institution from earlier cultures in the Middle East, Asia, and North Africa, the Greek and Roman worlds passed it along to medieval Europe, Byzantium, and the Arab world. A thriving trade in slaves linked Christian and Muslim communities surrounding the Mediterranean for centuries, drawing slaves not only from wars with each other but from Africa, Asia, and Eastern Europe, especially the Balkans and Caucasus. Indeed, the root word for slave in several languages, including English, refers to Eastern European Slavs taken in slave raids.[10] Even as slavery declined in medieval Europe, it still thrived on the continent's edges and revived in the early modern period as Italian, Spanish, and Portuguese entrepreneurs established plantation-style agricultural operations, especially for sugar production, on islands in the Mediterranean and, later, in the Atlantic off the African coast. These began drawing more slaves from sub-Saharan Africa, long a source for Arab slavery, and became the prototype for the massive slave colonies established in the New World, a region where many indigenous peoples enslaved each other and were enslaved, in turn, by European colonial powers. It was the arrival of European-style slavery in the Americas, especially when African slaves replaced indigenous ones decimated by disease, that brought the institution to its global apogee, creating a system that linked Europe, Africa, Asia, and the Americas in a worldwide market for slaves and the commodities they produced.

It was only at this point, when slavery had been around for so long and had developed into such a massive globally integrated system, that it faced any serious opposition. Sporadic slave revolts and occasional expressions of concern about the conditions of particular slaves had marked the institution's long history, but it wasn't until the late eighteenth century that anything like a full intellectual, social, and political challenge to slavery itself emerged. The rise of the abolitionist movement represented the first real opposition to slavery as such in world history. The movement began as a small voice, most notably in England, protesting slavery's inherent inhumanity and injustice. At first, it was rejected as sentimental foolishness, and later, as it grew stronger, slavery's defenders condemned it as utopian, religiously unorthodox, unpatriotic, and dangerous. Yet a mere century after its emergence, abolitionism had largely eliminated chattel slavery from much of the earth. Consider, for example, that on the eve of the American Revolution, slavery was a thriving, perfectly legal, socially acceptable, and economically crucial practice from Canada at the top of the Americas to Chile at their bottom tip, yet by 1888 it was abolished across the entire region, as Brazil became the last major New World slave society to give it up.[11] As Davis writes, this shift in one century away from an institution that had been with humanity for millennia represents "one of the most extraordinary events in history."[12]

* * *

Like war, slavery was long considered an inevitable part of the human condition, something that had always existed, and a necessary foundation for social order. Across its long history, common sense simply accepted the "naturalness and necessity of slavery," as the American George Fitzhugh put it in 1857.[13]

This view had deep roots. Classical philosophers did much to establish slavery's legitimacy by tying it to the proper ordering of society. Plato taught that a just and stable community required that those with reason rule over those without. His student Aristotle argued that those people who, like beasts of burden, lack sufficient reason "are by their nature slaves, and it is better for them to be ruled despotically." On his account, "The use made of slaves, too, departs but little from that made of other animals."[14]

Early Christian thinkers retained the association of slavery with social order, adding sin to the equation. Augustine wrote, "The prime cause, then, of slavery is sin, which brings man under the dominion of his fellow—that which does not happen save by the judgment of God." For Augustine, slavery was like war: a thing made necessary by the fallen nature of humanity. It was part of what the tranquility of order in the earthly city required, something "appointed by that law which enjoins the preservation of the natural order and forbids its disturbance."[15] Like Augustine, later thinkers such as Aquinas, Suárez, and Grotius all addressed slavery in terms strikingly similar to their defense of war. It would be unnecessary in a world without sin, but it is needed in the world as it is, one that requires hierarchy, force, and subordination to authority. Otherwise, lawlessness and disorder would reign, and all would be reduced to slavery. For such thinkers, moral realism demanded the recognition that slavery, like war, was necessary for a peaceful and secure order.[16]

In the same way that war's association with protecting a legitimate order can at times spill over into a kind of utopian belief in its ability to create a better world, epitomized, for example, by the faith Catholic teaching's neoconservative critics place in it, slavery too was often defended as an engine of social progress. As Davis details, from ancient Rome to the medieval Islamic world to Spain's conquest of the Americas, slave-owning civilizations always considered it a crucial foundation for their power and greatness, an essential tool of improvement for those who "regarded themselves as the carriers of light and truth."[17] One nineteenth-century defender called slavery "an integral link in the grand evolution of progressive society," something that would bring "the elevation and christianization of the dark races, the feeding and clothing of the world, the diminution of toil and the amelioration of all asperities of life, the industrial prosperity and the peace of nations, and the further glorious evolutions of Art, Science, Literature and Religion."[18]

Slavery's defenders, like just war proponents, drew heavily on Christianity. They pointed to the presence of slavery throughout the Bible, especially the Old Testament, and the failure of Jesus to condemn it explicitly. Specific passages, such as the curse of Ham in Genesis 9:20-27, or St. Paul's advice to slaves in Colossians 3:22-25, demonstrated that God marked those with dark skin to serve those with light skin, or that the authority of masters over slaves came from God. As with war, such religious sanction helped those shocked by the realities of slavery to set aside their moral qualms. When a young Englishman had his first sight of a brutal slave market in the West Indies, he took solace in the fact that "surely God ordained 'em for the use and benefit of us: otherwise his Divine Will would have been made manifest by some particular sign or token."[19] Christian just war theory itself provided one of the most frequent justifications for slavery. Building on the classical idea that it was an act of mercy to enslave rather than kill defeated enemies, Augustine endorsed taking slaves in a just war, a view subsequently adopted by popes and other religious leaders, Catholic and Protestant, down through the centuries.[20] This became a kind of catch-all rationale. Since those launching colonial wars usually cited ostensible just causes, they provided handy justifications for enslaving indigenous peoples. And, as the source of most global slaves shifted to Africa, those buying them from slave traders after overseas shipment routinely claimed their bondage had begun with warfare among faraway African tribes. The notion that all slaves had originated as prisoners of war was one of those pervasive fictions that owners throughout slave-holding societies, especially in the Americas, clung to reflexively, allowing them, as Davis writes, to become "dissociated from the violent act of enslavement" that produced their own human property, a dissociation similar to that of those who support war while closing their eyes to its realities.[21]

As abolitionists would later show, Christianity was always well-equipped to condemn slavery. Its images of mercy, nonviolence, liberation from bondage, moral equality, and shared membership in the Body of Christ that crossed lines of nation, race, or ethnicity were always standing ready to challenge slavery's brutal injustices. And, indeed, they did provide sources of hope and resistance to generations of Christian slaves themselves. Among nonslaves, however, their main effect was to prompt sporadic efforts at amelioration rather than abolition. Through its history, many Christians did try to comfort or improve the living conditions of slaves, usually in individual cases, but occasionally for larger groups as well. But this did not produce opposition to the institution of slavery itself. Indeed, in its later stages, slavery's defenders explicitly appealed to amelioration as a way to head off abolitionism, arguing that the institution should be made more humane rather than rashly eliminated entirely. Like just war theory's focus on limiting war and reducing its suffering, Christian thinkers carefully distinguished between slavery's unfortunate abuses, which should be minimized, and the legitimacy of the institution itself. Echoing claims that the injustices of particular wars do not render all wars immoral, Jesuit writers in the seventeenth and eighteenth centuries, for example, argued that particular abuses within slavery do not render all slavery unjust.[22]

Of course, the ameliorative impulse in Christianity had its limits, demonstrating the remarkable ability of institutionalized slavery, like war, to minimize and obscure its own realities. In 1711, when some South Carolina Baptists expressed concern about a member of their congregation who had castrated one of his slaves as punishment, church leaders warned against risking a rift among believers over such "light and Indifferent Causes."[23] Objections to enslaving and abusing indigenous peoples in the Americas by Catholic clerics, such as Bartolomé de Las Casas, while largely ineffective at the time, are rightly celebrated today. Less well-known, however, is his position that the best way to spare them inhumane treatment was to import enough African slaves to take their places as plantation labor.[24]

The most popular way to square Christianity with the practice of slavery was to point to its benefits for the slaves themselves. Recall how wars often cover their true nature with the moral veneer of a noble cause, how their defenders even claim to fight for good of the enemy community itself, much like a parent punishes a child out of love, to use Augustine's image. Such paternalism was central in defenses of slavery as well. In saving slaves from the barbarism, hunger, and paganism of their native lands, owners assumed they did their Christian duty by feeding, sheltering, converting, and caring for slaves as a part of their own families. One French ship captain claimed to treat the slaves he transported to the New World according to the Golden Rule.[25] Another defender said that the institution ensured that expressions of a slave's "animality are kept in restraint and he is compelled to lead an industrious, sober life, and certainly a more happy one than he would have if he was left to the free indulgences of his indolent savage nature."[26] On this view, when slaves resisted, they not only violated the social order ordained by God, but showed ingratitude as well. Sentencing slaves found guilty of plotting a revolt, a South Carolina court stated, "Servitude has existed under various forms, from the deluge to the present time, and in no age or country has the condition of slaves been milder or more humane than your own."[27] Thus do forms of institutionalized violence justify themselves through false appeals to the good of all, including even those subjected to that violence.

Given the centrality of religious orthodoxy in traditional understandings of slavery, it is no surprise abolitionists faced charges of rejecting it. Early Catholic opponents of slavery, for example, saw their work condemned by the Inquisition.[28] In language that closely parallels that later used by neoconservative critics of contemporary Catholic teaching on war and peace, abolitionists were accused of "forgetfulness" when it came to traditional Christianity, of substituting weak-minded enthusiasm and sentimentality for reason and moral clarity, and of smuggling progressive fashion into established religious doctrine. Those who dreamed of a world without slavery failed to recognize the reality of evil, sin, and disorder in the world, as well as the authority necessary to keep such things at bay, including that embodied in the age-old and divinely authorized practice of slavery.[29] This moral naiveté made abolitionism dangerous to peace and social stability. As the English Earl of Abingdon warned, "The Order, and Subordination, and Happiness of the whole habitable Globe is threatened."[30]

Just as supporters of war defend its necessity to a country's basic security, slavery's advocates considered its defense necessary to protect their society's very way of life. This view influenced even those who recognized the suffering the practice imposed on slaves. Echoing the same language long used to defend just wars, an eighteenth-century defender of slavery wrote, "Many things . . . which are repugnant to humanity, may be excused, on account of their necessity for self-preservation."[31] Like war, many considered slavery a necessary evil. This ultimately seemed to be Thomas Jefferson's view. While he famously expressed objections to slavery in theory, and freed some of his own enslaved offspring after his death, Jefferson consistently resisted actual efforts to end it across the board, always advising that abolition was unrealistically premature and would be "like abandoning children" not able to care for themselves. For him it was better to "await with patience the workings of an overruling providence." He advised a young slave owner struggling with his conscience to set aside moral reservations, saying, "I hope then, my dear sir, you will reconcile yourself to our country and its unfortunate condition." Jefferson even supported expanding slavery into new territories in the American West, though with the odd claim that doing so would weaken the institution and bring its eventual decline, a jump in logic similar to those who support fighting wars in the name of ending war.[32]

Slavery's most passionate defenders saw it as the bulwark against attacks on a superior way of life. On the eve of the American Civil War, George Fitzhugh contrasted the peace, stability, organic structure, and harmonious social relations of the South with the low wages, unemployment, crime, sexual license, and family breakdown of the so-called free North. The difference lay in slavery, which was "an indispensable police institution," one substituting caring authority and mutual benefit for "cruelty and tyranny" in social relationships, making it crucial for justice and "good order."[33] For those like Fitzhugh, abolitionists with no grasp of Southern life and blinded by their zeal for sentimental abstract principles were opening the door to disaster. Like pacifists accused of putting their faith in unrealistic alternatives to war guaranteed to fail, slavery's defenders considered abolitionists dangerously naïve, pushing a shift in social relations that would spark disorder, economic collapse, and violence.

Indeed, the specter of bloodshed was among the most powerful arguments against abolitionists, the equivalent of if-we-listen-to-the-pacifists-we'll-all-be-dead arguments when it comes to war. Slavery's defenders constantly circulated graphic descriptions of slave revolts, especially the violence following the Haitian Revolution, which served as a *de rigueur* challenge to abolitionists the way Hitler does to pacifists. These centered on lurid images of looting, torture, and whites killed in their beds. They suggested it was only slavery that kept the savage natural violence of African slaves at bay, and abolitionism threatened to unleash it upon innocent people across a defenseless society. One popular account from the British West Indies depicted white children impaled on stakes, white women raped on piles of their dead family members, and a pregnant women who saw her husband killed and decapitated before her baby was cut from her womb to be replaced by her husband's head. It concluded, "Such are thy triumphs, Philanthropy!"[34] South Carolina Governor James Henry Hammond argued that slavery's suppressing the "mud-sill" class was necessary for social order, and abolition's logical conclusion was social disintegration and anarchy "red with blood."[35] For another critic, emancipating slaves was a "proposal for the butchery of women and children, for scenes of lust and rapine, and of arson and murder."[36]

Debates about war obviously revolve around considerations of national security in the global arena, but it is remarkable how much debates about slavery did as well. Like war, slavery was clearly considered a tool of the state. Davis details how it "formed an integral part of the Atlantic imperial system" by the time abolitionism arose to challenge it.[37] As the American *Amistad* case illustrates, the global trade in slaves and the commodities they produced were subject to a web of international treaties, diplomatic maneuvering, and overlapping domestic laws. Great powers built alliances on pledges to return escaped slaves, or they plotted to undermine rivals by encouraging slave insurrections with promises of freedom in exchange for military aid. National leaders accepted the importance of slavery to their fundamental interests as a matter of course. It prevented the loss of white laborers and consumers at home, stimulated industries such as shipping and manufacturing, contributed to general economic growth, and generated tremendous wealth, which could be transformed into military strength to defend against enemies. An eighteenth-century English economist summed up the conventional wisdom: "The Negroe-Trade and the natural Consequences resulting from it, may be justly esteemed an inexhaustible Fund of Wealth and Naval Power to this Nation."[38]

In Britain, abolitionists were bitterly opposed on national security grounds. Their opponents claimed that abolition would amount to a kind of unilateral disarmament, shifting the international balance of power against Britain by ceding control of global slavery to France, Spain, Holland, the United States, and other rivals. Like pacifists charged with being unpatriotic, abolitionists were accused of opposing British power and being secretly loyal to France.[39] Even after Britain became the first great power to abolish the slave trade and, later, slavery itself from its possessions, critics pointed to how it only served to weaken the country. The *London Times* in 1850 lamented that "the sum of slavery has not been diminished" but only "transferred from us to more grasping pitiless and unscrupulous hands" so that "foreign slave-owners are establishing a monopoly of all the great staples of tropical produce."[40]

As for other countries, they clearly considered British-led efforts to abolish slavery worldwide a direct security threat. Slave-owning countries in Europe and the Americas saw it "as a flagrant violation of national sovereignty."[41] In 1790, a French National Assembly busy eliminating the entire edifice of feudalism took the time to declare abolitionism a form of treason.[42] American leaders, especially those from the South, branded Britain's antislavery efforts a plot to stop the westward expansion of the United States and seize Texas and Florida for itself. Its aim was to subvert the hard-won legacy of the American Revolution and destroy the international economic advantage slave societies enjoyed. According to Abel P. Upshur, the U.S. secretary of state in the 1840s, "England has ruined her own colonies, and like an unchaste female wishes to see *other* countries, where slavery exists, in a similar state." John C. Calhoun, a U.S. vice president, argued that Britain was out to destroy all slave societies that "have refused to follow her suicidal policy." And in South America, one Brazilian defender of slavery called international abolitionism "a crime, robbery, theft, and a communist plot."[43]

*   *   *

The evidence is overwhelming that chattel slavery's end did not result from some kind of economic determinism. Its abolition came when it was a thriving global institution, one that was enormously productive and profitable.[44] Great Britain in particular acted against its own interests in deciding to lead the global campaign against it. Prime Minister Benjamin Disraeli would later say that "the abolition of slavery was virtuous, but it was not wise" given the loss of power and wealth it meant for his country.[45]

Slavery's abolition was above all a moral revolution. Davis calls it "a profound transformation in moral perception" that finally led people to "see the full horror of a social evil to which mankind had been blind for centuries," one that "weakened the traditional screening mechanisms" that hid the "inherent contradictions of human bondage" and ultimately "removed slavery from the list of supposedly inevitable misfortunes of life."[46] Such a revolution faced long odds at its beginning. Slavery was so deeply institutionalized, so widely accepted as an unavoidable part of the world, so widely considered necessary for a peaceful and secure order, so entrenched by powerful social, economic, and political interests, that eliminating it from the earth seemed as far-fetched then as eliminating war from the earth does today.

It was Quakers, already among a lonely handful of sects advocating Christian pacifism, who launched the first sustained international protests against slavery as an institution. During the eighteenth century, they went from a denomination that was ambiguous about slavery, and included slave traders and owners among its numbers, to an outspoken witness against it. Quakers were soon joined by other Christians, especially those of a nonconformist and evangelical bent, in pointing to the long-standing but rarely before acknowledged truth that slavery was simply incompatible with Christianity.[47] They rejected the historical association of slavery with just war, original sin, and order and authority in a fallen world. These shifts were made possible by a declining emphasis on evil and sin as inescapable elements of the human condition. Instead, emerging religious voices stressed human dignity, universal benevolence, and the opportunity for individual and social redemption, one made possible by turning away from sinful practices such as slavery. These changes in religious ideas were joined by secular ones, rooted in the Enlightenment, also emphasizing moral equality, individual happiness, humanitarian concern, and historical progress. Both religious and secular trends combined to create an explosion of interest in social reform targeting a range of practices considered cruel, archaic, and corrosive to human flourishing. These included temperance initiatives, antidueling societies, public health and sanitation measures, prison reform, and campaigns against gender discrimination, capital punishment, and child abuse. Among these, abolitionism became increasingly important, attracting a growing number of supporters across social classes.

The eighteenth-century French intellectual Abbé Raynal wrote of slavery, "If the universality of a practice was proof of its validity, the case for usurpation, for conquest, for all manner of oppression would be made."[48] Breaking through the traditional acceptance of slavery as a historical given to be accepted with a shrug was a chief concern for abolitionists. One way was to force the public to see the humanity of slaves and the unjust suffering they endured as innocent persons created by God. Like pacifist writers and activists seeking to highlight the senseless slaughter of war, abolitionists turned to plays, novels, memoirs, essays, and public lectures to shine a light on the brutal realities of slavery. Especially powerful were accounts from former slaves themselves. These cut through theoretical debates over slavery with eyewitness reports by slavery's survivors, furnishing the public with riveting stories of slaves as real people with real, heartbreaking experiences, ones that exposed the abstraction-wrapped lies of slavery's defenders.

Another tactic was to emphasize the hypocrisy of societies purportedly dedicated to liberty and equality allowing slavery. From England to Revolutionary France to the United States, abolitionists pointed to the clash between slavery and the nation's constitutional ideals. One English critic of American slavery wrote, "If there be an object truly ridiculous in nature, it is an American patriot, signing resolutions of independency with the one hand, and with the other brandishing a whip over his affrighted slaves." And a 1786 petition from Frederick and Hampshire counties in the Virginia legislature stated, "That the Glorious and ever memorable Revolution can be Justified on no other Principles but what doth plead with greater Force for the emancipation of our Slaves in proportion as the oppression exercised over them exceeds the oppression formerly exercised by Great Britain over these States."[49]

This gulf between slavery and a country's core principles allowed abolitionists to flip the traditional equation of slavery with lawfulness and social order. The English abolitionist James Ramsay, for example, argued that slavery violated his country's ancient understandings of natural liberty, limited government, and the rule of law. It was an "artificial" and "unnatural" social arrangement, one amounting to the "negation of law" since it gave an owner despotic power and made him "his own legislator." Similarly, the American Senator Salmon Chase contrasted the rule of law, which upheld a person's natural liberty, and "the law of force, which made him a slave."[50] As Davis details, abolitionists increasingly made a convincing case that "slavery not only violated natural law but represented the supreme denial of those benevolent instincts which preserved society from anarchy."[51] Slave-owning regions, such as the West Indies and the American South, were described as corrupted by slavery—backward and disorderly societies marked by violence and brutality, lawlessness, fraud, dissolute living, coarse manners, and even bad roads, unpainted fences, and poorly maintained fields.

As with the process of ending other forms of institutionalized violence, changing social attitudes toward slavery prompted changes in government policy, which, in turn, further delegitimized slavery. Within individual countries, slavery was especially vulnerable to government action given how much its operation depended on a specific legal structure and enforcement action by public officials.[52] The abolitionist movement saw this and acted accordingly, emerging as a highly effective way to mobilize mass support for political change, especially in Britain. Like any such movement, it was marked by internal divisions. More radical voices focused on total and immediate abolition, including by violence if necessary, while moderates advocated working gradually through conventional politics in a series of steps leading up to abolition—ending the slave trade, stopping expansion into new territories, offering safe haven to fugitive slaves, long phase-out periods, compensating former owners, and so on. The way slavery ended in various countries at various times—early or late, sudden or gradual, violently or nonviolently—reflected these different considerations and the opposition strategies chosen by slavery's defenders.

Perhaps the biggest political obstacle to ending slavery was its international scope. Just because abolitionists could shut it down in one country didn't mean it wouldn't continue to flourish elsewhere, and, of course, it proved to be most entrenched where abolitionism was weakest—the American South, Cuba, Brazil, and elsewhere. Early international prohibitions were also notoriously easy to evade for countries opposed to abolition, and the incentives to continue benefiting from slavery while other countries gave it up were significant. As with war, then, abolishing slavery meant not simply working for its end in particular countries, but also forging an international consensus to eliminate a widespread and long-standing practice among the nations of the earth, including many clearly uninterested in going along.

This was a difficult and uneven process. It involved nations, such as Britain, as well as nonstate actors, such as international networks of abolition societies, working to establish moral norms, international agreements, monitoring bodies, and enforcement mechanisms. It meant cooperative efforts to intercept slave traders on the high seas and deny them safe havens. It meant targeting nations still supporting slavery with diplomatic pressure, economic sanctions, and political inducements. What this produced was a process where country after country eventually officially eliminated slavery. Sometimes internal conflicts turned bloody, as in the United States. Slaves themselves often brought pressure through either violent revolt, most famously in Haiti, or nonviolent noncooperation movements, as in the less well-known case of Brazil. Ultimately, most slave-owning countries gave it up out of self-interest, acting in response to international incentives, both positive and negative. But this laid the foundation for a growing moral consensus against the practice, one that put pressure on the remaining countries to renounce it, too. It eventually created a kind of tipping point where countries still practicing slavery become morally isolated. Their people, especially globally minded political and economic elites, came to see slavery as an embarrassing deviation from international norms, something dishonorable, backward, and harmful to their nation's international reputation.[53] The process was largely complete by the end of the nineteenth century, though some isolated countries around the globe held out well into the twentieth.

In acknowledging the dramatic achievements of abolitionism, it is important to recognize its moral limits. It certainly did not eliminate all forms of oppressive labor, and new institutionalized forms of coercive toil arose to fill the gap left by slavery. Debt-bondage, child labor, unfair wages, human trafficking, coercive apprenticeship arrangements, unsafe working conditions, forced marriage, and caste systems all survived or arose out of slavery's end, and many continue around the world today. Abolitionism also did not eliminate racism, including among abolitionists themselves. In many parts of the globe, formerly enslaved minorities faced institutionalized segregation, economic marginalization, political oppression, and violence, all injustices that continue in various forms in various places today as well. Finally, the repudiation of slavery by European powers flowed directly into the race to colonize Africa that immediately followed, something endorsed by many abolitionists, not to mention the Catholic Church and other religious bodies, and that resulted in massive violence and human suffering, the legacy of which also continues into the present.[54]

But in spite of the injustices it left behind and new forms of institutional violence that arose in its wake, the movement to abolish slavery was a remarkable success. In his biography of William Wilberforce, the great British antislavery leader, Eric Metaxas writes,

> There is hardly a soul alive today who isn't horrified and offended by the very idea of slavery. We seethe with moral indignation at it, and we can't fathom how anyone or any culture ever countenanced it. But in the world into which Wilberforce was born, the opposite was true. Slavery was as accepted as birth and marriage and death, was so woven into the tapestry of human history that you could barely see its threads, much less pull them out.[55]

Slavery was one of the most brutal forms of institutionalized violence the world has ever seen, one victimizing countless human beings through its long history. From something so widely practiced and considered natural, inevitable, and necessary for a just and peaceful order in a sinful world, abolitionism sparked a dramatic transformation that rendered slavery morally incomprehensible and dismantled its institutional infrastructure across the globe. Vestiges, successors, and related injustices survived its fall, but they do not negate the undeniable good that abolishing slavery as a routine worldwide practice did for humanity.

Notes

[1]This chapter relies primarily on Patterson 1982; Davis 1966, 1984, 1999, 2006; Appiah 2010, chap. 2; Andreas and Nadelmann 2006, chap. 1; Rodriguez 1999; and Meltzer 1993.

[2]Davis 1998, ix; and Keegan 1993, 343.

[3]Patterson 1999, ix.

[4]Patterson 1982, 7.

[5]See, for example, Davis 1999, chap. 1; and Davis 1966, chap. 3.

[6]Davis 2006, 193.

[7]Davis 2006, 107-09 and 118-19.

[8]Noonan 2002, 242.

[9]Davis 2006, 183 and 201.

[10]Patterson 1982, 154-56; and Noonan 2005, 48.

[11]Davis 2006, 142.

[12]Davis 1984, 108.

[13]Fitzhugh 1998, 277.

[14]Aristotle 1986, 22.

[15]Augustine 1950, book 19, chap. 15.

[16]Davis 1966, chaps. 3-4; and Davis 2006, chap. 2.

[17]Davis 1984, 23-24.

[18]Davis 1984, 23.

[19]Davis 1966, 202.

[20]Noonan 2005; Rodriguez 1997, xix; and Davis 2006, 41-65.

[21]Davis 1966, 166.

[22]Davis 1966, 191; and Davis 1999, 544-45.

[23]Davis 1966, 335.

[24]Davis 2006, 98.

[25]Davis 2006, 81.

[26]Davis 2006, 187.

[27]Davis 1999, 208.

[28]Davis 2006, 96.

[29]Davis 1966, 199 and chap. 7 generally; and Davis 1999, 531 and chap. 11 generally.

[30]Davis 1999, 345.

[31]Davis 1966, 396.

[32]Davis 1999, 176-82; and Davis 2006, 271.

[33]Fitzhugh 1998, 275.

[34]Davis 2006, 160.

[35]Davis 2006, 190.

[36]Davis 2006, 317.

[37]Davis 1999, 65.

[38]Davis 2006, 80.

[39]Metaxas 2007, especially chaps. 13-14.

[40]Davis 2006, 245.

[41]Davis 1984, 285.

[42]Davis 1999, 140.
[43]Davis 2006, 284-85 and 325 (italics in original).
[44]See, for example, Davis 2006, chap. 12; and Appiah 2010, chap. 3.
[45]Appiah 2010, 107.
[46]Davis 1999, 15 and 48.
[47]Metaxas 2007, 171.
[48]Davis 1966, 419.
[49]Davis 1999, 398 and 306-07.
[50]Davis 1999, 378 and 522.
[51]Davis 1999, 526.
[52]Nadelmann 1990, 497.
[53]For more on this process, see Ray 1989; Nadelmann 1990, 491-98; and Appiah 2010, chap. 3.
[54]Davis 1984, part 3, chap. 3.
[55]Metaxas 2007, xiii-xiv.

15

Lynching

In 1916, residents of Waco, Texas, lynched seventeen-year-old Jesse Washington, an African American accused on thin evidence of raping and killing a white woman. He was dragged through the streets by a chain to the town hall where schoolchildren and workers on their lunch break gathered to participate and watch. After his fingers, toes, ears, and penis were slowly cut off, he was suspended over a bonfire and burned alive. After he died, his body was again dragged through town, until eventually his head came loose and was taken by a group of boys who pulled out his teeth to sell as mementos.[1] There was a time, extending into the not-too-distant past, when such spectacles were a normal part of American life.[2]

Lynching is extrajudicial killing carried out by a group of people, usually openly and with community support. This kind of crowd violence outside normal legal proceedings has been common across human history and cultures. According to the historian Christopher Waldrep, the "practice must be as old as time."[3] It was certainly present from the earliest years of the United States. The term "lynching" itself likely comes from Revolutionary War–era Virginia, when a man or men named Lynch led violent reprisals against suspected traitors and criminals in the absence of functioning courts. Present throughout the young country, it was most common along the western frontier in the eighteenth and nineteenth centuries. It is best known, however, for its use against African Americans in the South during the century between the end of the Civil War and the modern civil rights movement, where at its height estimates were that someone was lynched once every four days.[4]

Lynchings were usually sparked by a particular crime or instance of outrageous behavior. These could be real, merely rumored, or completely fabricated. Sexual threats—rape, consensual liaisons, flirting, even a glance—were especially prominent as justifications for the practice in Southern racial lynching. Frontier lynching usually targeted those considered a danger to security and social order: outsiders, vagrants, gamblers, violent troublemakers, and racial or ethnic minorities. Sometimes calling for a lynch mob was a good way to remove a romantic rival, take over a plot of land, or cover one's own crime. In its Southern racial version, any African American was vulnerable, but its victims were most likely to be young black males, especially strangers, the unemployed, those not showing sufficient deference to white people (even in the face of taunts or abuse), and anyone suspected of sexual connections to a white woman. It also targeted African Americans threatening the racial order: political leaders advocating for civil rights, small business owners becoming too successful, workers organizing for higher wages, or farmers occupying coveted land. Fear of black political empowerment, for example, led to a spate of lynchings and antiblack riots in the Wilmington, North Carolina, area in 1898, where towns erected banners such as the one in Burlington that read "WHITE SUPREMACY—PROTECT US."[5] In many ways, lynching was merely an extension of the terror and lethal violence used during slavery to maintain social control over an area's black population.

Nathan Bedford Forrest, the first national leader of the Ku Klux Klan, an organization that helped spread lynching across the post–Civil War South, said of his experience as a Confederate General: "War means fightin', and fightin' means killin.'"[6] Like war, lynching centered on acts of terrible violence that were accepted, even celebrated, as part of its nature. Especially in its Southern racial version, lynching's victims were not just killed, but usually tortured and mutilated beforehand. In 1899, a large Georgia crowd cheered as a man named Sam Hose was stripped, castrated, and had his ears and fingers cut off. After about half an hour of torture, he was finally covered in oil and burned alive. A few years earlier, a Texas mob sealed a woman in a barrel, drove long nails through it, and rolled her up and down a hill until she was dead. A 1934 lynching victim in Florida was castrated and forced to eat his own genitals. In 1937, lynchers in Mississippi whipped two men with chains, gouged their eyes out with an ice pick, and slowly burned away their skin with a blowtorch before finally killing them. After getting into a fight with a shopkeeper who had slapped his mother, James Stephenson, a Second World War veteran, husband, and father of a young child, was lynched in Tennessee in 1946. Before being killed, his hands were cut off with a meat cleaver, his face and body burned by a blowtorch, and his eyes popped from their sockets.[7]

As in war, desecrating dead bodies was common. After being killed, victims were often dragged through the streets behind wagons or cars. Dead bodies were frequently shot or stabbed by community members long after death. In 1937, a Georgia mob broke into a funeral home where an alleged murderer and rapist killed by police lay. They paraded his body through town yelling "We got the nigger, we got the nigger!" before burning it on the town's black baseball field using wood torn from the bleachers.[8] Fingers, toes, ears, teeth, and penises were often kept by participants as lynching souvenirs, and photos of townspeople posing proudly with dead bodies were commonly sold as postcards. One example showed a group of young white boys standing below a lynched black man and featured the words "This fucking nigger was hung in Clanton, Alabama, Friday, August, 21, 1891, for murdering a little white boy in cold blood for 35-cents cash."[9]

Also like war, lynching's threshold for killing was very low, showing little regard for due process or collateral damage. The real motives behind particular lynchings were often thrill killings, personal grudges, or power grabs, motives that often remained obscure until later investigation by historians.[10] Lynching the wrong people was shockingly common, something casually accepted by those responsible as inevitable given its style of rough and quick justice. When, in 1893, two sisters in Kentucky were murdered, a black man named C. J. Miller was arrested for the crime, and a lynch mob gathered to kill him. Since no evidence actually linked him to the killings, and he didn't even match the description some witnesses gave of the suspect, the father of the murder victims, unsure of his guilt, asked the mob to hang rather than burn him to death since it would be wrong to inflict the more painful punishment on someone who might be innocent. After his lynching, later investigation did prove that Miller was indeed innocent of the crime.[11] In 1918, a Georgia mob, unable to find the black suspect they were looking for in connection with the murder of a white farmer, simply killed several other black men they ran across as substitutes. When one of their pregnant wives, Mary Turner, expressed outrage at the killing of her innocent husband, the local population was, in the words of the *Atlanta Constitution*, "angered by her remarks, as well as her attitude." As a result, she was taken by another mob, one including women and children, and, in the historian Philip Dray's description, "stripped, hung upside down by the ankles, soaked with gasoline, and roasted to death," though not before "a white man opened her swollen belly with a hunting knife and her infant fell to the ground, gave a cry, and was stomped to death."[12]

Lynching was a form of scripted violence with a larger social purpose. Dray writes that it "celebrates killing and makes of it a ritual, turning grisly and inhumane acts of cruelty into theater with the explicit intent that they be viewed and remembered."[13] As an institution, lynching's aim was to send a signal about power and the proper social order, not just to its specific victims but to the public at large. This is why bodies were left hanging, heads mounted on pikes, and body parts distributed as souvenirs or displayed in store windows. Defending white supremacy in 1903, Mississippi Governor James K. Vardman said, "If it is necessary, every Negro in the state will be lynched," a statement that served as both a warning for blacks and a call to action for whites.[14] Under lynching, generations of black families lived in fear, their children's memories haunted by images of mobs coming in the night, and generations of white families were participants, their children's memories filled with images of community-sanctioned torture and killing.

Indeed, one of the most shocking things about lynching was its public nature and level of popular participation. Word of a lynching would bring people from all around to enjoy the show. Ten thousand people witnessed one in Texas in 1893. Fifteen thousand showed up for one the previous year in Arkansas.[15] Sam Hose's lynching in rural Georgia drew so many Atlanta residents rushing from church that Sunday morning that the railroad chartered a special excursion train, and a special steamboat charter hurried people down the Mississippi to see C. J. Miller's Kentucky lynching.[16] There was tremendous social pressure to participate as entire families, neighborhoods, and towns turned out. It was considered an especially fun outing for children. For one 1917 Memphis lynching, parents sent notes to school asking that their children be excused for the day.[17] Many lynchings included festive parades in which victims themselves were pulled through the streets to the delight of onlookers. One 1911 lynching in Pennsylvania included ice cream sundaes, and a Mississippi eyewitness reported on another in 1903: "It was quite a gala occasion, and as soon as the corpse was cut down all the crowd betook themselves to the park to see a game of baseball."[18]

As with war, political leaders and the media reinforced the institution's legitimacy. Running for reelection as South Carolina's governor in 1912, Cole Blease printed campaign posters that read, "A Governor Who Lauds Lynching."[19] Following the lynching of two accused kidnappers in 1933, California's governor said, "If any one is arrested for the good job, I'll pardon them all."[20] Southern newspapers called for criminal suspects to be lynched, printing lurid details of their alleged crimes and linking them to the imagined ever-present threat of black violence. Before one Georgia lynching, a local paper called on readers to "remember that shocking degradation which was inflicted by the black beast, his victim swimming in her husband's warm blood as the brute held her to the floor."[21] Several years later, another Georgia paper wrote of the "duty of all men who appreciate a noble, innocent, true woman, of all men who love their homes, their mothers, their wives, their daughters, and their sweethearts, their friends and companions, to bend every effort and every energy, and every means of running down and capturing, and punishing to the fullest extent" any black assaults on white women.[22] Like war, euphemistic language often helped obscure the reality of lynching for newspaper readers. They wrote of "men of firmness and judgment" who "rid our community of all the pests of society," who did "orderly" work, and who acted with "tact," "dignity," "grace," and "military and administrative talent."[23]

As was the case with dueling, some local laws prohibited lynching but had little effect in practice. On the frontier, police and courts were often too distant or weak to stop it. In the South, they were often unwilling. Southern lynch mobs routinely took suspects from local jails without police protest, and police often participated in the lynching itself. One district attorney intervened with an 1893 Texas mob but only to insist that the suspect be returned to his jurisdiction, where the original crime took place, for lynching.[24] On those rare occasions when Southern lynchers were charged with a crime, grand juries refused to indict or trial juries refused to convict. They deemed actions by the accused "not unreasonable" or justifiable homicide, or they accepted far-fetched defense arguments, such as the body was not really that of the alleged victim, or that local black residents and their Northern allies had actually carried out the killing to make the community look bad.[25] After one Mississippi lynching, a local observer said, "You couldn't convict the guilty parties if you had a sound film of the lynching."[26]

* * *

Like war, lynching was widely defended as necessary to protect a peaceful and secure order under extraordinary circumstances. Especially where conventional law enforcement was too slow, too weak, or too lenient, lynching was portrayed as offering the only effective way to protect the innocent from those intent on mayhem. In 1782, the Virginia legislature indemnified lynchers when their actions were "justified from the imminence of the danger."[27] When a group of miners in Dubuque, Iowa, lynched a man for murder in 1834, defenders stated, "If there exists no means of application of the laws over that region, it then follows that their own safety and preservation depend on regulations of their own adoption."[28] The same California governor who promised to pardon members of a lynch mob that killed two kidnapping suspects praised the deterrent effect on other criminals: "They'll learn they can't kidnap in this state."[29] And defenders of an 1855 lynching in Wisconsin argued that "sickly sentimentalists" who had recently abolished capital punishment in the state had left the law with too little deterrent effect to protect communities, meaning the people themselves had to act in self-defense.[30]

Lynching's justifications were always tied closely to the threat of social corruption, disorder, and violence. Those lynched were cold-blooded, incorrigible criminals putting a community's very way of life in danger, while the lynchers themselves, like soldiers, were brave and noble defenders of public safety and peaceful order. One defender praised lynchers as "a kind of holy brotherhood, whose duty it was to purge the community of its unruly members."[31] Supporters contrasted the unbridled violence represented by those lynched with the firm but dignified force used by those who brought them to justice. After an 1892 lynching in Memphis, a local newspaper reported, "There was no whooping, not even loud talking, no cursing, in fact nothing boisterous. Everything was done decently and in order. The vengeance was sharp, swift and sure, but administered with due regard to the fact that people were asleep all around."[32]

The Southern defense of lynching was especially centered on the pervasive threat of black crime and the righteousness of using violence in response. When he heard lynching called an outrage on the floor of Congress, one representative from Alabama responded: "I call it justice."[33] For him and his fellow proponents, lynching was the only effective way to defend against the dangers posed by black violence, especially the rape of white women. Southerners warned that "schemes of hate, of arson, of murder and rape are being hatched in the dark depths"; that given this threat, there is "no other remedy"; and that lynching was a "necessary and proper" deterrent response.[34] An observer noted how parents would bring "their children to teach them how to dispose of negro criminals." One newspaper praised the lynching of an accused murderer and rapist by saying it was important to send the message that "there is protection in Georgia for women and children." And in 1897, Rebecca Felton gave a widely noted speech on the dangers black workers posed to white women on isolated farms, saying, "If it takes lynching to protect woman's dearest possession from drunken, raving human beasts, then I say lynch a thousand a week if it becomes necessary."[35]

As in defenses of war, proponents of racial lynching in the South appealed to the realities of human nature. By their account, black violence, especially the desire to rape white women, was rooted in blacks' basic condition as a brutish and inferior race, and whites were justified in using force to protect against such violence and maintain the racial authority that was part of the natural and divine order, something confirmed by both religious leaders and scientific studies of race at the time. Lynching was an unavoidable part of the age-old conflict between the races, a natural reaction to the inevitable threat posed by black criminal violence. One defender argued that "lynching for crime is the law of nature, and will go on," while another called it a "fixed and unchangeable law," one "written in the heart of a race that reveres its women next to God."[36] A Texas congressman called lynching a "racial instinct" that amounted "a call to the preservation of the race."[37]

Some defenders of lynching recognized its ugliness but endorsed it anyway. Like many just war proponents, they considered it a necessary evil that should be minimized but not recklessly abolished completely. One eyewitness to several lynchings remembered them as "distressing affairs" but claimed that "the safety of the better classes in those troublous times often demanded quick and determined action."[38] Particularly in the South, moderate whites were torn by their aversion to lynching's violence and their belief that it was necessary to social order and community self-defense. Echoing just war's language of just cause, last resort, and proportionality, they urged it be used only when necessary and that its violence be limited to only what was required to get the job done. Rather than rowdy celebrations and torture, they advocated "civilized lynching" done with sober dignity and minimum bloodshed. Following Jesse Washington's Waco lynching, some residents objected to his mutilation and burning, expressing instead the sentiment: "If only they had just hung him."[39]

Like advocates of a just war who acknowledge its suffering but put blame on the enemy for initiating it, lynchers often blamed its victims and their allies for forcing their hand. Typical was the view expressed by a Georgia newspaper: "The causes that led up to it were the recent criminal assaults made by brutal negroes on defenseless white women."[40] When a South Carolina mob killed a black postmaster and his baby daughter in 1898, supporters blamed federal postal officials for insisting on his appointment over local objections.[41] And in 1916, one Southern judge stated that "the best way to stop lynchings is to stop the crimes that provoke the lynchings."[42]

Those opposed to lynching faced criticism much like that leveled against pacifist critics of war. They were seen as foolishly utopian. One defender of lynching wrote that it "would be as easy to check the rise and fall of the ocean's tides" as to eliminate it, while another argued that protecting white women from black rape was "human nature, and it is quite the same the world over."[43] They were considered guilty of a "maudlin sentimentality" and of being "un-American."[44] Lynching's white critics, like pacifists accused of hypocritically opposing war only when safe from military danger, were charged with having the luxury of moral purity because they lived "where their wives and daughters are perfectly safe."[45] They were also accused of being traitors and conspiring with racial enemies, since most national antilynching efforts were led by African American activists. Like neoconservative critics of Catholic doctrine who argue that morally squeamish opponents of war are more concerned about the possibility of civilian casualties than the threat posed by communists or Islamic terrorists, lynching's defenders accused its opponents of caring more about brutal criminals than their innocent victims. One defender wrote that if lynching's critics "said as much to the negro concerning the enormity of rape as they say to the white people concerning the enormity of lynching, raping would become less common."[46]

Above all, opponents of lynching, black and white, were branded as dangerous. Like pacifists, their seditious ideas and naïve sentimentality threatened to get people killed. For its white Southern defenders, giving up lynching amounted to a kind of unilateral disarmament, a reckless renunciation of community self-defense that would leave the innocent open to unchecked violence. For them, a proposed federal law against lynching was a "bill to encourage rape," a blank check for "the ignorant negroes of the South" to "commit the foulest of outrages," and the "lynching of the Constitution itself."[47] Mississippi Senator Theodore Bilbo warned that it would "open the floodgates of Hell."[48]

*   *   *

Ending the widespread practice of lynching in the United States took a long campaign to change both minds and laws. Spearheaded by early African American civil rights activists, such as Ida B. Wells, Walter White, and James Weldon Johnson, the antilynching movement aimed to, in Johnson's words, save "black America's body and white America's soul."[49] Long portrayed as dangerous, utopian, anti-American, and procriminal, these activists and their white allies gradually undermined and then eliminated a brutally violent and unjust social institution, one that people still alive today experienced as a routine, socially accepted, and normal part of life in many parts of the country.

As with the campaign against slavery, a central goal for lynching's opponents was to force a complacent public to face the institution's vicious reality. While black America understood its nature all too well, much of white America, like people who easily overlook the civilian suffering in their nation's overseas wars, turned a blind eye to its violence. Over decades, the movement patiently worked to spread images and stories of actual lynchings and their victims, especially those wrongly accused and killed, through books, plays, lectures, newspapers, and radio. As

Johnson said, "The raw, naked brutal facts of lynching must be held up before the eyes of this country until the heart of this nation becomes sick, until we get a reaction of righteous indignation that will not stop until we have swept away lynching as a national crime."[50]

Gradually Americans, first outside the South but eventually there too, began to associate lynching not with the protection of peace and security but with lawlessness and disorder. In 1935, Senator Edward Costigan of Colorado declared, "No man can be permitted to usurp the combined functions of judge, jury and executioner of his fellow men," while several years later, U.S. Attorney General Tom Clark, condemning mob rule, stated, "Only due process of law sustains our claim to orderly self-government."[51] Rather than the calm and careful operation of justice under the law, lynching represented the frenzy of unrestrained, and often misdirected, vengeance. One newspaper reporter witnessing a Maryland lynching wrote, "I saw 3,000 men go mad with the blood lust tonight. I saw them take a human being and make of his body a holocaust of revenge."[52]

Thanks to the efforts of lynching's opponents, more and more Americans began to see it as something disgraceful and anachronistic. It stood in stark contrast to the values the country championed in the Second World War. President Franklin Roosevelt called it an example of "pagan ethics" that did not belong in our "modern civilization," while newspaper ads pointed out that the United States was the only country where people were still burned at the stake.[53] It took longer for such attitudes to spread in the South, but eventually white moderates and economic elites turned on the institution there too, seeing it as a regional embarrassment that was bad for business. White Southern women were especially crucial in joining local groups opposed to lynching, a movement that began as small and marginalized but eventually grew to challenge the ideological legitimacy of an institution that depended so heavily on claims to protect women. The Southern author Lillian Smith wrote that region's white women "did not need the chivalry of a lynching to protect them and did not want it."[54]

In addition to challenging social attitudes, the antilynching movement carried out a long campaign of political and legal pressure. On the local level, it pushed law enforcement officials to crack down on lynching and demonstrated how determined police action could easily and nonviolently disperse lynch mobs. While such efforts saw some isolated successes, local officials in the South resisted them bitterly, and lynching's opponents pinned greater hope on federal action to end the practice. The most visible goal on this front was a federal law against lynching, something that activists spent decades working for. One of the more shameful facts about American political history is that such a law never actually passed the U.S. Congress, going down to defeat again and again in the face of Senate filibusters by Southern conservatives and inaction by presidents, like Franklin Roosevelt, who condemned lynching in general but showed little interest in taking the political risks necessary to end it in practice. It was only with the modern civil rights movement and the pressure it placed on the national government that federal prosecutors, using long-neglected nineteenth-century statutes, began to prosecute lynching as a denial of constitutional rights. At the same time, federal courts began imposing stricter due process requirements on local police and judges in the South, while Southern juries finally showed a willingness to convict members of lynch mobs.

Like other forms of institutionalized violence, lynching in the United States faded away rather than ending abruptly. From its Southern heyday in the late nineteenth and early twentieth centuries, it became less common as social attitudes turned against it. After the Second World War, it gradually shifted from a public practice conducted in the open with broad social participation to a more clandestine form of violence, though one that still enjoyed significant tacit support, including from local law enforcement. By the 1960s, it was one of several terror tactics used against civil rights workers. As federal and then local law enforcement cracked down on such tactics and the civil rights movement achieved its legislative and judicial successes, lynching, as it had existed for well over a century, disappeared from American life.

Of course, this does not mean that racial injustice and violence disappeared. Lynching was only one element in a broader and long-standing pattern of racial oppression, some dimensions of which continue to this day. Our country is still marked by segregation, economic inequality, voter suppression, and other injustices tied to race. Perhaps most significant are massive racial inequities in the criminal justice system, from incarceration for drug crimes to capital punishment rates, that in many ways became more pronounced just as lynching faded away. As we have seen before, some waning forms of institutionalized violence can feed into newer ones, even if ending the older ones is still a significant accomplishment itself.

Echoes of lynching also still exist in some hate crimes, though these have a very different character than full-blown lynching. They tend to be rare, isolated, involve small numbers of people, and produce community condemnation rather than support. Contrast the 1916 community-wide, public, and festive lynching of Jesse Washington in Waco with the 1998 killing of James Byrd in Jasper, another Texas community, by two white men on a dark country road. The more recent case's isolated nature, national and local outcry, and swift prosecution and conviction of the killers demonstrate that while racial violence still exists, its scope has narrowed dramatically, and its institutional legitimacy has disappeared.

Notes

1 Dray 2002, 216-18; and Waldrep 2002, 154-55.
2 This chapter relies primarily on Dray 2002; and Waldrep 2002.
3 Waldrep 2002, 46.
4 Lepore 2010, 79.
5 Dray 2002, 122-27.
6 Dray 2002, 44.
7 All accounts from Dray 2002, 13, 103-04, 349, 359-60, and 375.
8 Dray 2002, 360-61.
9 Dray 2002, 103.
10 See, for example, Waldrep 2002, 65-66.
11 Dray 2002, 92-93.
12 Dray 2002, 245-46.
13 Dray 2002, xii.
14 Lepore 2010, 79.
15 Dray 2002, 77.
16 Dray 2002, 13 and 91.
17 Dray 2002, 232.
18 Dray 2002, 81-82.
19 Waldrep 2002, 121.
20 Dray 2002, 334.
21 Waldrep 2002, 120.
22 Dray 2002, 163.
23 Waldrep 2002, 53, 59, and 90.
24 Dray 2002, 77.
25 Dray 2002, 372, 376, and chap. 10.
26 Dray 2002, 439.
27 Waldrep 2002, 18.
28 Waldrep 2002, 28.
29 Dray 2002, 334.
30 Waldrep 2002, 91.
31 Waldrep 2002, 25.
32 Dray 2002, 62.
33 Waldrep 2002, 82.
34 Dray 2002, 133 and 168; and Waldrep 2002, 128.
35 Dray 2002, 78, 5, and 125.
36 Waldrep 2002, 116 and 128.
37 Dray 2002, 264.
38 Waldrep 2002, 51.
39 Dray 2002, 234 and 218.
40 Dray 2002, 166.
41 Dray 2002, 117.
42 Waldrep 2002, 116.
43 Dray 2002, 72 and 64.

[44]Waldrep 2002, 129 and 166.
[45]Dray 2002, 73.
[46]Dray 2002, 145.
[47]Dray 2002, 264-65.
[48]Lepore 2010, 80.
[49]Dray 2002, 234.
[50]Dray 2002, 258.
[51]Dray 2002, 356 and 382.
[52]Dray 2002, 322.
[53]Dray 2002, 258, 270, and 336.
[54]Dray 2002, 330.

16

Realism and Moral Progress

The last several chapters demonstrated how forms of institutionalized violence once thought inevitable, morally legitimate, and necessary for social order were actually none of these things. And these aren't the only examples.

Take the practice of binding women's feet in China.[1] This was an excruciatingly painful process of breaking bones in the foot and gradually mutilating it to keep it artificially small, leaving women who endured it permanently disabled. For a thousand years, this was an institution central to Chinese civilization, one closely tied to ideal images of femininity, beauty, grace, and social order. While most often associated with wealthy elites, the practice spread to all classes as well. Families considered it necessary for social status and a crucial way to protect a daughter's respectability, honor, and marriage prospects. Across its long history, sporadic laws against it proved ineffective. In the early twentieth century, however, it was finally abolished. Reformers successfully portrayed it as cruel, anachronistic, and internationally embarrassing. Both public opinion and government policy eventually turned against it.

Or consider piracy on the high seas.[2] While it still exists in a few places, it is nothing like the pervasive global institution it once was. For most of human history, the open sea was considered beyond the reach of law, an anarchic state of nature where people were on their own. Many communities depended on piracy for their livelihoods. Nations considered it crucial to national power and a legitimate weapon of war, using pirates as proxy military forces against enemies. Local laws against it were impossible to enforce, and a country's attempts to suppress piracy unilaterally were considered not only hopeless but also foolish given how its rivals would continue to exploit it. Yet from its height in the sixteenth through eighteenth centuries, piracy largely collapsed as an international phenomenon within a few decades. Its moral legitimacy plunged and nations joined with each other to institute one of the first effective global prohibition regimes, applying law and its enforcement to the high seas and denying pirates national sponsors, safe harbors, and ways to sell their stolen goods.

Capital punishment is another good example.[3] It too still exists in some countries but is a shadow of its former self. For most of human history and across almost all cultures, putting people to death was a routine and socially acceptable criminal justice practice. People were executed for burglary, blasphemy, adultery, forgery, poaching, heresy, sodomy, cutting down trees, picking pockets, fraud, and hundreds of other offenses. Usually designed as public spectacles, offenders were killed through a truly horrifying range of methods, most designed to maximize pain and degradation. A small sample includes crucifixion, burning, starvation or exposure in a body-shaped cage, attack by animals or insects, skin peeling, breaking on a wheel, drawing and quartering, and being slowly impaled by sharp objects through the rectum or other bodily openings. Capital punishment was justified, including by the Catholic tradition, in precisely the same terms as war: regrettable violence undertaken by legitimate authorities to uphold peace and the tranquility of order. Its opponents were considered naïve, irreligious, and blind to the reality of sin and evil in the world. In the words of early American death penalty supporters, since it was "so clearly a law of nature," and since murder "never has been, and never can be, checked by a slighter penalty than death," those seeking its abolition threatened to unleash a wave of violence against the innocent. One critic of Benjamin Rush, an early American death penalty opponent, said that he "has never had a brother, a wife, or a child murdered by the cruel hands of any ruffian. It is all theory with him."[4] Yet even given its long history of frequent use and deep social acceptance, the last century has seen capital punishment increasingly considered cruel and uncivilized. It has been abolished in the majority of countries around the world and dramatically limited in those, like the United States, that continue to use it, all without the violent crime waves its defenders always said this would produce.

Aside from capital punishment, the history of criminal justice is littered with cruel practices once considered necessary for law and order. Excruciating forms of torture were long a standard part of judicial questioning and punishment for those convicted. The rack, flogging, waterboarding, the stocks, crushing fingers and toes, branding, and a host of other brutal techniques were accepted as part of the normal operation of policing and the courts. While some countries still use torture against criminal suspects and political opponents, it is no longer a routine and widely accepted practice. The very fact that those who still use it feel compelled to do so in secret and lie about it reveals the shift in moral attitudes toward torture. Another long-standing practice in the history of law enforcement was debtor's prisons. These held people in often brutal conditions for as long as it took for them to pay money they owed to creditors, and such harsh treatment was accepted as necessary for a functioning economy. Once such prisons were replaced by bankruptcy laws and far more humane legal sanctions for indebtedness, it became clear how unnecessary their harshness was.

What is remarkable about all these institutions, including the ones we examined in more detail over the previous chapters, is how they are part of a larger trend toward a dramatically less violent world. Given reports we routinely see of the terrible things people do to each other around the globe, this may strike some as strange, but, as scholars such as Steven Pinker and Pieter Spierenburg have recently detailed, it is true nonetheless.[5] Take murder rates, which are measured as the annual number of homicides per 100,000 people. Around the time war and slavery emerged in human societies, the rate was likely well over one hundred and remained high for nonstate peoples up into the twentieth century. Medieval and early modern Europe saw it fluctuate between fifty and one hundred, and colonial America was probably around one hundred, too. Over the last several centuries, however, it has steadily declined to a global average of between six and nine today, with the United States coming in at around four and Europe at one.[6] These are stunning declines in lethal violence. Even the most violent neighborhoods in the United States today have far lower murder rates than those found through much of human history.

Modernity has brought similar declines in both the rates and social legitimacy of other forms of violence, particularly in the developed world. Declining rates of rape coincide with a shift away from seeing it as a kind of property crime against fathers or husbands, or a moral offense akin to adultery, to an act of violence against women as persons, one that violates their basic human rights and is properly subject to criminal sanction. Rates of spousal abuse have also declined, as a practice formerly considered both appropriate and private has lost social legitimacy and is now considered a matter for police intervention. Modernity has brought similar shifts in the world of children. Harsh corporal punishment, laboring in brutal conditions, and routine beatings by other children have all gone from being accepted parts of childhood to injustices in need of redress, ones subject to social pressure and government regulations that have made children's lives much less violent. Religious pogroms, racial and ethnic riots, and socially endorsed violence against homosexual persons have all declined under conditions of modernity as well. Even formerly popular entertainments such as cat burning, bear baiting, bare knuckle boxing, and arranged battles among males from rival villages, neighborhoods, or professions with knives or clubs are now widely considered cruel and shocking. This in no way implies that things such as rape, child abuse, ethnic violence, or animal fighting have disappeared—only that they and similar forms of violence have all dramatically declined in the modern world, especially among the most developed countries. As Pinker writes, "It is easy to forget how dangerous life used to be, how deeply brutality was once woven into the fabric of daily existence."[7]

Declines among various forms of institutional and interpersonal violence over the last few centuries have been closely linked. Those who study this trend point to several factors.[8] Modernity has been associated with a gradual civilizing process. Ideas about manners and acceptable behavior around such things as bodily functions, eating, hygiene, and interpersonal conflicts have created higher levels of social discipline. Norms expecting people to exercise self-restraint and impulse control have become stricter. Such changes have gone hand in hand with growing economic complexity, prosperity, urbanization, and education. Another related factor has been the emergence over the last several centuries of a powerful humanitarian ethic, one marked by an expanding circle of empathy, a concern for the suffering of people we don't necessarily know personally, even those on the other side of the world. The spread of novels, plays, magazines, and, more recently, television, film, and on-line technology has provided intimate stories and images of the misery, injustice, and struggles facing others beyond our immediate social circle. While we often take this for granted today, it is something that would have made little sense to most people across the ages. As Charles Taylor writes, "We live in an extraordinary moral culture, measured against the norm of human history, in which suffering and death, through famine, flood, earthquake, pestilence, or war, can awaken worldwide movements of sympathy and practical solidarity."[9]

Growing humanitarian sympathy and action have been closely tied to the increasing importance attached to ideas about the moral equality, dignity, rights, and bodily integrity of individual persons over the last several centuries. This is why many of the efforts against various forms of violence have been so closely connected. Those working to end slavery, dueling, capital punishment, lynching, violence against women, animal cruelty, child abuse, and other injustices have overlapped considerably, and relied on very similar appeals over the history of such movements. In his biography of William Wilberforce, Eric Metaxas shows how he linked his antislavery work to a range of other reform efforts, seeing them as part of a unified "reformation of manners" to make society less cruel, violent, and disorderly.[10] These movements were successful not just in changing individual behavior, but public policy as well. Modernity is also marked by the increasing ability and willingness of the state to use its police powers to protect a growing circle of people from violent abuse, upholding their individual dignity and rights as part of a peaceful and just social order.

When it comes to violence, then, things really can get better. Ordinary human life is far less violent than it once was. Indeed, Pinker concludes that "today we may be living in the most peaceable era in our species' existence."[11] This reality of improvement is reason to rejoice, but it does not mean that we inhabit some kind of entirely just and nonviolent utopia. There is a critical difference between moral progress and moral perfection. It is entirely realistic to work for progress without expecting perfection, just as perfection's impossibility does not render progress illusionary. Ending trials by ordeal and combat was a good thing, even if they were replaced in part by judicial torture, just as dramatically reducing torture has been a blessing for humanity, even if it is not entirely gone. The world is better off without chattel slavery, even if forms of labor coercion and exploitation remain. The fact that lynching survived slavery, just as racial injustice and violence survived lynching, does not mean ending slavery and lynching were not immense moral achievements. Ending the vendetta and its successor the duel did not eliminate conflicts, including violent ones, from human relationships, but we are nonetheless better off without them.

Opponents of these various forms of institutionalized violence consistently faced charges of being unrealistic and foolishly utopian, but what their critics always missed was the fact that we can make moral progress without achieving moral perfection. Abolishing a particular injustice does not mean ushering in a realm of perfect justice. Moral improvement does not require overcoming all instances of violence, abuse, conflict, selfishness, exploitation, and all the other failings humanity suffers from. Even as the materials offered by the human condition remain the same, we can clearly use them to construct communities that are better or worse. The crooked timber of humanity can never make a flawless social structure, but that doesn't mean some can't be sounder than others, something we know from historical experience. This is why the ways in which violence is or is not socially institutionalized is so important. In a society that has slavery, an ordinary person, one possessing the average admixture of virtue and vice, is perfectly capable of owning slaves. It doesn't require exceptional moral depravity. But in a society without slavery, an ordinary person possessing the average admixture of virtue and vice would never think of enslaving another human being. In such a society, rejecting slavery does not require exceptional moral goodness. The same is true of other forms of institutionalized violence.

So the reason moral progress is realistic is that it is entirely possible to change such institutions, even abolish them, without radically changing human nature itself.

This is also why we still need politics. Because moral progress cannot rely on moral perfection, because we are still dealing with the crooked timber of humanity, we cannot eliminate the need for political power. As we have seen, abolishing institutional violence is a self-reinforcing process of changing both social attitudes and public policies. Precisely because the human capacity for violence, abuse, exploitation, and so on remains, state action to restrain such capacities is still necessary. Dueling ended because many people concluded it was wrong, but also because others wanted to avoid going to prison or being cashiered from the army. Lynching ended because many people turned against it, but also because others perfectly happy to continue doing it feared the legal consequences. Abolishing slavery or piracy or capital punishment around the world has not simply been a process of changing moral attitudes within countries, but also one of bringing political pressure, providing incentives, and enforcing sanctions, all designed to convince countries reluctant to give up such things to do so anyway. Abolishing institutionalized violence, then, certainly means transforming moral beliefs, but it also means making it in people's self-interest to go along, at least until the institution itself fades far enough into the past that people no longer seriously consider it, and this is something that requires political action.

* * *

This kind of belief in moral progress without moral perfection is exactly the blend of hope and realism found in contemporary Catholic doctrine. As the peacemaking agenda we explored in chapter 4 illustrates, the Catholic tradition teaches that there are universal moral values that have the potential to transform the world for the better. At the same time, the reality of sin means the earthly realm will never achieve the perfect peace promised by God's kingdom, something that makes continuing attempts at gradual improvement through moral persuasion and political reform necessary.

On some matters, the Catholic tradition views modernity with suspicion—the rise of secularism, moral relativism, or new assaults on human life made possible by technology, for example. On others, however, it finds much to applaud. Human rights, democracy, moral equality, the dignity of the human person, solidarity, and humanitarian concern are all central to Catholic teaching today. Acknowledging and celebrating the growth of such values, it praises, in the words of *Gaudium et Spes*, the modern world's "keener sense of human dignity," the "growing discovery and vindication" of human rights, and "the birth of a new humanism."[12] As John Paul II puts it, "The fact that men and women in various parts of the world feel personally affected by the injustices and violations of human rights committed in distant countries, countries which perhaps they will never visit, is a further sign of a reality transformed into awareness, thus acquiring a moral connotation."[13]

John Paul II writes that "man, who was created for freedom, bears within himself the wound of original sin, which constantly draws him toward evil and puts him in need of redemption."[14] This is why sin will always "contaminate" the "social sphere" to some extent.[15] But this in no way prevents the reality of progress within the fallen world. The Second Vatican Council speaks to civilization's "advance toward maturity," and the "task of constructing for all men everywhere a world more genuinely human."[16] John Paul II invokes Catholicism's "optimistic view of history" and states, "However imperfect and temporary are all the things that can and ought to be done through the combined efforts of everyone and through divine grace, at a given moment of history, in order to make people's lives 'more human,' nothing will be lost or will have been in vain."[17] In spite of the reality of sin in the world, beliefs in the possibility of "social progress" are not "vain flights of fancy" according to Paul VI.[18] *Gaudium et Spes* argues that while "on pilgrimage toward the heavenly city," we have a duty to "work with all men in the building of a more humane world," and that "while earthly progress must be carefully distinguished from the growth of Christ's kingdom, to the extent that the former can contribute to the better ordering of human society, it is of vital concern to the Kingdom of God."[19] Echoing this call for improvement on this side of the kingdom, John Paul II writes in *Sollicitudo rei Socialis*,

> The Church well knows that no temporal achievement is to be identified with the Kingdom of God, but that all such achievements simply reflect and in a sense anticipate the glory of the Kingdom, the Kingdom which we await at the end of history, when the Lord will come again. But that expectation can never be an excuse for lack of concern for people in their concrete personal situations and in their social, national and international life, since the former is conditioned by the latter, especially today.[20]

In other words, the impossibility of moral perfection is never a legitimate excuse to give up on moral progress.

While the inevitable reality of sin does not make progress toward a more nonviolent and humane world impossible, it does make it difficult, something certainly confirmed by the movements to abolish institutionalized violence detailed over the last several chapters. John XXIII writes in *Pacem in Terris*, "If there is to be any improvement in human institutions, the work must be done slowly and deliberately from within."[21] And in calling for the abolition of "structures of sin," John Paul II calls it "a task which demands courage and patience."[22] This is consistent with the traditional Catholic emphasis on engaging the world through mainstream institutions and conventional politics. The reality of sin makes both moral conversion and political power necessary for progress, and it means such progress will rarely come easy. Improvements are incremental and uneven, coming in stops and starts, and demanding compromises and settling for partial victories along the way. This is the difficult road taken by those seeking to gradually undermine, weaken, and ultimately abolish entrenched forms of institutional violence. And it is the way we can eventually do away with war, leaving a world far from perfect, but one nonetheless better for its absence.

Notes

[1]I rely here on Appiah 2010, chap. 2.
[2]I rely here on Lane 1998; Ritchie 1986, chap. 10; Andreas and Nadelmann 2006, chap. 1; and Nadelmann 1990, 486-91.
[3]I rely here on Cawthorne 2006; Bae 2007; Megivern 1997; and Banner 2002.
[4]Banner 2002, 116, 114, and 106.
[5]Pinker 2011; and Spierenburg 2008.
[6]Pinker 2011, chap. 3.
[7]Pinker 2011, 1.
[8]Again, Pinker 2011 and Spierenburg 2008 are most helpful here.
[9]Taylor 1999, 25.
[10]Metaxas 2007, chap. 6.
[11]Pinker 2011, xxi.
[12]Second Vatican Council 1965, nos. 73, 41, and 55.
[13]John Paul II 1987, no. 38.
[14]John Paul II 1991a, no. 25.
[15]Second Vatican Council 1965, no. 25.
[16]Second Vatican Council 1965, no. 25.
[17]John Paul II 1987, nos. 31-47.
[18]Paul VI 1967, nos. 34 and 79.
[19]Second Vatican Council 1965, nos. 57 and 39.
[20]John Paul II 1987, no. 47.
[21]John XXIII 1963, no. 162.
[22]John Paul II 1991a, no. 38.

SECTION IV

ENDING WAR

The Path to Abolition

Speaking in Coventry, England, in 1982, John Paul II declared, "War should belong to the tragic past, to history, it should find no place on humanity's agenda for the future."[1] While its neoconservative critics dismiss contemporary Catholic teaching's calls to end war as an idealistic delusion, doing so is by no means impossible. While long and difficult, there is a realistic path away from war open to humanity. Indeed, it is one we are already on, and, while there is no guarantee we will see it through, it is entirely within our power to do so.

As other forms of institutionalized violence show, abolitionism of any kind is based on the reality of moral progress without moral perfection. It is possible to rid ourselves of war without ridding ourselves of international conflict and injustice. The pursuit of national self-interest by states can still exist in a world without war. So can greed, hostility, suspicion, and ambition. Just as abolishing slavery didn't end racism or labor exploitation, and abolishing the duel didn't end conflicts over romance or reputation, abolishing war will produce a better world, but not one of perfect peace and justice. We can eliminate war and improve human life without fundamentally changing our fallen nature and the discontents it still brings.

Understanding this reality helps avoid both fatalism, accepting war as an inescapable feature of the human condition, and utopianism, expecting a world without wrongdoing and strife. Realism does not mean complacency, and rejecting war does not mean ignoring the world as it is. A realistic abolitionism also argues against what Kenneth Himes labels the "sectarian withdrawal" of some pacifist traditions, the tendency to reject not only participation in war but all forms of ordinary political power as inherently corrupting. Abolishing war doesn't mean turning away from the state and its legitimate role in protecting Augustine's "tranquility of order."[2]

The quest to eliminate war, like eliminating other forms of deeply rooted institutionalized violence in human history, is a lengthy and uneven process, one demanding ongoing efforts to shift both cultural attitudes and public policies. It means working through mainstream social institutions and conventional politics; great ends often demand modest and pragmatic means. Abolishing war is not about eliminating the conflicts that drive it so much as gradually replacing it with other institutionalized ways to address those conflicts. And ending war does not end the need for government power to uphold peace, justice, and stability. A world without war is still one in need of policing, of rewards and punishments for behavior, of ways to resolve disputes and enforce compliance.

Interestingly enough, a realistic path toward war's abolition also has the potential to render theoretical debates about just war and pacifism moot. In considering the case against war offered by Erasmus, Stanley Hauerwas writes that no "particular theological beliefs are required for such a position."[3] He means this as a criticism, that Erasmus does not center his pacifism specifically on discipleship to Jesus Christ. But if humanity is finally to set aside war, it will be arguments like those of Erasmus, ones expressed in universal terms and relying on mainstream political action, that will have to carry the day. Campaigns against other forms of institutionalized violence certainly drew on deep religious commitments for support, but their success relied upon also reaching people who didn't necessarily share those commitments. Supporting the steps necessary to abolish war does not require a radical form of discipleship, embracing Christianity, or any particular religious beliefs at all. It doesn't even require pacifism. Many people who believe in the possibility of war's justness would nonetheless be perfectly happy to see it eliminated from human affairs. The end of trials by ordeal or slavery left plenty of unresolved philosophical and theological disputes in their wake, but such disputes lost their relevance as their subjects faded into history. Moral disagreements about the legitimacy of war would be far less important if we could manage to just get rid of it altogether, a development almost all participants in such disputes would presumably welcome.[4]

* * *

So what are the prospects for ending war? An answer must begin with what we have already accomplished. It turns out that, perhaps without realizing it, humanity has become far less warlike compared to the past. This doesn't guarantee we will continue moving away from war, but it does help reveal the path open for doing so.

Measuring long-term trends in warfare is a complicated process, and it gets more difficult the further back researchers go, but the overall direction is clear: a decline in the frequency and lethality of war is part of the long-term reduction in violence that we examined in the last chapter.[5] On a per capita basis, the earliest kind of war found in many prestate tribes and chiefdoms was extraordinarily lethal. Perhaps 15 percent of each generation was killed in chronic low-level warfare, a rate that would equal about a million war deaths each and every year for the contemporary United States. For modern equivalents, only the exceptionally deadly violence of the kind found in Eastern Europe during the Second World War approaches the normal casualty rate for this kind of prestate war.[6] Following the rise of states, war trends fluctuate, but they show an overall decline across the last few centuries, one that is masked by the two world wars during the first half of the twentieth century, which created a temporary spike in an otherwise downward long-range trajectory.

The last half-century has seen the most dramatic retreat from warfare across the globe. War's frequency, duration, and rate of battle deaths have all declined since the conclusion of the Second World War, and this trend accelerated with the Cold War's end over two decades ago. The last three decades have seen annual battle deaths drop 75 percent, even as the global population sharply increased. The world is averaging almost half as many armed conflicts today as it did during the late 1980s, and the wars we do fight kill fewer people than they did during the Cold War.[7] While still a long way from being abolished, warfare has now declined to levels unprecedented since its invention.

These trends reflect striking declines in certain types of war. Warfare between great powers has accounted for the lion's share of its death and destruction over much of human history, but in what political scientist Robert Jervis calls "the single most striking discontinuity that the history of international politics has anywhere provided," war between world powers has essentially stopped.[8] The only case after the Second World War is sixty years ago, when the United States and China fought against each other in the Korean War.[9] Equally remarkable is the virtual disappearance of wars over territory, which historically accounted for around 80 percent of the total. Wars to conquer neighboring states, secure overseas colonies, and redraw international boundaries have gone from being routine to being extraordinarily rare since the Second World War.[10]

In fact, interstate wars of any kind, those fought between two or more countries, have declined dramatically over the last half-century, though the United States in its willingness to invade other countries is an important exception to this trend. While such interstate conflicts once accounted for most wars, the vast majority today are civil wars fought within states.[11] It is these kinds of conflicts that present the biggest remaining challenge to reducing war further toward abolition. While civil wars have shown some decline over the last several decades—the number of major ones in Africa dropped from seven to four between 2001 and 2010, for example—it has been slower and more uneven than for war generally.[12] Parts of the world are still plagued by cycles of chronic low-intensity armed conflict within weak or failed states. As John Mueller details, many of these conflicts are "opportunistic predation" by small and undisciplined groups of "criminals, bandits, and thugs."[13] On his account, noble-sounding causes based on ideology, ethnicity, or religion are often mere covers for insurgency groups more interested in looting, smuggling, and other forms of organized crime. While such conflicts can still unleash terrible death and destruction, especially on civilian populations, they differ significantly from the much larger and better organized armed conflict traditionally associated with war. Indeed, Mueller refers to them as the "remnants of war," a kind of blend of warfare and organized crime that is left over after most other forms of war have seen such remarkable reductions.

The dynamics driving war's overall decline are complex, but their general shape is familiar from other forms of institutionalized violence we have considered. Start with social attitudes. Much like broad-based social opposition to slavery as such only emerged about a century before its fall, attitudes toward war have undergone similar shifts. While pacifism has been around for millennia, a broader-based and more general war aversion, even among those who consider it an unfortunate if rare necessity, has only emerged in the last century or so as a significant social force in many countries.[14] While a romantic belief in the goodness of war itself was once common—Alex de Tocqueville said it "almost always widens a nation's mental horizons and raises its heart," while John Ruskin believed it "the foundation of all the high virtues and faculties of man"—such sentiments are rare today.[15] Beginning in the late-nineteenth century and accelerating in the wake of the First World War, a cultural skepticism toward war in general, if not always particular wars, began to grow. This shift is evident in the emergence of more critical treatments of war in art, literature, and the teaching of many religious traditions. It is also closely tied to the growth of humanitarian concern for suffering, human rights, and individual dignity around the world. While this general process of war aversion obviously still has a long way to go, it does mark, as John Keegan notes in his global history of the institution, "a profound change in civilization's attitude toward war."[16] And as we saw in chapter 4, the Catholic tradition has been especially supportive of this shift, not only in its own increasingly powerful condemnations of war, but in praising how humanity, in the words of John XXIII in *Pacem in Terris*, is "becoming more and more convinced that any disputes which may arise between nations must be resolved by negotiation and agreement, not by recourse to arms."[17]

Like other forms of institutionalized violence, a general shift in social attitudes has gone hand in hand with a series of more specific institutional changes in both domestic and international affairs that have done much to reduce war and have the potential to do even more. What is remarkable about these changes is how closely they overlap with contemporary Catholic teaching's peacemaking agenda. Recall its basic priorities: strengthening global political authority and international law to promote closer cooperation among nations; democracy, the rule of law, human rights, and protections for vulnerable national minorities; a growing appreciation for the power of nonviolence; global development that includes widely shared economic growth as well as improvements in basic human security and well-being; and robust conflict resolution and peacekeeping efforts lead by networks of states, intergovernmental organizations, and civil society groups.

As we will see in chapters that follow, it turns out that these are the very factors helping drive the decline of war, ones that have the potential to push it even further toward abolition. They are also the very ones ridiculed by Catholic teaching's neoconservative critics as foolishly sentimental, feckless, cowardly, secularist, anti-American, and dangerous. But while such critics dismiss the Catholic peacemaking agenda as hopelessly utopian, a wealth of social scientific research confirms that it is actually a powerfully realistic blueprint for eliminating war. Pursuing its priorities has done much to reduce war already, and it offers a path to make further progress toward ensuring that war joins ordeals, trials by combat, vendettas, duels, slavery, lynching, and a host of other examples of institutional violence as practices once thought inevitable but now recognized as immoral anachronisms rightly discarded by humanity.

Notes

[1]United States Conference of Catholic Bishops 1983, no. 219.
[2]Himes 1991, 338.
[3]Hauerwas 1988, 155.
[4]Stassen 2008, introduction; Hauerwas 2011, 45-46; and Koontz 1996, 169-73.
[5]Pinker 2011, especially chaps. 5-6; Goldstein 2011, especially chaps. 2 and 9; Mueller 2004; Wallensteen 2007, chaps. 2 and 4; Ramsbotham, Woodhouse, and Miall 2005, chap. 3; Potts and Hayden 2008, chap. 7; and Dyer 2004, 94-97.
[6]Dyer 2004, 94.
[7]Goldstein 2011, 5-6 and 13; Hewitt 2010; and Pinker 2011, 305.
[8]Jervis 2002, 1.

[9]Pinker 2011, 225.

[10]Pinker 2011, 251 and 259; and Goldstein 2011, 278-79.

[11]Doyle and Sambanis 2006, 11; Goldstein 2011, 237; Pinker 2011, chap. 6; and Mueller 2004, chaps 5-6.

[12]Horgan 2012, 137; and Goldstein 2011, 237.

[13]Mueller 2004, 1.

[14]Pinker 2011, chap. 3; Mueller 2004, chap. 2; and Cortright 2008.

[15]Tocqueville 1969, 649; and Ruskin 2008, 70.

[16]Keegan 1993, 58.

[17]John XXIII 1963, no. 126.

18

Global Political Authority

Perhaps the biggest obstacle to abolishing war is the unilateral problem. Like other types of institutionalized violence, it is tough to give up if others are unwilling to go along. A medieval family wanting to avoid vendettas found it difficult if other families insisted on attacking its members. Plenty of nineteenth-century American politicians or German army officers opposed to dueling nonetheless considered it impossible to refuse a challenge from others who did not share that opinion. Many nations thought independently renouncing slavery or piracy would leave them at the mercy of those who did not. Supporters of torture, capital punishment, and trials by ordeal and combat all argued that abolition would leave them defenseless against crime and social chaos.

This fear of unilateral disarmament is one reason movements to eliminate institutionalized violence do not rely on moral persuasion alone. Changes in social attitudes are crucial, but they must work together in a mutually reinforcing cycle with effective enforcement mechanisms targeting those who remain unmoved. These mechanisms are usually a blend of existing and newly emerging forms of social and political authority. Recall how officials seemed powerless to stop dueling until shifting attitudes gave them enough legitimacy to do so, or the way trials by ordeal and combat were suppressed by changing church practices and evolving judicial structures. Vendettas and lynching often flourished where political institutions were too weak and underdeveloped to stop them, and they were only abolished when such institutions became mature enough to act effectively against them.

This is why contemporary Catholic doctrine consistently links its calls to end war with the need to strengthen global political authority. While some nations do seem to have turned away from war unilaterally—Japan, Costa Rica, several Scandinavian countries—this is often with the implicit promise of military protection from a stronger power, and most countries around the world are unwilling to completely renounce war as long as it may expose them to military risk from others. The Catholic tradition's answer to this security dilemma is to support an international system of governance capable of enforcing global norms against war, much as domestic governments act to prevent bloodshed between private citizens. In *Centesimus Annus*, John Paul II argues that just as "in individual States a system of private vendetta and reprisal has given way to the rule of law, so too a similar step forward is now urgently needed in the international community."[1]

This position is easily caricatured as calling for some kind of global superstate that will abolish all national governments and rule the world directly. Critics usually reject it outright, raising either the specter of a United Nations world dictatorship or labeling it foolishly utopian. Reacting to Benedict XVI's *Caritas in Veritate*, George Weigel calls its strong support for strengthening global political authority a "fantasy," one whose continuing place in magisterial teaching amounts to "one of the enduring mysteries of the Catholic Church."[2] Here again, however, contemporary Catholic doctrine is more sensible and realistic than its neoconservative critics admit. In drawing a parallel to the rise of the modern state within countries, Catholic teaching is pointing to how new political institutions can emerge over time in response to violence and disorder. This process can also happen on the international level, but without duplicating those same institutions. More effective global governance does not require a single world superstate; indeed John Paul II explicitly rejects such an interpretation.[3] Instead, it is possible to develop more diffused and multidimensional forms of effective authority within a gradually evolving international realm.

There is a popular notion that international affairs necessarily unfold in a state of nature, one where countries must rely on self-help, doing whatever is necessary to pursue and protect their national interests, including war. But this is not the case. Researchers studying the international arena have shown how shared institutions, norms, and cultural meanings powerfully shape the behavior of individual states within it, providing the basis for how they view the actions of others, make judgments, and decide what is reasonable and acceptable. This process also shapes how states take on certain identities and define their national interests in the first place. As international institutions, norms, and cultural meanings shift, so too do the identities, interests, and behavior of states. This does not guarantee peace. An international context in which common institutions, values, and perceptions center on war, competition for resources, suspicion, and hostility can easily lead to cycles of armed conflict. But the context in which states interact with each other need not go in that direction. It can instead support greater trust, reciprocity, and peaceful conflict resolution. As such values become institutionalized, simply part of the normal way states understand their international roles and what counts as acceptable behavior in their interactions with each other, they become mutually reinforcing. This process does not depend on tightly centralized power to control behavior. Instead, authority is spread across a wide array of structures and expectations that actors increasingly accept as simply the way things properly work. These actors also become more willing to use a variety of tools to require compliance from others. The deeper, stronger, and more multidimensional such a process becomes, the more potential it has to uphold norms against warfare.[4]

The decline of war has coincided with the emergence of just such a development in the international order. Since the Second World War, the world has seen the emergence of a much more sophisticated and coherent international community, one that is both the source and target of diffuse but growing global political authority. This authority does not replace national sovereignty, but it does constrain and shape its exercise through an overlapping network of institutions linking individual states to both intergovernmental and nongovernmental organizations (IGOs and NGOs). These institutions range from global bodies such as the United Nations, the World Bank, and the International Criminal Court; to regional organizations such as the European Union, the Association of Southeast Asian Nations, and a host of more specific bodies regulating everything from fishing to transportation systems; to free trade zones such as that established by the North American Free Trade Agreement; to development and advocacy organizations such as Catholic Relief Services, Doctors without Borders, Greenpeace, and Human Rights Watch.

Such institutions are the basis for a growing "complex multilateralism," a web of interaction relying on cooperation and reciprocity and established by ongoing contact among government officials, international diplomats, civil society groups, media organizations, social movements, businesses, scientists, cultural leaders, and others engaged in regular transnational collaboration.[5] It is this long-term trend that best captures Catholic teaching's concern for global political authority. Pointing to a growing sense of being a single world community and the need for greater "international order," the Second Vatican Council calls for "countries to cooperate more advantageously and more closely together and to organize together international bodies and work tirelessly for the creation of organizations which will foster peace."[6] Paul VI endorses "setting up structures in which the rhythm of progress would be regulated with a view to greater justice" in the international community, and John Paul II urges a "greater degree of international ordering" and celebrates the proliferation of IGOs and NGOs dedicated to doing so.[7]

Complex multilateralism's network of institutions helps foster the emergence of global norms. In some cases, these are values spread informally through ongoing international interaction to the point where they are internalized and, in the words of political scientist Alexander Wendt, "become taken for granted rather than objects of calculation."[8] In other cases, they are formally embodied in international laws, treaties, agreements, and organizational charters. From the role of the Universal Declaration of Human Rights and the Helsinki Accords in spreading a commitment to human rights, to that of the General Agreement on Tariffs and Trade in promoting free trade, formal statements of norms are a powerful way to deepen their global legitimacy. This is why Benedict XVI says the growth of international law is so closely tied to a "commitment to strengthening the profound human content of international norms."[9]

Norms spread partly through their inherent attractiveness—the moral force of human rights or the practical benefits of free trade, for example—but the international community also enforces them with a range of specific tools. Diplomatic isolation and negative international attention put pressure on states not wanting to be seen as "an outlaw in the community of nations."[10] More specific sanctions can include import and export embargoes, freezing assets, and travel bans. These are matched by positive incentives such as diplomatic recognition or support in other areas, favorable trade deals, debt relief, technology transfers, membership in regional organizations, and development aid. None of these enforcement mechanisms are guaranteed to succeed. It is difficult, for example, for them to remove a country's regime entirely. But they do have an impressive record of success in modifying behavior, especially if multiple methods are used in combination, they are tied to specific demands, and they enjoy broad multilateral support.[11] Wendt shows how external pressure brought by international sanctions and incentives can produce "repeated compliance" by targeted states, something that eventually leads them to "internalize" the norms of a particular institution. He writes, "Even if states initially comply with this institution for reasons of coercion or self-interest, continuing adherence over time will tend to produce conceptions of identity and interest which presuppose its legitimacy, making compliance habitual or second nature. External constraints become internal constraints, so that social control is achieved primarily through self-control."[12]

This process of establishing, enforcing, and internalizing global norms is the very one that targeted piracy in the eighteenth century, slavery in the nineteenth, and a host of issues since.[13] While certainly more effective in some cases than others, it is responsible for significant changes in the international landscape and has the potential to do more. The international community relies on it to enforce free trade agreements, coordinate infectious disease responses, and counter environmental threats such as the manufacture of ozone-depleting chemicals. It has driven the dramatic decline of capital punishment around the world, even in the face of significant opposition to abolition in most countries.[14] It has made possible certain things we now take for granted, such as the smooth delivery of international mail or the extradition of criminals from one country to another, something once seen as violating a state's integrity but now considered a routine "normative responsibility of governments."[15]

Even something as central to national sovereignty as law enforcement has seen a dramatic rise in international coordination to address the global nature of smuggling, human trafficking, money laundering, counterfeiting, and other crimes.[16]

The spread of global norms also has much to do with the decline of war. It has contributed to the remarkable drop in the legitimacy of wars to expand borders or secure overseas colonies. Much of the world now exists in "zones of peace" where such a war is inconceivable, where stronger countries that could easily absorb weaker neighbors for their land, resources, and industry don't even think of doing so.[17] Even though the United States has had a variety of economic and environmental conflicts with Canada and could easily defeat the Canadian military in a war, any American leader proposing an invasion would be considered joking or mad.[18] Consider too the issue of a nation's outstanding debts. Their collection was once a routine cause for war, but such action is now rejected as too absurd to seriously consider.[19] Even as an ongoing debt crisis following the 2008 world financial meltdown threw European countries into sharp conflict, there was never a remote possibility that Germany or France would invade Greece or Spain. Military coups provide another instance. As the norm of peaceful transitions of power has spread, their global rate has dropped by half since the end of the Cold War.[20]

Another example is weapons of mass destruction. International relations scholars have found evidence that a strong norm against the use of nuclear and biological weapons has significantly influenced state behavior since the end of the Second World War, including the phenomenon of countries losing wars while still refusing to use them.[21] Indeed, there are many countries around the world that could easily develop nuclear weapons but have not, and since the mid-1960s, as many countries have given them up as have joined the nuclear club.[22] The United States and Russia, who together account for well over 90 percent of the world's nuclear weapons, have reduced their stockpiles by two-thirds since the end of the Cold War.[23] None of this is to say that nuclear and biological weapons do not remain a serious threat, especially the prospect of their spread to new countries or terrorist groups, but only that global norms have shown the potential to control them.

Obviously, norms developed and implemented by the international community are not an instant cure for the world's problems. They have done much good, but their effectiveness is uneven and often incomplete. Some issues prove more difficult to address than others. For war in particular, progress so far is important but there is still a long way to go. What this process demonstrates, however, is that the international community does have the ability to better police itself. Despite being dismissed by its neoconservative critics, Catholic doctrine's emphasis on global political authority is informed by moral realism. Global affairs still require the exercise of power, but this power need not involve war. It can instead operate through a rich array of still-maturing global institutions, ones developing both the legitimacy and the enforcement power to uphold international law and order. Better global policing is a realistic alternative to war.[24]

Notes

[1]John Paul II 1991a, no. 52.

[2]Weigel 2009b.

[3]John Paul II 2003a, no. 6.

[4]For this perspective, usually referred to as constructivism within the field of international relations, see Wendt 1992, 1999; and Katzenstein 1996. For its relation to Christian, including Catholic, understandings of war and peace, see Shadle 2011; Neufeldt 2007; and Schroeder 2008.

[5]Morgan 2006, chap. 8; and Wendt 1999, chap. 7.

[6]Second Vatican Council 1965, nos. 33, 83-84, and 88.

[7]Paul VI 1971, no. 45; John Paul II 1987, no. 43; John Paul II 2000; and John Paul II 2004.

[8]Wendt 1999, 310-11.

[9]Benedict XVI 2008, 13.

[10]Toulmin 1992, 288.

[11]See, for example, Kupchan 2010; Cortright 2007; and Lopez 2008.

[12]Wendt 1999, 360-61.

[13]Nadelmann 1990; and Andreas and Nadelmann 2006, chap. 1.

[14]Bae 2007.

[15]Nadelmann 1990, 501-02.

[16]Andreas and Nadelmann 2006.

[17]Goldstein 2011, chap. 11; and Ramsbotham, Woodhouse, and Miall 2005, chap. 3.

[18]Wendt 1999, 300.

[19]Ray 1989, 432.

[20]Goldstein 2011, 244; and Wallensteen 2007, 127.

[21]Price and Tannenwald 1996; and Morgan 2006, 81.

[22]Pinker 2011, 272-73.

[23]Goldstein 2011, 18.

[24]For an excellent collection of essays on this theme, see Schlabach 2007c.

19

Democracy, the Rule of Law, and Nonviolence

In his 2003 annual peace message, John Paul II calls the spread of democracy around the world "one of the great dynamics of contemporary history."[1] This process is central to Catholic teaching's peacemaking agenda. And with good reason. The gradual expansion of democratic norms across the globe is a key factor driving the worldwide decline of war.[2]

The existence of a democratic peace is one of the most powerful findings in political science. With theoretical roots in the work of Immanuel Kant, empirical studies have consistently uncovered a remarkable absence of war between democracies.[3] Especially over the last two centuries, which correspond to the rise of modern democracy, democratic regimes rarely if ever get into wars with each other. This does not necessarily mean that democracies will avoid wars against nondemocracies, as plenty of examples in the historical record demonstrate, though there is evidence that democracies are less prone to war overall compared to their nondemocratic counterparts. The upshot, then, is that democratic regimes are generally less warlike than nondemocratic ones and almost never make war on each other.

This phenomenon creates the possibility for an expanding zone of peace as the number of democratic countries grows. The more countries that embrace democracy, the less likely war becomes. This seems to be precisely what has happened in recent decades. Since the Second World War, the decline of armed conflict has coincided with an increase in the percentage of the world's countries that are democratic. The number of democracies has more than doubled since the early 1970s. They went from being outnumbered by autocracies during much of the Cold War, to being about even by its end, to becoming a majority of the world's countries in the years since, now standing at around 60 percent.[4] This is real progress, but the news is not all good. There are still plenty of nondemocratic regimes, the rapid increase in the number of democracies following the Cold War's end has slowed in the last decade, and some countries, Russia for example, have slipped back toward autocracy.[5]

Another challenge the democratic peace faces in reducing war is the transition problem. As countries move from autocracy toward democracy, they often go through a period of instability and social strain. While scholars disagree about its significance, there is evidence that such transitions can actually increase the risk of both interstate and civil war.[6] There are several factors at work here. Young democracies are subject to score settling by new leaders and sabotage by old ones. They often see rising nationalist figures mobilizing support through an aggressive foreign policy or scapegoating minorities within the country, especially ones associated with the old regime. Emerging religious parties sometimes seem more interested in theocracy than democracy, a problem particularly pressing in the Middle East. New democracies also tend to have immature political institutions, ones less capable of delivering basic security, government services, and reliable conflict resolution. Their combination of new openness and the remaining tools of repression increase the risk that leaders will see elections as zero-sum games to monopolize power and national resources, turning to corruption, patronage, and violence to gain and maintain control. Once countries become mature democracies, they are more stable and less prone to war than autocracies, but the transition can be difficult, and there is a risk countries can be stuck between the two for long periods or slide back into autocracy.

The problems facing many new democracies are the same ones that make weak and failed states generally more prone to war: an absence of law and order. As John Mueller writes, "To a very substantial degree, the amount of warfare that persists in the world today—virtually all of it civil war—is a function of the extent to which inadequate government exists."[7] Such countries, almost always among the world's poorest, lack the ability to provide security, stability, and basic public functions such as courts, schools, power, and clean drinking water. They cannot deliver a minimum level of responsive and accountable government. This failure opens up a power vacuum filled by warlords, militias, and organized crime syndicates that the civilian population has little choice but to turn to for basic protection. Corruption, plunder, and violence flourish. Even large atrocities can be carried out by relatively small and otherwise easily controlled groups of people.[8] The answer to this kind of situation is not more war, but better policing and more responsive governance. It lies in building the basic state capacity necessary to provide security, uphold the rule of law, and deliver essential services.

What all this means is that the potential for democracy to reduce war involves more than merely rejecting autocracy and scheduling elections.

As the Catholic peacemaking agenda makes clear, real democracy also requires establishing social order through the rule of law. This means a government that is effective and accountable to its citizens, one that upholds human rights, protects vulnerable minorities, and respects a vibrant and free civil society. This is the kind of democracy that undermines war and one the international community can help cultivate around the globe.

The primary engine of democratization comes from within countries, and because democratic values have universal appeal, the internal potential is always there.[9] What it often needs is external support, and there is much the international community can do to provide it. What virtually everyone who studies democratization concludes, however, is that war is an especially poor way to do this.[10] While it can sometimes pave the way for democracy, as with Germany and Japan following the Second World War, its success rate is far below that of more gradual and less dramatic alternatives. These involve steady, patient, and multidimensional action to both spread and deepen democracy worldwide.

This process has two broad dimensions. The first is opening up more autocratic states to democratization, something research shows is difficult but not impossible.[11] With a few exceptions, such as North Korea, most autocracies are part of the web of institutions that structure the international community. They depend on global connections—the United Nations, the International Monetary Fund, regional bodies—for their power and prosperity. Their economic and political interests—energy, trade, environmental factors, access to technology, border disputes—are powerfully shaped by transnational concerns and relationships. Their citizens, connected to the world through economic ties, consumer goods, entertainment, and social media, are not walled off from international norms. This leaves such countries open to significant pressure by others in the international community. While a single method, economic sanctions for example, is often insufficient, a steady campaign of multiple tools, focusing on penalties, incentives, and international attention, can have a significant impact.

Many of these states actually have gaps in their autocratic structures. They have elections, if usually rigged; civil society groups, if usually harassed; a press, if usually censored; and independent religious communities, if usually repressed. International pressure to widen these gaps by allowing greater freedom of assembly, the press, or religious practice can provide more space for democratic energy to build. Additionally, overt and covert financial and technical assistance from states, intergovernmental organizations, and nongovernmental organizations (NGOs) to groups inside target countries—religious communities, underground political parties, democracy activists, independent journalists—can have a big impact. The emphasis here is not suddenly decapitating a regime, but gradually building enough external and internal pressure to transform it, a process that has worked from South Africa to the Philippines to Chile to Poland and other former Soviet satellite states.

The second dimension comes next. It focuses on strengthening state capacity and the full range of democratic institutions in countries making the transition to democracy, what Benedict XVI calls the critical task of "consolidating constitutional, juridical and administrative systems."[12] Such democratic consolidation may be even more challenging than creating the opening for democracy in the first place, but here too research shows there is much the international community can do to help.[13] Individual states, regional bodies, NGOs, foundations, and aid donors can all make vital contributions to reduce the risk of both warfare and regression back to autocracy. Acting quickly once a transition is under way and remaining committed to support throughout the process significantly increases the chances of success. So too does channeling financial and technical support through civil society as well as state institutions. It is local activists, human rights groups, NGOs, journalists, unions, religious organizations, and civic education groups that will provide both the initiative and accountability that democratic governance requires.

Transitions are sometimes hurt by holding elections too quickly, before an infrastructure of political parties, a free press, an independent judiciary, and an open civil society are in place. While in no way an excuse to delay elections indefinitely, helping build up such institutions ahead of elections is crucial. Running legitimate elections is also complex, especially for countries unused to them. This is where assistance in writing fair election laws, establishing sound procedures and accurate voter rolls, and running the actual balloting is important. Success in nations ranging from Peru to Indonesia to South Africa proves it can be done.

Countries in democratic transitions also struggle to establish basic elements of the rule of law: constitutional protections for human rights; clear criminal, civil, and commercial codes; independent and efficient courts; due process procedures; and policing that is impartial and responsive rather than corrupt and abusive. Such failures severely undermine democratic legitimacy, and outside assistance has proven it can make a big difference, not only in helping to reform legal systems, but in providing basic legal aid to citizens trying to navigate them, something done with promising results in countries such as Bangladesh, Kenya, the Philippines, and El Salvador. One particular challenge for the rule of law is the question of what to do about abuses under the previous regime. Many citizens want people associated with it held responsible, but such figures are also potential spoilers who could derail a peaceful transition to democracy if threatened. Interestingly, it seems the best way to increase the long-term prospects for democracy and human rights in countries undergoing democratic transitions is a balanced mix of initial amnesties followed later by accountability measures, such as trials or truth commissions, focusing especially on top officials in the former regime.[14] External assistance can be critical in helping establish this process within countries.

Those who study international efforts to assist during transitions to democracy stress that there is no standard set of political institutions that fit all cases. Political arrangements must match specific circumstances and attract local support. For example, there is evidence that parliamentary systems are more stable than presidential ones during transitions, but constitutional structures will vary depending on the country. It is also important to keep in mind that building up state capacity does not necessarily mean centralizing power. Depending on national conditions, strong local governments with broad participation can strengthen democratic legitimacy, increase government responsiveness, and reduce the risk of violence by separatist groups, something seen in Ghana and India for example. What is most important is that political structures allow broad participation by all social groups, have built-in checks and balances, and provide for effective delivery of government services, something that civil service reforms emphasizing a smaller workforce, better pay and training, and more transparency and accountability can help accomplish.

Mueller points out that if you want a formula to build stable democracies, it is hard to beat Canada's popular slogan: "Peace, Order and Good Government."[15] Such democracies dramatically reduce the risk of war, so supporting their spread and development is a critical part of abolishing it from the world. Working with local stakeholders, there are tools the international community can use to do so. These tools do not guarantee success in every case, but they have proven effective in many, and far more effective than military means. And given that they receive a fraction of the resources devoted to preparing for and fighting wars, they have the potential to do much more.

* * *

A critical element in democracy's potential to undermine war is how it institutionalizes nonviolence. John Paul II writes, "Honesty in the supply of information, equity in legal systems, openness in democratic procedures give citizens a sense of security, a readiness to settle controversies by peaceful means, and a desire for genuine and constructive dialogue, all of which constitute *the true premises of a lasting peace*."[16] Democracy relies on values of respect, toleration, and compromise. Its social pluralism, open civil society, limited state, and checks and balances all decentralize and disperse power, making its exercise an ongoing process of dialogue and negotiation at different levels. Conflict is still present, but it is channeled into nonviolent forms. The consolidation of such institutions and the norms they embody is why mature democracies are so much less likely to experience civil wars and why they do not consider war a legitimate option in disputes with each other. In R. J. Rummel's terms, democracy itself represents "a method of nonviolence," one standing in sharp contrast to the violent centralized repression of autocratic regimes.[17]

One of the most remarkable things about the spread of democratic norms around the world is the growing use over the last century of nonviolent direct action as an alternative to war, one that can effectively challenge and defeat democracy's opponents.[18] This, of course, is a trend contemporary Catholic teaching strongly supports. John Paul II praises it in *Centesimus Annus* and *Evangelium Vitae* as "effective," inspiring, and one of the "signs of hope" in building a culture of life.[19] It is also one Catholic teaching's neoconservative critics frequently dismiss as a utopian expression of a "fraudulent pacifism." This is even though most people who turn to nonviolent action are not themselves pacifists, and it is grounded in a thoroughly realistic understanding of power.

Any leader's authority depends on the willingness of others to go along. As Gene Sharp, one of the leading theorists of nonviolence, writes, "Every ruler needs the skill, knowledge, advice, labor, and administrative ability of a significant portion of subjects."[20] Usually this is not an issue: people believe in their leaders; accept the legitimacy of the system; follow out of habit; or go along to avoid prison, torture, or death. But it also represents a crucial vulnerability for rulers. If enough people stop following their commands, their power disintegrates. Nonviolent resistance capitalizes on this by mobilizing campaigns of noncooperation. Mass protests, strikes, boycotts, sit-ins, and similar tactics can cripple regimes and undermine their legitimacy. Those that respond with violence often see their authority undermined even further. In an instance of what Sharp calls "political jiu-jitsu," regime violence can lead to increased opposition, declining support by external allies as disgust at the sight of unarmed protesters being beaten or killed grows, and eroding cooperation among the regime's own personnel.[21] When a regime's rank and file, its civil servants, police, and soldiers, refuse to carry out its orders, including orders to arrest or shoot protestors, its authority collapses completely.

Nonviolent resistance offers no guarantee of success. It can fail in the face of violent repression, as attempts from China to Iran show. But it has also amassed an impressive record of success against both internal and external oppressors. It turns out that while violent repression has what Dustin Ells Howes calls "a veneer of dependability," in actual practice it is relatively ineffective if enough people refuse to be moved by it.[22] Regimes that rely on violence to crush dissent are far less stable than those that enjoy genuine legitimacy. While Mohandas Gandhi's movement against British rule in India is the most famous, nonviolent campaigns have removed dictators and foreign occupiers, including ones with a history of brutal and widespread violence, in Chile, Lithuania, South Africa, Ukraine, Tunisia, Serbia, and a host of other countries. The Catholic Church played an especially important role in successful campaigns in Poland, the Philippines, and East Timor. And beyond individual instances, researchers comparing hundreds of cases of both violent and nonviolent resistance movements against domestic dictators and foreign occupiers have found that nonviolent ones have nearly double the success rate, even in the face of violent repression. They are not only more likely to defeat opponents, but the democratic norms embedded in their methods make a successful transition to sustainable democracy in the aftermath of the campaign more likely.[23] Far from being a utopian illusion, then, the evidence is overwhelming that nonviolent action is a much more realistic tactic for achieving freedom, democracy, and human rights than war.

Like other methods of democracy promotion, nonviolent direct action receives only a fraction of the planning, coordination, and money devoted to war, even as it proves itself a more effective alternative. While some nonviolent campaigns can lose local legitimacy if they have too close an association with external support, most benefit from at least some level of quiet assistance from the international community. This includes focusing global attention on their cause and the regime's repression, as well as providing training, funding, and technology where needed. Aside from specific campaigns, more action by both states and NGOs to research and spread information about effective methods of nonviolent direct action can help develop the tools activists around the world can draw upon in their struggles for democratic values, something Catholic teaching has long called for.[24] Supporting nonviolence, then, is an important part of an international agenda on behalf of the interrelated causes of democracy promotion and war abolition.

Notes

1. John Paul II 2003a, no. 4.
2. Pinker 2011, chaps. 5-6; and Goldstein 2011, chap. 11.
3. Russett and Oneal 2001; Russett 1993, 2008; Rummel 1997; Doyle 1986; Ward and Gleditsch 1998; and Hook 2010.
4. Sørensen 2008, chap. 2; Diamond, L. 2008a; and Russett and Oneal 2001, 123-24.
5. Kurlantzick 2008, 2011; and Diamond, L. 2008a.

⁶Mansfield and Snyder 2005; Ward and Gleditsch 1998; Hegre et al. 2001; Diamond, L. 2008a; and Russett and Oneal 2001, chaps. 2-3.

⁷Mueller 2004, 172.

⁸Mueller 2004, 100 and 114; Horgan 2012, 65; and Goldstein 2011, 84.

⁹Diamond L. 2008b, chap. 1.

¹⁰Wallensteen 2007, 109; McFaul 2010; Wittes 2008; Deudney and Ikenberry 2009; Russett 2008; Hook 2010; and Kaplan 2008, chaps. 5-6.

¹¹For overviews of democracy promotion and more on the specific elements that follow here, see Sørensen 2008; Wittes 2008; McFaul 2010; Deudney and Ikenberry 2009; Hook 2010; Diamond L. 2008a, 2008b; and Katzenstein 1996, chap. 1.

¹²Benedict XVI 2009a, no. 41.

¹³For overviews of democratic consolidation and more on the specific elements that follow here, see Cheema 2005; McFaul 2010; Carothers 2006, 2009; Mansfield and Snyder 2005; Mueller 2004, chap. 9; Diamond, L. 2008a, 2008b; Power 2009; Zakaria 2007; Russett 2008; and Hook 2010.

¹⁴Olsen, Payne, and Reiter 2010.

¹⁵Mueller 2004, 179.

¹⁶John Paul II 2003a, no. 8 (italics in original).

¹⁷Rummel 1997.

¹⁸For overviews of nonviolent action and its specific elements that follow here, see Sharp 1985, 1990a, 1990b, and 2005; Ackerman and Duvall 2000; Schell 2003; Cartwright and Thistlethwaite 2008; and Kohl 1990.

¹⁹John Paul II 1991a, no. 23; and John Paul II 1995a, no. 27.

²⁰Sharp 1990a, 26.

²¹Sharp 1985, 116.

²²Howes 2009, 117.

²³Stephan and Chenoweth 2008; Chenoweth and Stephan 2011; and Katatnycky and Ackerman 2005.

²⁴See, for example, United States Conference of Catholic Bishops 1993.

20

Development, Trade,
and International Integration

War is not exclusive to the poorest parts of the globe, but it is concentrated there. The poorer the country, the greater its risk for war, especially civil war. The world's least developed nations are the ones most likely to be trapped in cycles of armed conflict, while strong economic growth and rising per capita gross domestic product are associated with dramatic reductions in the odds of war breaking out.[1] Economic development, then, offers a powerful mechanism to further reduce war where it is most prevalent, making support for such development by the international community a key element in the process of abolishing it. Catholic social teaching is correct when it calls development another name for peace.

Unfortunately, there is no simple formula for boosting economic growth in the developing world. Several decades worth of development assistance by individual states, international bodies, and aid groups have shown the need to recognize both the complexity and limits of such efforts.[2] Poorly tailored aid to impoverished countries can create dependency, stifle local innovation, and feed government corruption. Plenty of it has historically been wasteful and ineffective.[3] If captured and controlled by local warlords to feed and equip their militias or plunder natural resources, for example, aid can even intensify armed conflict.[4]

At the same time, there has been remarkable progress in the developing world over the last several decades. Global poverty has been dropping since 1970, and strong growth in poor regions, particularly Africa, since 2000 has produced rising income levels.[5] The number of people living in absolute poverty, those living on less than $1.25 per day, has dropped by half in the last twenty years.[6] Aside from income, other areas of life have seen even more dramatic improvements. Since the middle of the twentieth century, life expectancy has risen, infant mortality has been cut in half, and primary school enrollment has doubled. Among sub-Saharan Africans, for example, literacy is now 61 percent, twice what it was in 1970. The economist Charles Kenny calls these global trends "historically unprecedented progress in the quality of life."[7]

Development efforts by the international community are by no means the only factor driving this progress, but they have made important contributions, and there is more they can do. Development experts disagree on a great deal of specifics, but some basic lessons about aid emerge from their work.[8] First, it is best to avoid simple, one-size-fits-all solutions in favor of multidimensional approaches that target specific countries or problems. The most successful aid is varied, pragmatic, and context driven. Second, aid is often spread too widely and thinly. More tailored and concentrated efforts get better results. Third, better coordination, evaluation, and accountability are critical. Especially promising are randomized clinical trials, much like the process for testing the effectiveness of drugs, in identifying specific interventions that work and deserve international support. Finally, aid efforts should focus more intentionally on the countries most in need but use a more diverse set of tools in doing so. The least developed nations tend to suffer from multiple and interconnected problems—poverty, slow growth, political instability, weak governance, cycles of violence, disease, inadequate education, geographical isolation, poor soil or climate, and dependence on primary commodity exports such as oil or diamonds. Development is difficult under such conditions, and it requires multiple interventions targeting different problems to be successful. In this way, economic development is inseparable from political and social development, which, of course, is the approach also championed by Catholic social teaching. As Benedict XVI writes in *Caritas in Veritate*, "*authentic human development*" goes beyond economic factors alone to address "*the whole of the person in every single dimension*."[9] This understanding of development points to three main areas for international assistance: state capacity, human capital, and economic fundamentals.

As we saw in the last chapter, there is much the international community can do to strengthen effective democratic governance, human rights, the rule of law, and a free civil society. These are not only good in their own right, but also important foundations for long-term economic growth and prosperity. A free and stable society with inclusive, responsive, and accountable political institutions promotes the innovation, entrepreneurship, and foreign investment that economic progress requires—while weak institutions, clientelism, and rulers intent on extracting rather than building wealth only sabotage it.[10] This is why reducing corruption and building up a culture of respect for the rule of law is so important to successful development efforts, and researchers have identified a host of effective mechanisms for doing so.[11] On the international level, these include bans on commodities, such as diamonds, from conflict areas and accounting procedures to make tracking revenues from oil, gas, mining, and other key resources more transparent. Indeed, there is a growing network of international anticorruption nongovernmental organizations, industry trade groups, global rankings, and laws by major trading nations that are beginning to have real impacts. On the local level, more targeted efforts include random municipal audits, support for investigative journalism, independent anticorruption agencies, public information (giving parents information about levels of funding that should be reaching local schools, for example), strong whistleblower protections, and tying incentives for civil servants to anonymous citizen feedback on their responsiveness.

Investing in basic human well-being—reliable access to food, clean water, shelter, health care, and education—is another important foundation for long-term economic growth and prosperity. As Kenny details, it is also the area where international development assistance has had the most dramatic success.[12] It has helped spread basic knowledge about sanitation, breastfeeding, agricultural techniques, and effective rehydration after diarrhea. It has relied on relatively cheap methods—antibiotics, bed nets, vaccines, pit latrines, cement floors, water pumps, de-worming medication, more efficient cooking stoves—to make remarkable improvements in human health and well-being. For example, small steps, such as providing uniforms or paying parents a token sum for regular school attendance by their kids, can dramatically increase education enrollment, while making midwives available in rural areas produces big drops in the percentage of women who die during childbirth. Such efforts have proven remarkably successful, even as the resources devoted to them are tiny compared to military spending. Eradicating smallpox worldwide or river blindness in western Africa both cost less than a single advanced American warplane.[13]

Especially important to such efforts in the years ahead is action to promote sustainability and environmental protection.[14] This is a key theme in the Catholic peacemaking agenda. Benedict XVI asks, "Can we remain indifferent before the problems associated with such realities as climate change, desertification, the deterioration and loss of productivity in vast agricultural areas, the pollution of rivers and aquifers, the loss of biodiversity, the increase of natural catastrophes and the deforestation of equatorial and tropical regions?"[15] On his account, refusal by the developed world to act on issues such as global warming is producing intolerable suffering in the developing world. Environmental destruction is closely tied to problems such as refugees, disease, food security, and access to water. Fortunately, there is little evidence that scarce resources directly increase the risk of war in today's world.[16] They have, however, played a role in warfare during previous periods of human history and could do so again.[17] And, aside from direct connections to armed conflict, the impact of environmental stress on human well-being and economic development in the poorest parts of the world warrants a significant international response in and of itself.

Since development aid cannot easily produce strong economic growth on its own, most researchers focus instead on helping to build the basic foundations for such growth.[18] In addition to good governance and human capital, these include more traditionally economic factors, such as infrastructure, that connect rural areas to the cities and the entire country to the outside world; a free, though properly regulated, market that does not rely on exporting a single commodity; and macroeconomic stability in the areas of employment, inflation, and public debt. Measures to more effectively connect citizens to the market in poor countries include better access to banking to make their assets more secure and productive, clear property rights and titles to land to encourage entrepreneurship and provide collateral, and microfinance initiatives.

Perhaps the most important factor in boosting economic growth in poor countries is better integration into global markets. As demonstrated by a host of rapidly developing nations around the world, international trade has the potential to reduce poverty dramatically and raise gross domestic product. For example, if the African share of global exports rose only 1 percent, the continent would bring in far more than it receives in aid each year.[19] The crucial thing, however, is that greater participation in global trade be a gradual and fair process. Too often free trade means sudden shock therapy for developing nations—demands that they open their markets, slash public budgets, and remove protections for local industries—while the developed world maintains its own economic subsidies, particularly in agriculture, that rig the game in its favor.[20] This is something criticized by popes from Paul VI to Benedict XVI.[21] Instead, as the developed world opens its own markets more fully, the international community should work to steadily phase in greater participation in trade by the least developed nations, including allowing some protections and subsidies to remain in place to help them nurture vulnerable domestic enterprises and move away from exporting only raw materials.

In addition to its ability to increase economic growth, trade has an even more direct benefit in efforts to reduce war. Like the theory of the democratic peace, the idea that closer trade relationships will reduce the likelihood of armed conflict among countries is an old one. It is also one that now has considerable empirical support. Research demonstrates that countries linked more closely by trade are less likely to go to war against each other, and openness to trade puts a country at lower risk for war generally.[22] Independent of other factors, then, trade reduces warfare, and the more trade links nations of the world together, the less likely war becomes. Increasing global trade is one of those factors driving the decline of war, and it has the potential to continue doing so as the international community works to extend its benefits more fully to the least developed countries.

In an ever more globalized world, trade is one of the primary drivers of closer international integration, as capital, labor, consumer goods, energy, technology, and media images all flow across borders. Countries have established a network of intergovernmental bodies to help control such flows and regulate the economic disputes that inevitably arise. As we have seen, these intergovernmental organizations (IGOs) have also moved well beyond trade issues to address a whole variety of regional and global concerns: security, pollution, law enforcement, natural resource management, and so on. And it turns out that this is yet another factor with a significant and independent impact on declining rates of armed conflict. The more a country participates in IGOs, regardless of their subject matter, the lower its risk of experiencing warfare.[23]

Increasing participation in IGOs, especially among the least developed countries as a condition of development assistance, is therefore an important priority for the international community.[24] It has also long been a goal in Catholic social teaching's peacemaking agenda since, in Drew Christiansen's terms, "interdependence is desirable because it contributes to the historical realization of the essential unity of the human family."[25] John Paul II, for example, calls in *Sollicitudo rei Socialis* for "new regional organizations inspired by criteria of equality, freedom and participation in the comity of nations—as is already happening with promising results."[26] He is right to see such potential. International relations scholars have shown how involvement in IGOs increases the capacity of countries to act collectively. Shared knowledge of each other's intentions allows for ongoing negotiation and reciprocal self-restraint, which, in turn, builds trust and norms of mutual aid. This shapes the identity and interests of states in ways that reduce warlike behavior. This process is gradual and often uneven, but it has proven effective in helping to create growing zones of peace in many parts of the world.[27] As Alexander Wendt points out, even without a strong centralized authority, norms constructed in such ongoing interactions create "assurance that the members of that community will not fight each other physically, but will settle their disputes in some other way."[28]

The most dramatic example of this process in action is Europe. War was a regular feature of European life for centuries, including civil wars, wars between states, and wars of colonial expansion around the globe. During the first half of the twentieth century, this warlike history culminated in two great armed conflicts that killed tens of millions. Since then, however, war has disappeared from most of the continent in what the historian James Sheehan calls "a slow, silent revolution," one "as dramatic as any other in European history."[29] Rather than following a particular plan, the course of European integration has been gradual, incremental, and decentralized. It has relied on a web of regional agreements and organizations that slowly brought its members closer together to address common concerns.[30] While national sovereignty has not disappeared in Europe, it has become significantly limited, existing alongside authority embodied in larger regional bodies, just as a common European identity now exists alongside still strong national ones. The process is an excellent example of how norms expressed through emerging international institutions can transform state identity, interests, and behavior. In 1990, the president of the soon-to-be-reunited Germany said, "Today, sovereignty means participating in the international community."[31]

From the very beginning, European integration was seen as a way to promote democracy, trade, and cooperation while also suppressing war, something evident in its original principles, as well as in later incorporation of countries such as Greece, Spain, Portugal and, eventually, former Soviet bloc countries.[32] Even on the rare occasions that war has broken out on the continent, as it did in the still unintegrated Balkans during the 1990s, it has not spread to the rest of Europe, as was the norm through much of its history. Integration still comes with plenty of problems; the post-2008 financial crisis brought the biggest economic challenge to the project since its beginning. Power and conflict have not disappeared from European affairs. What has changed, however, is the view that war is a legitimate option.

For all its continuing difficulties, European integration reveals how democracy, trade, and IGOs can all reinforce each other. As political scientists Bruce Russett and John Oneal detail, while each of these factors reduces the likelihood of war on its own, the "magnitude of their combined effect is, however, particularly striking."[33] When the three combine to form a virtuous circle, peace becomes much more likely, a peace that, in turn, strengthens each factor even more. This is why action by the international community to help spread and deepen such a dynamic around the world is crucial to the task of abolishing war.

Notes

[1]Collier 2007, chap 2; and Goldstein 2011, chap. 11.
[2]Kenny 2011c.
[3]Moyo 2009.
[4]Gourevitch 2010; Polman 2010; and Fisman 2012.
[5]Pinkovskiy and Sala-i-Martin 2010; and Kenny 2011b.
[6]Kenny 2011a.

[7]Kenny 2011c, 9, 12, 75, and 80.

[8]See, for example, Riddell 2007; Sachs 2005; Collier 2007; Bryant and Kappaz 2005; Banerjee and Duflo 2011; Cohen and Easterly 2009; Weaver, Rock, and Kusterer 1997; and Kenny 2011c, chap. 9.

[9]Benedict XVI 2009a, no. 11 (italics in original).

[10]Acemoglu and Robinson 2012; and Cheema 2005.

[11]Banerjee and Duflo 2011, chap. 10; Cheema 2005, chap. 3; McFaul 2010, 202-03; Kenny 2011c, 168-72; and Applebaum 2012.

[12]Kenny 2011c.

[13]Kenny 2011c, 123-25 and 175-76.

[14]Bronkema, Lumsdaine, and Payne 2008.

[15]Benedict XVI 2010, no. 4.

[16]Horgan 2012, chap. 3; and Pinker 2011, 376.

[17]LeBlanc and Register 2003; Potts and Hayden 2008; and Keegan 1993, chap. 1.

[18]Sachs 2005; Collier 2007; Bryant and Kappaz 2005; Banerjee and Duflo 2011; and Acemoglu and Robinson 2012.

[19]Bryant and Kappaz 2005, chap. 4.

[20]Bryant and Kappaz 2005, chap. 4; and Sachs 2005.

[21]See, for example, Paul VI 1967, nos. 58-60; and Benedict XVI 2009a, nos. 58-59.

[22]Russett and Oneal 2001; Russett 2008; Pinker 2011, chaps. 5-6; Goldstein 2011, chap. 11; and Cortright 2007.

[23]Russett and Oneal 2001; Russett 2008; Pinker 2011, chaps. 5-6; Goldstein 2011, chap. 11; and Cortright 2007.

[24]Cortright 2007; and McFaul 2010, chap. 6.

[25]Christiansen 2005, 231.

[26]John Paul II 1987, no. 45.

[27]Wendt 1999, chaps. 6-7; Morgan 2006, chap. 8; Goldstein 2011, chap. 11.

[28]Wendt 1999, 299.

[29]Sheehan 2008, xx.

[30]Morgan 2006, chap. 8.

[31]Sheehan 2008, 201.

[32]Sheehan 2008, 186-97.

[33]Russett and Oneal 2001, 193.

21

Conflict Resolution and Peacekeeping

In its summary of Catholic teaching's peacemaking agenda, the *Compendium of the Social Doctrine of the Church* calls on the international community "to work together to resolve conflicts and promote peace, re-establishing relationships of mutual trust that make recourse to war unthinkable."[1] This process has three dimensions: stopping armed conflicts before they break out, ending ones already under way, and preventing those just ended from restarting. Failures in all three areas are common, as cases such as Rwanda, Bosnia, Somalia, and Lebanon demonstrate. But there is also a growing list of successes. The international community is getting better at preventing warfare and upholding peace, and this increasing capacity is a big factor in the worldwide decline of war, one with the potential to move us even closer to war's global abolition.[2]

Resolving disputes before they escalate into war means relying on diplomacy and negotiation. Often this happens during routine face-to-face contacts among nations, but for more serious conflicts, it increasingly involves third parties acting as mediators. These can be individual countries, regional bodies, nongovernmental organizations, global political figures, or religious organizations.[3] John Paul II, for example, helped mediate a border dispute early in his papacy between Chile and Argentina that was moving toward war.[4] Sometimes mediation, which is a nonbinding process producing voluntary agreements, gives way to binding arbitration proceedings by international tribunals. The most significant of these is the International Court of Justice, established by the United Nations to handle disputes between countries and an institution frequently endorsed by Catholic teaching.[5] Formal mediation and arbitration mechanisms are being incorporated into international laws and the charters of intergovernmental organizations (IGOs) at a growing rate, creating a norm for their use that countries, especially those who are not great powers, are turning to with increasing frequency.[6]

While these conflict resolution methods do not guarantee success, researchers have established their growing effectiveness in preventing both interstate and civil wars.[7] Even though they can be long, frustrating, and contentious, they do provide a way for parties to communicate their grievances, signal their intentions, and seek common ground. Skilled diplomats and mediators, working in either formal proceedings or informally behind the scenes, can help parties moderate their claims, institute confidence-building measures, save face, and engage in cycles of reciprocal self-restraint. This process has the ability to transform a conflict, where each party aims for victory, into a shared problem, where parties work together on a solution. It removes the security dilemma in which parties see concessions as dangerous, allowing them to more safely signal their willingness to deescalate and thereby reduce the perception of threat to each other, something done, for example, when Ukraine gave up nuclear weapons on its territory during its peaceful break from the Soviet Union.[8]

It is important to realize that this process need not rely on good will alone. International pressure in the form of sanctions and incentives is often necessary to bring parties to the table and keep negotiations moving. Closing the deal frequently requires outside security guarantees and pledges of aid. While messy, such conflict resolution efforts have prevented war between countries such as Nigeria and Cameroon, India and Pakistan, Egypt and Israel, Botswana and Namibia, and Ecuador and Peru. It has helped control civil conflict in countries from Estonia to Kenya to Canada. It kept the partition of Czechoslovakia into two independent countries from devolving into war, something routine through much of the region's history. Especially encouraging are efforts by scholars to develop models that use early warning signs to forecast escalating conflict early enough to intervene.[9] Such early action has been crucial to preventing violent conflict erupting in places such as Macedonia and Central African Republic.

One of the most successful methods for preventing the outbreak of civil wars is the spread, often through international pressure, of certain political and economic responses to grievances by vulnerable ethnic and religious minorities within countries. Historically, many countries responded to such grievances with repression, which often sparked a violent response from minority groups, leading to an escalating cycle of civil war. Since the Cold War's end, however, countries have increasingly turned to more nonviolent and democratic measures. These include political incorporation and formal power-sharing structures for formerly excluded groups; regional autonomy, language recognition, and religious liberty for groups concerned with preserving a traditional homeland, culture, or religious identity; and economic development, land reform, and better access to jobs and education for formerly disadvantaged groups. Such methods have done much to reduce the likelihood of war.[10]

Another war prevention measure of particular concern to Catholic social teaching is disarmament. Detailing threats to the dignity of life in *Evangelium Vitae*, John Paul II writes, "And what of the violence inherent not only in wars as such but in the scandalous arms trade, which spawns the many armed conflicts which stain our world with blood?"[11] Efforts to reduce the flow of arms to potential war zones, including small arms such as Kalashnikov rifles that are so deadly in the developing world, help deescalate tensions, while international bans on certain types of arms—nuclear and biological weapons, cluster bombs, landmines—help reinforce global norms against war. The Vatican has called for a legally binding "international regime" to control and reduce arms worldwide.[12] Unfortunately, while much of the globe has come to support such efforts, the United States remains one of their chief obstacles and the world's largest arms supplier.[13] Shifting U.S. policies in this area could have a significant impact for the better.

Ending wars once they are under way is more difficult than preventing them in the first place, but here too the international community has had considerable success.[14] Mediators have helped end wars in Ethiopia, Nicaragua, East Timor, Cambodia, Guatemala, Liberia, Indonesia, and a host of other countries. The Catholic Community of Sant'Egidio has helped broker a successful peace process in several countries, most notably Mozambique, and the parties to the conflict in Northern Ireland turned to the Clonard monastery to pass back-channel communications during their negotiations.[15] These mediators rely on the same types of methods we saw in efforts to prevent war in the first place, only now they push parties in an armed conflict toward an end to hostilities. This usually requires a ceasefire, which allows more space to negotiate, followed by a comprehensive peace agreement. Such agreements don't always hold, but they do have a better rate of success in establishing long-term peace than cease-fires alone, stalemates, or even outright military victory by one side. The United Nations in particular has a good track record of securing these kinds of agreements.[16]

International efforts to help end wars, especially civil wars, are closely connected to the idea of a "responsibility to protect." This principle argues that national sovereignty is limited by the duty of states to safeguard rather than violate the basic dignity and security of their citizens. If they fail in this responsibility, the international community can assume it, taking action to prevent mass violence and other gross violations of human rights within countries. This principle emphasizes alternatives to war as its primary methods, but most versions do endorse military intervention as a last resort, even while warning that it is not an excuse for unilateral wars that ignore international law, such as the U.S. invasion of Iraq.[17]

This is an example of how pacifists and nonpacifists who share a commitment to abolishing war can disagree on the appropriate methods. Some nonpacifists see a limited role for military interventions in helping clean up what remains of war in the world today, especially by bringing order and stability to regions where it is still chronic.[18] In its current form, Catholic social teaching also remains open to such interventions as long as they respond to a sufficiently grave humanitarian threat, operate under international law, and strictly follow just war principles such as last resort, proportionality, and discrimination.[19] For pacifists, however, even the worthiness of the cause does not justify resorting to military means given the kinds of killing inevitably found in warfare. Military interventions also risk further legitimizing war, even as their effectiveness is frequently overstated. Such interventions fail up to 80 percent of the time by some measures, often making conflicts last longer and sparking new insurgency campaigns against outside powers in addition to the violence already present before the intervention.[20]

Ending a war by no means guarantees peace. Up to half of them will restart within a few years.[21] Indeed, frequent recurrences are the primary challenge to further progress in reducing war. The annual rate of new wars is down to historic lows—in many years not a single new one breaks out—but old ones that restart remain a persistent problem. Of the thirty-nine armed conflicts that became active in the 2000s, thirty-one were recurrences.[22] Preventing such recurrences, then, offers the best method to undermine the wars that remain in today's world.

The good news here is that doing so is entirely possible. The international community is becoming increasingly successful in breaking the cycle of war through postconflict peacekeeping initiatives.[23] While its failures get much of the attention, successes far outnumber them and have helped establish peace in countries such as El Salvador, East Timor, Namibia, Croatia, Nicaragua, Cyprus, and Mozambique. Especially over the last two decades, both the United Nations and smaller regional bodies have developed multidimensional operations that emphasize not just keeping warring factions separated, but helping provide the basic security, effective governance, democratic institutions, and economic development that make lasting peace possible. In his investigation of such efforts, Joshua Goldstein remarks, "Considering how few funds and resources they get, these international peace operations have succeeded remarkably well."[24] Studies show that the presence of external peacekeeping operations reduces the chance that war will recur by at least half, and even up to over 80 percent depending on circumstances.[25]

Research by the RAND Corporation demonstrates that international peacekeeping is both cheaper and more effective in instituting long-term peace and democracy than military invasions and occupations.[26]

Successful operations depend on negotiating a cease-fire and peace accord, and then putting personnel in place quickly to begin implementing it. The most significant early threats to a sustainable peace are disorder, factions convinced their rivals are cheating, and spoilers looking to sabotage the process. Peacekeepers respond by providing security, preventing natural resources from being looted, overseeing disarmament and demobilization, monitoring compliance with the peace agreement's provisions, and delivering humanitarian assistance and basic services in a timely manner. Such measures inspire confidence in the process, reassure factions, and convince people they have more to gain by cooperating than resisting. Certain factors increase success rates. For example, a greater role for women in the postconflict peace process increases the chances it will succeed.[27] After civil wars, a mix of amnesties, trials, and truth commissions reduces the risk of recurrence, and international peacekeepers make such measures more likely.[28] Politically, building democratic institutions helps address underlying grievances nonviolently and makes it possible to co-opt one-time enemies into the new system, as when former rebel armies in El Salvador and Mozambique transformed themselves into successful political parties.[29] Economically, the timing of aid matters. Postconflict societies have the potential for rapid catch-up growth, and research shows that aid can help with this, but while such aid often floods in early and fades quickly, growth potential develops more slowly and peaks about five years after the conflict's end, just as aid is running out. Aid that increases with growth potential and fades out only after a full decade is more effective.[30]

While successful in many cases, experts emphasize that there is still plenty of room for improvement in international peacekeeping. Organizations, especially the United Nations, need greater capacity to handle larger and more complex operations. This requires better planning, coordination, and local knowledge. It also means more funding and personnel. The average U.S. household contributes $700 per year to the military but only $2 to peacekeeping efforts, and the entire UN workforce is smaller than that of Starbucks Coffee.[31] Too many missions suffer from slow deployments, unclear mandates, and peacekeepers that are poorly trained, paid, and disciplined. It is also important that operations be designed to avoid merely allowing militias or insurgency groups time to reorganize and reequip themselves before resuming the war.[32] Many of these problems point to the need for standing peacekeeping forces, instead of today's efforts that are usually ad hoc and assembled on the fly for each conflict. As Goldstein points out, it is always better to have a fire department in place before the fire starts.[33]

As with the case of military interventions to stop a civil war, pacifist support for peacekeeping after a conflict's conclusion emphasizes the danger of its spilling over into warfare. To remain both effective and morally legitimate, peacekeeping must conform to a policing rather than military model. While the two can at times blend into each other, they are distinct; as the old saying goes, the existence of twilight does not mean we can't distinguish between night and day. Policing and war, as we saw in chapter 8, rely on very different understandings of their core functions, their relationship to law and due process, and the appropriate use of deadly force, especially when and against whom it can be used. Peacekeepers may on occasion have to resort to force to protect themselves and others from immediate attack, but as long as this conforms to the rules of engagement central to legitimate policing, it will remain morally permissible.[34] Peacekeeping that becomes a form of counterinsurgency warfare retains the morally impermissible features of war itself, even as it undermines global norms against war and is less effective at establishing a just and lasting peace.[35]

Indeed, it is a policing-based understanding of peacekeeping that has the potential to transform the very image of soldiers from warriors trained to kill for their country to men and women charged with ensuring human security in the face of disorder, humanitarian crises, and natural disasters, both at home and abroad. This is what the pacifist William James has in mind in his call, a century ago, for a "moral equivalent of war," and what is happening to the self-understanding of national defense forces in countries such as New Zealand today.[36] Just as the abolition of trials by ordeal and combat transformed the role of judges, the abolition of war promises to transform the very idea of soldiers.

Notes

[1]Pontifical Council for Justice and Peace 2004, no. 499.

[2]Goldstein 2011; Pinker 2011, 313-16; and Wallensteen 2007, 74 and 86-87.

[3]Bercovitch 2007; and Sampson 2007.

[4]Russett and Oneal 2001, 40.

[5]Bilder 2007; and United States Conference of Catholic Bishops 1993.

[6]Wallensteen 2007, 266.

[7]Kupchan 2010; Wallensteen 2007; Ramsbotham, Woodhouse, and Miall 2005; Brion-Meisels et al. 2008; and Morgan 2006, chap. 9.

[8]Wallensteen 2007, 88; and Wendt 1999, 362-63.

[9]Gurr 2000; Hewitt, Wilkenfeld, and Gurr 2010; Goldstein 2011, chap. 12; Wallensteen 2007, 244 and 259-66; and Ramsbotham, Woodhouse, and Miall 2005, chap. 4.

[10]Gurr 2000; and Wallensteen 2007, chap. 7.

[11]John Paul II 1995a, no. 10.

[12]Pontifical Council for Justice and Peace 1994.

[13]Green and Stassen 2008; Winright 2011; Mathews 2009; and Keefe 2010.

[14]Goldstein 2011; Wallensteen 2007; and Ramsbotham, Woodhouse, and Miall 2005.

[15]Marazziti 2012; Ramsbotham, Woodhouse, and Miall 2005, 169; and Goldstein 2011, 101.

[16]Doyle and Sambanis 2006; and Wallensteen 2007, chap. 2.

[17]Evans 2009.

[18]See, for example, Mueller 2004.

[19]John Paul II 2000, no. 11; John Paul II 1993b; Pontifical Council for Justice and Peace 1994; and United States Conference of Catholic Bishops 1993. See also Christiansen 1999b.

[20]Regan 2000; Doyle and Sambanis 2006, 44; and Ringsmose 2008.

[21]Collier 2007, chap. 2; and Collier 2008.

[22]Hewitt 2010; and Hewitt, Wilkenfeld, and Gurr 2010, 1.

[23]Goldstein 2011; Dobbins et al. 2005; Dobbins 2007; Dobbins et al. 2007; Doyle and Sambanis 2006; Hoeffler 2010; Rubin 2008; Collier 2008; Wallensteen 2007; Ramsbotham, Woodhouse, and Miall 2005; and Morgan 2006, chaps. 10-12.

[24]Goldstein 2011, 7.

[25]Goldstein 2011, 105; and Pinker 2011, 313-16.

[26]Dobbins et al. 2005; and Dobbins 2007.

[27]Caprioli, Nielsen, and Hudson 2010.

[28]Olsen, Payne, and Reiter 2010, chap. 7.

[29]Goldstein 2011, chap. 4.

[30]Hoeffler 2010; and Collier 2008.

[31]Goldstein 2011, 310-12.

[32]Gourevitch 2010; and Goldstein 2011, chap. 7.

[33]Goldstein 2011, chap. 12.

[34]Horgan 2012, 165-67.

[35]Cohen 2010; and Schlabach 2007b.

[36]James 2005; Horgan 2012, 170; and Keegan 1993, conclusion.

22

A Last Word: Terrorism

For many people, particularly Americans following the attacks of September 11, 2001, the existence of terrorism serves as proof that war is still necessary. As long as there are those willing and able to massacre the innocent in such ways, we will need military force to defend against them. On their account, terrorism is a prime example of why it is dangerously utopian to hope for a world without war.

Contemporary Catholic teaching consistently condemns terrorism. John Paul II calls it a "crime against humanity" and an attack on social order.[1] And the church's just war framework still allows for military responses. In their statement following the September 11 attacks, the U.S. Bishops acknowledge "the right and duty of a nation and the international community to use military force if necessary to defend the common good by protecting the innocent against mass terrorism." Such action, however, is always a last resort, limited by international law and the principles of just war, and packaged with the tradition's primary emphasis on a "wide range of non-military measures," ones centering on better law enforcement, international conflict-resolution, and using the church's global peacemaking agenda to address terrorism's underlying causes.[2]

Catholic doctrine's neoconservative critics readily embrace the possibility of war while disparaging the rest of the package as feckless and hopelessly naïve. An editorial in *First Things*, running soon after the U.S. Bishops' statement, urges decisive military action and ridicules those advocating nonviolent responses as "dumb" for suggesting "aggression should be resisted by hugging a terrorist."[3] George Weigel calls the view that terrorism is best considered a crime countered through law enforcement, rather than an act of war countered through military action, "dangerous nonsense," and he scorns those who emphasize a link between global injustice and terrorism as thinking it "can be understood in terms drawn primarily from the patios of the therapeutic society."[4]

A closer look at terrorism and its countermeasures, however, clearly shows how ineffective war is compared to alternative methods. Far from proving war's necessity, terrorism proves how counterproductive and dispensable it is.

What do we know about terrorism? It is not an ideology itself, but rather a tactic many groups use for a variety of causes. It's also been around a long time. Spreading fear through brutal acts of violence against civilian targets in order to advance a particular agenda is nothing new. Terrorism is a form of asymmetrical warfare. It is used by radical groups too militarily, politically, or socially weak to use other means effectively. One reason groups who can rely on other methods avoid terrorism is because it almost never works. Terrorist campaigns tend to be short lived, lasting only eight years on average, and fewer than 5 percent actually accomplish any significant goals.[5] Rates of global terrorism have been on a long-term decline since the end of the Cold War, though there was a temporary bump from 2001 to 2006 with the September 11 attacks and the beginning of subsequent wars in Afghanistan and Iraq. Suicide attacks are only a small percentage of all terrorist strikes, but they account for more than half of the casualties and are themselves growing in frequency, even as terrorist activity overall continues to decline.[6]

While usually proclaiming themselves protectors of the oppressed, terrorists are often middle class and well educated. Suicide bombers are not depressed or mentally ill. For jihadist groups in particular, many recruits experience a sense of rootlessness and alienation, especially those living in Western countries outside the Muslim world. Not necessarily religious to begin with, such recruits are attracted to social networks that provide a sense of belonging and connect local and personal grievances such as discrimination, lack of economic mobility, or a crisis of identity to a larger global cause. These networks tend to pull already social marginalized recruits into a self-contained echo chamber where the most radical voices dominate, creating a narrative of worldwide Muslim victimization.[7]

Terrorist groups, then, depend upon a sense of grievance to unite their members. Such grievances can be exaggerated, distorted, or even entirely invented, but they can also be real, even if they in no way excuse the goals and methods of terrorists. Terrorist groups use factors such as poverty, tyranny, or ethnic and religious oppression to gain support from at least a portion of the local population. This support is critical because it gives them a source of recruits and funding, as well as safe places to hide, plan, and gather materials.[8] The most dangerous terrorist groups are ones large and cohesive enough to carry out major attacks. As Eli Berman's research demonstrates, these are most likely to be religious-based groups, such as Hamas or Hezbollah, that can attract support and prevent defection by cultivating a powerful and distinctive identity, as well as monopolizing the delivery of social services, such as education, health care, and financial assistance, to the communities they claim to champion.[9]

Given the death and destruction they cause, understanding suicide attacks better is especially important in developing effective responses to terrorism. Studying every case going back three decades, over two thousand of them, Robert Pape and James Feldman find that over 95 percent of them are a direct response to military occupation of a disputed territory. This remarkably consistent dynamic links not only jihadist groups, but secular ones such as the Tamil Tigers and the Kurdistan Workers Party (PKK). They write, "Simply put, military occupation accounts for nearly all suicide terrorism around the world since 1980."[10]

This is one reason nearly all those who study terrorism point to the ineffectiveness of war as a response.[11] Findings by Seth Jones and Martin Libicki are typical: "Our analysis suggests that there is no battlefield solution to terrorism. Military force usually has the opposite effect from what is intended."[12] Since terrorists blend into the civilian population and avoid pitched battles, targeting them with military might is virtually impossible. Instead, invasions and occupations, such as those undertaken in Afghanistan and Iraq following the September 11 attacks, actually increase terrorism by alienating the local population and boosting support for terrorist groups. In fact, fighting terrorism through war rather than other means is precisely the response terrorist groups want.[13] Their tactics are designed to invite military retaliation, not only because it is less effective and can increase support for their cause, but also because it validates their self-image as soldiers fighting a just war. War, especially against a strong military power, gives them the credibility and status they seek as self-proclaimed defenders of an oppressed population.

The folly of the American response to the attacks of September 11 was to immediately embrace war rather than policing. Ignoring those with experience fighting terrorism, including the lessons learned by countries with a longer history in such struggles, the Bush administration, with the strong support of Catholic doctrine's neoconservative critics, focused almost single-mindedly on military means, even seeing traditional legal methods and restraints, such as laws against torture, as liabilities.[14] This was exactly the wrong approach, since law enforcement methods are far more effective in fighting terrorism than military ones.[15] Such methods refuse to give terrorists the war they want. A more low-key, patient, ongoing criminal justice strategy denies them the glory they seek, treating them as common criminals rather than warriors and denying them a critical recruiting tool.[16] It also undermines the sense that anti-terrorism efforts are targeting entire communities, allowing community policing techniques to cultivate local knowledge, relationships, and tips, something the British, for example, learned was crucial in their long campaign against terrorism in Northern Ireland.[17] Such methods can be effective on both the domestic and international levels. The difficult work of identifying suspects, infiltrating and disrupting networks, and cutting off recruits, money, and weapons is too fine grained for military means. It takes intelligence, investigation, and close collaboration among police across national borders.

In a statement to the United Nations decades before the September 11 attacks, Paul VI calls for "the institutionalization on an international scale of police measures against terrorism."[18] As the criminologist Mark Hamm details, such international policing targets a key vulnerability of terrorists since "crimes are the lifeblood of terrorist groups."[19] Terrorists need money to continue their operations and almost all groups turn to organized crime to get it, including jihadist groups such as al Qaeda. Smuggling, extortion, bank robbery, kidnapping, tax evasion, money laundering, human trafficking, credit card scams, immigration violations, forged documents, and counterfeiting are all routine activities for terrorist organizations. Targeting such activities disrupts operations and preempts larger attacks. This is especially important since terrorists, being in the business for an ideological cause, actually make poor criminals, ones prone to lots of mistakes, and when they turn to experienced criminals for assistance, they open themselves up to infiltration and prosecution for participating in criminal conspiracies. Targeting the organized crime that keeps them operating and their ongoing need to illegally get people and materials across international borders provides key points of attack that have proven remarkably successful in dismantling such groups. Hamm concludes that "the most successful method of both detecting and prosecuting cases of terrorism is through the pursuit of conventional criminal investigations."[20] The openness of democratic societies does give terrorists opportunities to attack, and no amount of security will completely stop those committed to acts of violence against persons, especially if they are willing to lose their own lives in the process. But as Audrey Kurth Cronin shows in her research, democracies have a pretty good track record fighting terrorism. They do so most effectively by avoiding a short-term cycle of attacks and reactions, especially military ones, focusing instead on longer-term strategies to undermine and dismantle terrorist groups, or at least minimize their harm until they collapse on their own, as most groups do fairly quickly.[21] This is less dramatic than war, but it works better. It is also consistent with John Paul II's warning that democracies should not "*justify a renunciation of the principles of the rule of law*" in fighting terrorism or forget that the "guilty must be correctly identified, since criminal culpability is always personal and cannot be extended to the nation, ethnic group or religion to which the terrorists may belong."[22]

In addition to more effective policing at both the domestic and international levels, Catholic doctrine consistently emphasizes the need to address the underlying causes of terrorism. Here is John Paul II again, writing a few months after the September 11 attacks: "International cooperation in the fight against terrorist activities must also include a courageous and resolute political, diplomatic and economic commitment to relieving situations of oppression and marginalization which facilitate the designs of terrorists. The recruitment of terrorists in fact is easier in situations where rights are trampled upon and injustices tolerated over a long period of time."[23] Such language is especially objectionable to Catholic teaching's neoconservative critics. Weigel, for example, calls concern with economic deprivation and other root causes of terrorism "distasteful" and a "detour from reality."[24]

It is true that addressing the conflicts and grievances that give rise to terrorist campaigns is not an automatic solution, but it does hold considerable potential. The key here is distinguishing between hard-core, committed members of a terrorist organization and its more loosely affiliated sympathizers. In most cases, negotiating with hard-core elements in the organization itself is misguided.[25] Their demands are often unreasonable and unjust, and direct concessions set a bad precedent for other terrorist groups. Terrorist organizations also have a vested interest in continuing the conflict that justifies their existence. This is why they work so hard to sabotage reconciliation and reform efforts. Peace and justice put them out of business.

What resolving underlying disputes and discontent can do, however, is break off the weaker support network among their communities that terrorists need to operate.[26] It drains the swamp that sustains them. It was only when a political settlement in Northern Ireland reversed the marginalization and second-class status of its Catholics that the Irish Republican Army lost its support among the Catholic population and largely collapsed. It was only after the Turkish government took seriously the Kurdish minority's complaints about discrimination, economic deprivation, and the need for cultural autonomy that they could successfully isolate and contain the PKK.[27] Foreign aid targeting education, health care, civil society promotion, and conflict prevention has proven successful in decreasing terrorism, while military aid has the opposite effect.[28] Breaking the hold terrorist groups have over local populations by competing with them to provide basic security and social services is another successful strategy.[29] So too is co-opting more moderate elements of movements that have terrorist wings by bringing them into the political system, leaving their more radical colleagues isolated and subject to criminal prosecution.[30] Such strategies are especially promising in empowering the moderate and prodemocracy majorities in much of the Islamic world caught between corrupt dictators and radical jihadist groups.[31] Even in developed Western countries themselves, successfully defeating jihadist terrorism from within means addressing discrimination and marginalization within local Muslim communities, something the United States does a far better job of than Europe.[32] In other words, the evidence shows that the Catholic peacemaking agenda of democracy, rule of law, human rights, economic development, and peaceful conflict resolution can do much to undercut the forces that breed and sustain terrorist groups.

*   *   *

So we don't need to keep war around to defeat terrorism. It is a particularly ineffective approach compared to its alternatives. Indeed, the same methods of global policing and peacemaking that have such potential to undermine war can do the same for terrorism. The two, however, are not necessarily a package deal. A world without war is certainly one in which terrorism, like other forms of political violence, can still exist, confirming again that eliminating war will not bring perfect peace and justice. But this should not minimize the real good finally abolishing war will do. It is one of the great scourges of human history, one that systematically slaughters the innocent and leaves a path of lawlessness, disorder, and suffering in its wake. Long sustained by lies about its righteousness and inevitability, it is neither. As we have seen, abolishing it is possible, even if difficult. Like other forms of institutionalized violence, it requires an incremental and multidimensional effort toward gradual elimination. And the progress the international community has already made in delegitimizing and reducing war offers reason for hope. This may turn out to be a temporary lull before war's dramatic comeback, but it may also be a stage in its eventual fall.

Recall how between lynching's heyday of routine and celebratory spectacle killings in front of entire communities and its abolition decades later, it went through a middle phase, one where lynchings still occurred, but they were fewer, more isolated, and clandestine, even while still enjoying tacit if somewhat embarrassed public support. The movement to abolish global slavery had a similar middle stage where world opinion had turned against it and many countries had abolished it, but some regions defensively held onto it considerably longer in the face of international pressure. It is possible that today's "remnants of war" are akin to these similar remnants of lynching and slavery, ones that while still causing terrible injustice and suffering, turned out to be the final gasps of forms of institutionalized violence whose abolition we now take for granted.[33] War may not take this path, but ensuring that it does is certainly a realistic option open to humanity.

If so, good riddance.

Notes

[1] John Paul II 2002, nos. 3-4.

[2] United States Conference of Catholic Bishops 2001.

[3] *First Things* 2001.

[4] Weigel 2011a; and Weigel 2007, 58.

[5] Cronin 2009.

[6] LaFree, Dugan, and Cragin 2010; and Pape and Feldman 2010, 5.

[7] Sageman 2008; Aslan 2009, especially chap. 6; Hari 2009; and Wright 2006, 344.

[8] Dumas 2003.

[9] Berman 2009.

[10] Pape and Feldman 2010, 10. See also Pape 2006.

[11] Cronin 2009; Berman 2009; Sageman 2008; Pape and Feldman 2010; Pape 2006; and Mueller 2006.

[12] Jones and Libicki 2008, xvii.

[13] Sageman 2008; Aslan 2009; Dyer 2004, chap. 10; and Wright 2006, 203, 246, and 374-75.

[14] See, for example, Mayer 2009a; and Kaplan 2008.

[15] See, for example, Jones and Libicki 2008; Mueller 2006; Rosen 2008; and Wright 2006.

[16] Sageman 2008; and Aslan 2009.

[17] Sageman 2008, 155.

[18] Paul VI 1977, 254.

[19] Hamm 2007, 2.

[20] Hamm 2007, 16.

[21] Cronin 2009.

[22] John Paul II 2004, no. 8; and John Paul II 2002, no. 5 (italics in original).

[23] John Paul II 2002, no. 5.

[24] Weigel 2007, 6; and Weigel 2003a, 25.

[25] Cronin 2009.

[26] Dumas 2003; and Ramsbotham, Woodhouse, and Miall 2005, chap. 11.

[27] Stassen 2007.

[28] Young and Findley 2011; and Wright 2011.

[29] Berman 2009.

[30] Jones and Libicki 2008.

[31] Aslan 2009; and Esposito 2002.

[32] Ackerman 2005; Sageman 2008; and Aslan 2009, chap. 6.

[33] Mueller 2004.

References

Acemoglu, Daron, and James Robinson. 2012. *Why Nations Fail: The Origins of Power, Prosperity, and Poverty*. New York: Crown.

Ackerman, Peter, and Jack DuVall. 2000. *A Force More Powerful: A Century of Nonviolent Conflict*. New York: Palgrave.

Ackerman, Spencer. 2005. "Religious Protection." *The New Republic*. December 12.

Allen, John L., Jr. 2000. *Pope Benedict XVI: A Biography of Joseph Ratzinger*. New York: Continuum.

Allen, John L., Jr. 2003. "Pope's 'Answer to Rumsfeld' Pulls No Punches in Opposing War." *National Catholic Reporter Online*. February 14. http://www.natcath.org/NCR_Online/archives/021403/021403e.htm.

Ambrose. 391. *On the Duties of the Clergy*. New Advent. http://www.newadvent.org/fathers/34011.htm.

America. 2011. "Conscience in the Mud." October 31.

Anderson, John Lee. 2009. "The Most Failed State." *The New Yorker*. December 14.

Anderson, John Lee. 2011. "Death of the Tiger." *The New Yorker*. January 17.

Andreas, Peter, and Ethan Nadelmann. 2006. *Policing the Globe: Criminalization and Crime Control in International Relations*. Oxford: Oxford University Press.

Anscombe, Elizabeth. 1970. "War and Murder." In *War and Morality*, ed. Richard A. Wasserstrom, 42-53. Belmont, CA: Wadsworth.

Appiah, Kwame Anthony. 2010. *The Honor Code: How Moral Revolutions Happen*. New York: W. W. Norton.

Applebaum, Anne. 2012. "Why the Anti-Corruption Movement Is the New Human Rights Movement." *Slate*. December 13. http://www.slate.com/articles/news_and_politics/foreigners/2012/12/anti_corruption_movement_protests_riots_and_marches_across_the_globe_are.html.

Aquinas, Thomas. 1947. *Summa Theologica*. Trans. Brothers of the English Dominican Province, vol. 2. New York: Benziger Brothers.

Aristotle. 1986. *Politics*. Trans. Hippocrates G. Apostle and Lloyd P. Gerson. Grinnell, IA: Peripatetic Press.

Aslan, Reza. 2009. *How to Win a Cosmic War: God, Globalization, and the End of the War on Terror.* New York: Random House.

Augustine. 1950. *The City of God.* Trans. Marcus Dods, D.O. New York: Modern Library.

Augustine. 1964. *On Free Choice of the Will.* Trans. Anna S. Benjamin and L. H. Hackstaff. Indianapolis: Bobbs-Merrill.

Bacevich, Andrew J. 2005. *The New American Militarism: How Americans Are Seduced by War.* Oxford: Oxford University Press.

Bae, Sangmin. 2007. *When the State No Longer Kills: International Human Rights Norms and the Abolition of Capital Punishment.* Albany: State University of New York Press.

Banerjee, Abhijit V., and Esther Duflo. 2011. *Poor Economics: A Radical Rethinking of the Way to Fight Global Poverty.* New York: Public Affairs.

Banner, Stuart. 2002. *The Death Penalty: An American History.* Cambridge, MA: Harvard University Press.

Barstow, David. 2008. "Behind TV Analysts, Pentagon's Hidden Hand." *New York Times.* April 20.

Bartlett, Robert. 1986. *Trial by Fire and Water: The Medieval Judicial Ordeal.* Oxford: Oxford University Press.

Benedict XVI. 2007. *World Day of Peace Message.* http://www.vatican .va/holy_father/benedict_xvi/messages/peace/documents/hf_ben-xvi_mes_20061208_xl-world-day-peace_en.html.

Benedict XVI. 2008. *World Day of Peace Message.* http://www.vatican .va/holy_father/benedict_xvi/messages/peace/documents/hf_ben-xvi_mes_20071208_xli-world-day-peace_en.html.

Benedict XVI. 2009a. *Caritas in Veritate.* http://www.vatican.va/holy_father/benedict_xvi/encyclicals/documents/hf_ben-xvi_enc_20090629_caritas-in-veritate_en.html.

Benedict XVI. 2009b. *World Day of Peace Message.* http://www.vatican .va/holy_father/benedict_xvi/messages/peace/documents/hf_ben-xvi_mes_20081208_xlii-world-day-peace_en.html.

Benedict XVI. 2010. *World Day of Peace Message.* http://www.vatican .va/holy_father/benedict_xvi/messages/peace/documents/hf_ben-xvi_mes_20091208_xliii-world-day-peace_en.html.

Bercovitch, Jacob. 2007. "Mediation in International Conflicts: Theory, Practice, and Developments." In *Peacemaking in International Conflict: Methods and Techniques*, rev. ed., ed. I. William Zartman, 163-94. Washington, DC: United States Institute of Peace.

Berman, Eli. 2009. *Radical, Religious, and Violent: The New Economics of Terrorism.* Cambridge, MA: MIT Press.

Bernstein, Richard, and Mark Landler. 2005. "Few See Taint in Service by Pope in Hitler Youth." *New York Times.* April 21.

Bica, Camillo C. 1999. "Another Perspective on the Doctrine of Double Effect." *Public Affairs Quarterly* 13 (2): 131-39.

Biddle, Stephen D. 2004. *Military Power: Explaining Victory and Defeat in Modern Battle.* Princeton, NJ: Princeton University Press.

Bilder, Richard D. 2007. "Adjudication: International Abritral Tribunals and Courts." In *Peacemaking in International Conflict: Methods and Techniques,* rev. ed., ed. I. William Zartman, 195-226. Washington, DC: United States Institute of Peace.

Boggs, Carl. 2005. *Imperial Delusions: American Militarism and Endless War.* Lanham, MD: Rowman & Littlefield.

Bourke, Joanna. 1999. *An Intimate History of Killing: Face to Face Killing in 20th Century Warfare.* New York: Basic Books.

Bourke, Joanna. 2006. "Barbarization vs. Civilization in Time of War." In *The Barbarization of Warfare,* ed. George Kassimeris, 19-38. New York: New York University Press.

Brady, Bernard V. 2008. *Essential Catholic Social Thought.* Maryknoll, NY: Orbis Books.

Brion-Meisels, Steven, Meenakshi Chhabra, David Cortright, David Steele, Gary Gunderson, and Edward LeRoy Long, Jr. 2008. "Use Cooperative Conflict Resolution." In *Just Peacemaking: The New Paradigm for the Ethics of Peace and War,* new ed., ed. Glen H. Stassen, 71-97. Cleveland: Pilgrim Press.

Bronkema, David, David Lumsdaine, and Rodger A. Payne. 2008. "Foster Just and Sustainable Economic Development." In *Just Peacemaking: The New Paradigm for the Ethics of Peace and War,* new ed., ed. Glen H. Stassen, 132-52. Cleveland: Pilgrim Press.

Bryant, Coralie, and Christina Kappaz. 2005. *Reducing Poverty, Building Peace.* Bloomfield, CT: Kumarian Press.

Cady, Duane L. 1989. *From Warism to Pacifism: A Moral Continuum.* Philadelphia: Temple University Press.

Cahill, Lisa Sowle. 1994. *Love Your Enemies: Discipleship, Pacifism, and Just War Theory.* Minneapolis: Fortress Press.

Caprioli, Mary, Rebecca Nielsen, and Valerie M. Hudson. 2010. "Women and Post-Conflict Settings." In *Peace and Conflict 2010,* ed. J. Joseph Hewitt, Jonathan Wilkenfeld, and Ted Robert Gurr, 91-102. Boulder, CO: Paradigm Publishers.

Carothers, Thomas, ed. 2006. *Promoting the Rule of Law Abroad: In Search of Knowledge.* Washington, DC: Carnegie Endowment for International Peace.

Carothers, Thomas. 2009. "Rule of Law Temptations." *The Fletcher Forum of World Affairs* 33 (1): 49-61.

Cartwright, John, and Susan Thistlethwaite. 2008. "Support Nonviolent Direct Action." In *Just Peacemaking: The New Paradigm for the Ethics of Peace and War*, new ed., ed. Glen H. Stassen, 42-56. Cleveland: Pilgrim Press.

Catechism of the Catholic Church. 1994. 2nd ed. Vatican City: Libreria Editrice Vaticana.

Cawthorne, Nigel. 2006. *Public Executions: From Ancient Rome to the Present Day.* Edison, NJ: Chartwell Books.

Ceadel, Martin. 1987. *Thinking about Peace and War.* Oxford: Oxford University Press.

Chandrasekaran, Rajiv. 2010. "Petraeus Reviews Directive Meant to Limit Afghan Civilian Deaths." *Washington Post.* July 9.

Chaput, Charles J., O.F.M., Cap. 2008. *Render unto Caesar: Serving the Nation by Living Our Catholic Beliefs in Political Life.* New York: Doubleday.

Cheema, G. Shabbir. 2005. *Building Democratic Institutions: Governance Reform in Developing Countries.* Bloomfield, CT: Kumarian Press.

Chenoweth, Erica, and Maria J. Stephan. 2011. *Why Civil Resistance Works: The Strategic Logic of Nonviolent Conflict.* New York: Columbia University Press.

Christiansen, Drew, S.J. 1999a. "Peacemaking and the Use of Force: Behind the Pope's Stringent Just-War Teaching." *America.* May 15.

Christiansen, Drew, S.J. 1999b. "What We Must Learn from Kosovo: Military Intervention and Humanitarian Aid." *America.* August 28.

Christiansen, Drew, S.J. 2005. "Commentary on *Pacem in Terris (Peace on Earth)*." In *Modern Catholic Social Teaching: Commentaries and Interpretations*, ed. Kenneth R. Himes, O.F.M., 217-43. Washington, DC: Georgetown University Press.

Christopher, Paul. 1999. *The Ethics of War and Peace: An Introduction to Legal and Moral Issues.* 2nd ed. Upper Saddle River, NJ: Prentice Hall.

Clough, David, and Brian Stiltner. 2007. *Faith and Force: A Christian Debate about War.* Washington, DC: Georgetown University Press.

Cochran, David Carroll. 1996. "War-Pacifism." *Social Theory and Practice* 22 (2): 161-81.

Cohen, Jessica, and William Easterly, eds. 2009. *What Works in Development: Thinking Big and Thinking Small.* Washington, DC: Brookings Institution Press.

Cohen, Michael A. 2010. "The Myth of a Kinder, Gentler War." *World Policy Journal* 27 (1): 75-86.

Colby, Elbridge A. 2011. "Keeping the Peace." *First Things.* January.

Collier, Paul. 2007. *The Bottom Billion: Why the Poorest Countries Are Failing and What Can Be Done about It.* Oxford: Oxford University Press.

Collier, Paul. 2008. "Postconflict Economic Policy." In *Building States to*

Build Peace, ed. Charles T. Call and Vanessa Wyeth, 103-17. Boulder, CO: Lynne Rienner Publishers.

Collingham, Lizzie. 2012. *The Taste of War: World War Two and the Battle for Food*. New York: Penguin.

Cortright, David. 2007. "Sanctions and Stability Pacts: The Economic Tools of Peacemaking." In *Peacemaking in International Conflict: Methods and Techniques*, rev. ed., ed. I. William Zartman, 385-418. Washington, DC: United States Institute of Peace.

Cortright, David. 2008. *Peace: A History of Movements and Ideas*. Cambridge: Cambridge University Press.

Cronin, Audrey Kurth. 2009. *How Terrorism Ends: Understanding the Decline and Demise of Terrorist Campaigns*. Princeton, NJ: Princeton University Press.

Cronin, Rev. Michael, M.A., D.D. 1922. *The Science of Ethics, Volume II: Special Ethics*. 2nd ed. New York: Benziger Brothers.

Crowley, Michael. 2010. "Our Man in Kabul?" *The New Republic*. March 25.

Curran, Charles E. 2002. *Catholic Social Teaching, 1891-Present: A Historical, Theological, and Ethical Analysis*. Washington, DC: Georgetown University Press.

Cyprian. 1903. "Epistle I." In *The Ante-Nicene Fathers*, ed. Alexander Roberts, D.D., and James Donaldson, LL.D., 275-80. New York: Charles Scribner's Sons.

Davidson, Amy. 2011. "Asleep in Afghanistan." *The New Yorker Close Read Blog*, May 16. http://www.newyorker.com/online/blogs/closeread/2011/05/asleep-in-afghanistan.html.

Davis, David Brion. 1966. *The Problem of Slavery in Western Culture*. Oxford: Oxford University Press.

Davis, David Brion. 1984. *Slavery and Human Progress*. Oxford: Oxford University Press.

Davis, David Brion. 1998. "The Problem of Slavery." Introduction to *A Historical Guide to World Slavery*, ed. Seymour Drescher and Stanley L. Engerman. Oxford: Oxford University Press.

Davis, David Brion. 1999. *The Problem of Slavery in the Age of Revolution, 1770-1823*. New ed. Oxford: Oxford University Press.

Davis, David Brion. 2006. *Inhuman Bondage: The Rise and Fall of Slavery in the New World*. Oxford: Oxford University Press.

Deats, Paul. 1980. "Protestant Social Ethics and Pacifism." In *War or Peace? The Search for New Answers*, ed. Thomas A. Shannon, 75-92. Maryknoll, NY: Orbis Books.

Deudney, Daniel, and G. John Ikenberry. 2009. "The Myth of the Autocratic Revival: Why Liberal Democracies Will Prevail." *Foreign Affairs* 88 (1): 77-93.

Diamond, Jared. 2008. "Vengeance Is Ours." *The New Yorker*. April 21.

Diamond, Larry. 2008a. "The Democratic Rollback." *Foreign Affairs* 87 (2): 36-48.

Diamond, Larry. 2008b. *The Spirit of Democracy: The Struggle to Build Free Societies throughout the World*. New York: Henry Holt.

Dobbins, James. 2007. *Testimony: A Comparative Evaluation of United Nations Peacekeeping*. Santa Monica, CA: RAND Corporation.

Dobbins, James, Seth G. Jones, Keith Crane, and Beth Cole DeGrasse. 2007. *The Beginner's Guide to Nation-Building*. Santa Monica, CA: RAND Corporation.

Dobbins, James, Seth G. Jones, Keith Crane, Andrew Rathmell, Brett Steele, Richard Teltschik, and Anga R. Timilsina. 2005. *The UN's Role in Nation Building: From the Congo to Iraq*. Santa Monica, CA: RAND Corporation.

Dorr, Donal. 1983. *Option for the Poor: A Hundred Years of Vatican Social Teaching*. Maryknoll, NY: Orbis Books.

Douglas, Mary. 1986. *How Institutions Think*. Syracuse, NY: Syracuse University Press.

Douglass, James W. 1968. *The Non-violent Cross: A Theology of Revolution and Peace*. New York: MacMillan.

Doyle, Michael W. 1986. "Liberalism and World Politics." *American Political Science Review* 80 (4): 1151-63.

Doyle, Michael W., and Nicholas Sambanis. 2006. *Making War and Building Peace: United Nations Peace Operations*. Princeton, NJ: Princeton University Press.

Dray, Philip. 2002. *At the Hands of Persons Unknown: The Lynching of Black America*. New York: Modern Library.

Duffey, Michael K. 1995. *Peacemaking Christians: The Future of Just Wars, Pacifism, and Nonviolent Resistance*. Kansas City, MO: Sheed & Ward.

Dula, Peter. 2004. "The War in Iraq: How Catholic Conservatives Got It Wrong." *Commonweal*. December 3.

Dumas, Lloyd J. 2003. "Is Development an Effective Way to Fight Terrorism?" In *War after September 11*, ed. Verna V. Gehring, 65-74. Lanham, MD: Rowman & Littlefield.

Dyer, Gwynne. 2004. *War: The Lethal Custom*. Rev. ed. New York: Carroll & Graf.

Egan, Eileen. 1980. "The Beatitudes, the Works of Mercy, and Pacifism." In *War or Peace? The Search for New Answers*, ed. Thomas A. Shannon, 169-87. Maryknoll, NY: Orbis Books.

Egan, Eileen. 1993. "Peacemaking in the Post-Just War Age." In *Studying War—No More? From Just War to Just Peace*, ed. Brian Wicker, 59-63. Grand Rapids: Eerdmans.

Elliott, Justin. 2011. "Santorum: What Does McCain Know about Torture?" Salon.com. May 17. http://www.salon.com/2011/05/17/santorum_mccain_enhanced_interrogation/.

Elshtain, Jean Bethke, ed. 1992. *Just War Theory*. New York: New York University Press.

Erasmus, Desiderius. 1972. "An Essay on War." In *Bellum: Two Statements on the Nature of War*, ed. William Royall Tyler. Barre, MA: Imprint Society.

Erasmus, Desiderius. 1990. "A Complaint of Peace." In *The Erasmus Reader*, ed. Erika Rummel, 288-314. Toronto: University of Toronto Press.

Erdely, Sabrina Rubin. 2013. "The Rape of Petty Officer Blumer." *Rolling Stone*. February 14. http://www.rollingstone.com/politics/news/the-rape-of-petty-officer-blumer-20130214?print=true.

Esposito, John L. 2002. *Unholy War: Terror in the Name of Islam*. Oxford: Oxford University Press.

Evans, Gareth. 2009. *The Responsibility to Protect: Ending Mass Atrocity Crimes Once and for All*. Washington, DC: Brookings Institution Press.

Ferguson, Niall. 2006. "Prisoner Taking and Prisoner Killing: The Dynamics of Defeat, Surrender and Barbarity in the Age of Total War." In *The Barbarization of Warfare*, ed. George Kassimeris, 126-58. New York: New York University Press.

Filkins, Dexter. 2011a. "After the Uprising." *The New Yorker*. April 11.

Filkins, Dexter. 2011b. "The Journalist and the Spies." *The New Yorker*. September 19.

Finkel, David. 2009. *The Good Soldiers*. New York: Farrar, Straus and Giroux.

Finnis, John. 1996. "The Ethics of War and Peace in the Catholic Natural Law Tradition." In *The Ethics of War and Peace: Religious and Secular Perspectives*, ed. Terry Nardin, 15-39. Princeton, NJ: Princeton University Press.

Finnis, John, Joseph M. Boyle Jr., and Germain Grisez. 1987. *Nuclear Deterrence, Morality, and Realism*. Oxford: Oxford University Press.

First Things. 2001. "In a Time of War." December.

Fisman, Ray. 2012. "Food for Naught: Does Sending Food Aid to Struggling Nations Do More Harm Than Good?" *Slate*. February 1. http://www.slate.com/articles/business/the_dismal_science/2012/02/international_aid_does_sending_food_to_struggling_nations_do_more_harm_than_good_.single.html#pagebreak_anchor_2.

Fitzhugh, George. 1998. "Cannibals All!" In *American Political Thought*, 4th ed., ed. Kenneth M. Dolbeare, 271-80. Chatham, NJ: Chatham House Publishers.

Ford, John C., S.J. 1960. "The Hydrogen Bombing of Cities." In *The State of the Question: Morality and Modern Warfare*, ed. William J. Nagle, 98-103. Baltimore: Helicon Press.

Ford, John C., S.J. 1970. "The Morality of Obliteration Bombing." In *War and Morality*, ed. Richard A. Wasserstrom, 15-41. Belmont, CA: Wadsworth.

Fry, Douglas P. 2007. *Beyond War: The Human Potential for Peace.* Oxford: Oxford University Press.

Fullinwider, Robert K. 1975. "War and Innocence." *Philosophy and Public Affairs* 5 (1): 90-97.

Geltzer, Joshua A. 2009. *U.S. Counter-Terrorism Strategy and al-Qaeda: Signalling and the Terrorist World-View.* New York: Routledge.

George, Robert. 2011. "The Worst Protest Song Ever." *Mirror of Justice Blog*, April 24. http://mirrorofjustice.blogs.com/mirrorofjustice/2011/04/the-worst-protest-song-ever.html.

Gilbert, G. M. 1947. *Nuremberg Diary.* New York: Farrar, Straus.

Glenny, Misha. 2008. *McMafia: A Journey through the Global Criminal Underworld.* New York: Knopf.

Goldstein, Joshua S. 2011. *Winning the War on War: The Decline of Armed Conflict Worldwide.* New York: Dutton.

Gourevitch, Philip. 2010. "Alms Dealers." *The New Yorker.* October 11.

Green, Barbara, and Glen Stassen. 2008. "Reduce Offensive Weapons and Weapons Trade." In *Just Peacemaking: The New Paradigm for the Ethics of Peace and War*, new ed., ed. Glen H. Stassen, 177-200. Cleveland: Pilgrim Press.

Grisez, Germain. 1970. "Toward a Consistent Natural-Law Ethics of Killing." *The American Journal of Jurisprudence* 15: 64-96.

Grisez, Germain, and Russell Shaw. 1980. *Beyond the New Morality: The Responsibilities of Freedom.* Rev. ed. Notre Dame, IN: University of Notre Dame Press.

Groeger, Lena. 2011. "The Dead, the Dollars, the Drones: 9/11 Era by the Numbers." *Wired.* September 9. http://www.wired.com/dangerroom/2011/09/dangerroom_911toll_0909/all/1.

Grossman, Dave. 2009. *On Killing: The Psychological Cost of Learning to Kill in War and Society.* Rev. ed. New York: Little, Brown.

Grotius, Hugo. 2005. *The Law of War and Peace.* Trans. Francis W. Kelsey. Lonang Institute. http://www.lonang.com/exlibris/grotius/index.html.

Gumbleton, Thomas J. 1991. "Peacemaking as a Way of Life." In *One Hundred Years of Catholic Social Thought: Celebration and Challenge*, ed. John A. Coleman, S.J., 303-16. Maryknoll, NY: Orbis Books.

Gurr, Ted Robert. 2000. *Peoples Versus States: Minorities at Risk in the New Century.* Washington, DC: United States Institute of Peace Press.

Halbertal, Moshe. 2009. "The Goldstone Illusion." *The New Republic.* November 18.

Hallock, Dan. 1999. *Bloody Hell: The Price Soldiers Pay.* Farmington, PA: Plough Publishers.

Hamm, Mark S. 2007. *Terrorism as Crime: From Oklahoma City to Al-Qaeda and Beyond.* New York: New York University Press.

Hari, Johann. 2009. "Renouncing Islamism: To the Brink and Back Again." *The Independent* (London). November 16.

Hartigan, Richard S. 1965. "Noncombatant Immunity: Its Scope and Development." *Continuum* 3 (3): 300-14.

Hassan, Nasra. 2001. "An Arsenal of Believers." *The New Yorker.* November 19.

Hauerwas, Stanley. 1988. "Epilogue: A Pacifist Response to the Bishops." In *Speak Up for Just War or Pacifism: A Critique of the United Methodist Bishops' Pastoral Letter "In Defense of Creation,"* by Paul Ramsey, 149-82. University Park: Pennsylvania State University Press.

Hauerwas, Stanley. 2011. *War and the American Difference: Theological Reflections on Violence and National Identity.* Grand Rapids: Baker Academic.

Hedges, Chris. 2002. *War Is a Force that Gives Us Meaning.* New York: Anchor Books.

Hegre, Håvard, Tanja Ellingsen, Scott Gates, and Nils Petter Gleditsch. 2001. "Toward a Democratic Civil Peace? Democracy, Political Change, and Civil War, 1816-1992." *American Political Science Review* 95 (1): 33-48.

Hehir, J. Bryan. 1980. "The Just War Ethic and Catholic Theology: Dynamics of Change and Continuity." In *War or Peace? The Search for New Answers,* ed. Thomas A. Shannon, 15-39. Maryknoll, NY: Orbis Books.

Hehir, J. Bryan. 1992. "Just War Theory in a Post-Cold War World." *Journal of Religious Ethics* 20 (2): 237-57.

Hewitt, J. Joseph. 2010. "Trends in Global Conflict, 1946-2007." In *Peace and Conflict 2010,* ed. J. Joseph Hewitt, Jonathan Wilkenfeld, and Ted Robert Gurr, 27-32. Boulder, CO: Paradigm Publishers.

Hewitt, J. Joseph, Jonathan Wilkenfeld, and Ted Robert Gurr, eds. 2010. *Peace and Conflict 2010.* Boulder, CO: Paradigm Publishers.

Himes, Kenneth R., O.F.M. 1991. "Pacifism and the Just War Tradition in Roman Catholic Social Teaching." In *One Hundred Years of Catholic Social Thought: Celebration and Challenge,* ed. John A. Coleman, S.J., 329-44. Maryknoll, NY: Orbis Books.

Himes, Kenneth R. O.F.M. 2008. "Working for Peace." In *We Hold These Truths: Catholicism and American Political Life,* ed. Richard W. Miller, 63-74. Ligouri, MO: Ligouri Publications.

Hoeffler, Anke. 2010. "State Failure and Conflict Recurrence." In *Peace and Conflict 2010*, ed. J. Joseph Hewitt, Jonathan Wilkenfeld, and Ted Robert Gurr, 65-78. Boulder, CO: Paradigm Publishers.

Holland, Barbara. 2003. *Gentleman's Blood: A History of Dueling from Swords at Dawn to Pistols at Dusk*. New York: Bloomsbury.

Hollenbach, David, S.J. 1983. *Nuclear Ethics: A Christian Moral Argument*. New York: Paulist Press.

Holmes, Robert L. 1989. *On War and Morality*. Princeton, NJ: Princeton University Press.

Holmes, Robert L. 1990. "General Introduction." In *Nonviolence in Theory and Practice*, ed. Robert L. Holmes, 1-6. Belmont, CA: Wadsworth.

Holmes, Robert L., and Barry L. Gan, eds. 2005. *Nonviolence in Theory and Practice*. 2nd ed. Long Grove, IL: Waveland Press.

Hook, Steven W. 2010. *Democratic Peace in Theory and Practice*. Kent, OH: Kent State University Press.

Horgan, John. 2012. *The End of War*. San Francisco: McSweeney's Books.

Howard, Michael. 2008. *War and the Liberal Conscience*. New York: Columbia University Press.

Howes, Dustin Ells. 2009. *Toward a Credible Pacifism: Violence and the Possibilities of Politics*. Albany: State University of New York Press.

Hull, Richard. 2000. "Deconstructing the Doctrine of Double Effect." *Ethical Theory and Moral Practice* 3 (2): 195-207.

International Rescue Committee. 2007. *Measuring Mortality in the Democratic Republic of Congo*. http://www.rescue.org/sites/default/files/resource-file/IRC_DRCMortalityFacts.pdf.

James, William. 2005. "The Moral Equivalent of War." In *Nonviolence in Theory and Practice*, 2nd ed., ed. Robert L. Holmes and Barry L. Gan, 176-85. Long Grove, IL: Waveland Press.

Jervis, Robert. 2002. "Theories of War in an Era of Leading-Power Peace." *American Political Science Review* 96 (1): 1-14.

John XXIII. 1961. *Mater et Magistra*. http://www.vatican.va/holy_father/john_xxiii/encyclicals/documents/hf_j-xxiii_enc_15051961_mater_en.html.

John XXIII. 1963. *Pacem in Terris*. http://www.vatican.va/holy_father/john_xxiii/encyclicals/documents/hf_j-xxiii_enc_11041963_pacem_en.html.

John of Salisbury. 1979. *Policraticus: The Statesman's Book*. Abr. and ed. Murray F. Markland. New York: Frederick Ungar Publishing.

John Paul II. 1984. *Reconciliation and Penance*. http://www.vatican.va/holy_father/john_paul_ii/apost_exhortations/documents/hf_jp-ii_exh_02121984_reconciliatio-et-paenitentia_en.html.

John Paul II. 1987. *Sollicitudo rei Socialis*. http://www.vatican.va/holy_
father/john_paul_ii/encyclicals/documents/hf_jp-ii_enc_30121987_
sollicitudo-rei-socialis_en.html.

John Paul II. 1989. *World Day of Peace Message*. http://www.vatican
.va/holy_father/john_paul_ii/messages/peace/documents/hf_jp-
ii_mes_19881208_xxii-world-day-for-peace_en.html.

John Paul II. 1990. *World Day of Peace Message*. http://www.vatican
.va/holy_father/john_paul_ii/messages/peace/documents/hf_jp-
ii_mes_19891208_xxiii-world-day-for-peace_en.html.

John Paul II. 1991a. *Centesimus Annus*. http://www.vatican.va/holy_
father/john_paul_ii/encyclicals/documents/hf_jp-ii_enc_01051991_
centesimus-annus_en.html.

John Paul II. 1991b. "War, a Decline for Humanity." *Origins* 20 (33):
525-31.

John Paul II. 1991c. "The Pope's Letters to Bush and Hussein." *Origins*
20 (33): 534-35.

John Paul II. 1991d. "We Are Not Pacifists." *Origins* 20 (36): 625.

John Paul II. 1993a. *World Day of Peace Message*. http://www.vatican
.va/holy_father/john_paul_ii/messages/peace/documents/hf_jp-
ii_mes_08121992_xxvi-world-day-for-peace_en.html.

John Paul II. 1993b. "Principles Underlying a Stance toward Unjust
Aggressors." *Origins* 22 (34): 583-87.

John Paul II. 1994. *World Day of Peace Message*. http://www.vatican
.va/holy_father/john_paul_ii/messages/peace/documents/hf_jp-
ii_mes_08121993_xxvii-world-day-for-peace_en.html.

John Paul II. 1995a. *Evangelium Vitae*. http://www.vatican.va/holy_
father/john_paul_ii/encyclicals/documents/hf_jp-ii_enc_25031995_
evangelium-vitae_en.html.

John Paul II. 1995b. *World Day of Peace Message*. http://www.vatican
.va/holy_father/john_paul_ii/messages/peace/documents/hf_jp-
ii_mes_08121994_xxviii-world-day-for-peace_en.html.

John Paul II. 1996. *World Day of Peace Message*. http://www.vatican
.va/holy_father/john_paul_ii/messages/peace/documents/hf_jp-
ii_mes_08121995_xxix-world-day-for-peace_en.html.

John Paul II. 1998. *World Day of Peace Message*. http://www.vatican
.va/holy_father/john_paul_ii/messages/peace/documents/hf_jp-
ii_mes_08121997_xxxi-world-day-for-peace_en.html.

John Paul II. 1999. *World Day of Peace Message*. http://www.vatican
.va/holy_father/john_paul_ii/messages/peace/documents/hf_jp-
ii_mes_14121998_xxxii-world-day-for-peace_en.html.

John Paul II. 2000. *World Day of Peace Message*. http://www.vatican
.va/holy_father/john_paul_ii/messages/peace/documents/hf_jp-
ii_mes_08121999_xxxiii-world-day-for-peace_en.html.

John Paul II. 2002. *World Day of Peace Message.* http://www.vatican
.va/holy_father/john_paul_ii/messages/peace/documents/hf_jp-
ii_mes_20011211_xxxv-world-day-for-peace_en.html.

John Paul II. 2003a. *World Day of Peace Message.* http://www.vatican
.va/holy_father/john_paul_ii/messages/peace/documents/hf_jp-
ii_mes_20021217_xxxvi-world-day-for-peace_en.html.

John Paul II. 2003b. "The International Situation Today." *Origins* 32
(33): 543-45.

John Paul II. 2004. *World Day of Peace Message.* http://www.vatican
.va/holy_father/john_paul_ii/messages/peace/documents/hf_jp-
ii_mes_20031216_xxxvii-world-day-for-peace_en.html.

John Paul II. 2005. *World Day of Peace Message.* http://www.vatican
.va/holy_father/john_paul_ii/messages/peace/documents/hf_jp-
ii_mes_20041216_xxxviii-world-day-for-peace_en.html.

Johnson, Chalmers. 2004. *The Sorrows of Empire: Militarism, Secrecy,
and the End of the Republic.* New York: Holt.

Johnson, James Turner. 1987. *The Quest for Peace: Three Moral Traditions in Western Cultural History.* Princeton, NJ: Princeton University
Press.

Johnson, James Turner. 2005. "Just War, As It Was and Is." *First Things.*
January.

Johnstone, Brian. 1986. "Noncombatant Immunity and the Prohibi-
tion of the Killing of the Innocent." In *Peace in a Nuclear Age: The
Bishops' Pastoral Letter in Perspective,* ed. Charles J. Reid, 305-22.
Washington, DC: Catholic University of America Press.

Jones, Seth G., and Martin C. Libicki. 2008. *How Terrorist Groups
End: Lessons for Countering al Qa'ida.* Santa Monica, CA: RAND
Corporation.

Kahn, Paul W. 2002. "The Paradox of Riskless Warfare." *Philosophy &
Public Policy Quarterly* 22 (3): 2-8.

Kaplan, Fred. 2008. *Daydream Believers: How a Few Grand Ideas
Wrecked American Power.* Hoboken, NJ: John Wiley & Sons.

Kaplan, Lawrence. 2011. "Vietnamization." *The New Republic.* March
24.

Kassimeris, George. 2006. "The Barbarization of War: A User's Manual."
In *The Barbarization of Warfare,* ed. George Kassimeris, 1-18. New
York: New York University Press.

Katatnycky, Adrian, and Peter Ackerman. 2005. *How Freedom Is Won:
From Civic Resistance to Durable Democracy.* Washington, DC:
Freedom House.

Katzenstein, Peter J., ed. 1996. *The Culture of National Security: Norms
and Identity in World Politics.* New York: Columbia University Press.

Kavanaugh, John F., S.J. 2001. *Who Count as Persons? Human Identity and the Ethics of Killing.* Washington, DC: Georgetown University Press.

Keefe, Patrick Radden. 2010. "The Trafficker." *The New Yorker.* February 8.

Keegan, John. 1993. *A History of Warfare.* New York: Vintage Books.

Kenny, Charles. 2011a. "The Price Is Right." *Foreign Policy.* July 18. http:// foreignpolicy.com/articles/2011/07/18/the_price_is_right?page=0,0.

Kenny, Charles. 2011b. "Club for Growth." *Foreign Policy.* October 24. http://www.foreignpolicy.com/articles/2011/10/24/club_for_ growth?page=0,0.

Kenny, Charles. 2011c. *Getting Better: Why Global Development Is Succeeding—And How We Can Improve the World Even More.* New York: Basic Books.

Khatchadourian, Raffi. 2009. "The Kill Company." *The New Yorker.* July 6 and 13.

Khatchadourian, Raffi. 2010. "No Secrets." *The New Yorker.* June 7.

Kiernan, V. G. 1988. *The Duel in European History: Honour and the Reign of Aristocracy.* Oxford: Oxford University Press.

Kinder, Donald R., and Cindy D. Kam. 2009. *Us against Them: Ethnocentric Foundations of American Opinion.* Chicago: University of Chicago Press.

Kleinig, John. 1996. *The Ethics of Policing.* Cambridge: Cambridge University Press.

Kohl, Marvin. 1990. "Toward Understanding the Pragmatics of Absolute Pacifism." In *In the Interest of Peace: A Spectrum of Philosophical Views,* ed. Kenneth H. Klein and Joseph C. Kunkel, 227-36. Wakefield, NH: Longwood Academic.

Kolbert, Elizabeth. 2011. "Peace in Our Time." *The New Yorker.* October 3.

Koontz, Theodore J. 1996. "Christian Nonviolence: An Interpretation." In *The Ethics of War and Peace: Religious and Secular Perspectives,* ed. Terry Nardin, 169-96. Princeton, NJ: Princeton University Press.

Krauthammer, Charles. 2006. "The Truth about Torture." In *Torture: A Collection,* rev. ed., ed. Sanford Levinson, 307-16. Oxford: Oxford University Press.

Kupchan, Charles A. 2010. *How Enemies Become Friends: The Sources of Stable Peace.* Princeton, NJ: Princeton University Press.

Kurlantzick, Joshua. 2008. "Monsters' Ball." *The New Republic.* October 8.

Kurlantzick, Joshua. 2011. "The Great Democracy Meltdown." *The New Republic.* June 9.

Kyle, Chris. 2012. *American Sniper: The Autobiography of the Most Lethal Sniper in U.S. Military History.* New York: HarperCollins.

La Civilta Cattolica. 1991. "Modern War and the Christian Conscience." *Origins* 21 (28): 450-55.

LaFree, Gary, Laura Dugan, and R. Kim Cragin. 2010. "Trends in Global Terrorism, 1970-2007." In *Peace and Conflict 2010*, ed. J. Joseph Hewitt, Jonathan Wilkenfeld, and Ted Robert Gurr, 51-64. Boulder, CO: Paradigm Publishers.

Lammers, Stephen E. 1990. "Approaches to Limits on War in Western Just War Discourse." In *Cross, Crescent, and Sword: The Justification and Limitation of War in Western and Islamic Tradition*, ed. James Turner Johnson and John Kelsay, 51-78. New York: Greenwood Press.

Lane, Kris E. 1998. *Pillaging the Empire: Piracy in the Americas, 1500-1750*. Armonk, NY: M. E. Sharpe.

LeBlanc, Steven A., and Katherine E. Register. 2003. *Constant Battles: Why We Fight*. New York: St. Martin's Press.

Lepore, Jill. 2010. "The Uprooted." *The New Yorker*. September 6.

Lichtenberg, Judith. 1994. "War, Innocence, and the Doctrine of Double Effect." *Philosophical Studies* 74 (3): 347-64.

Lopez, George A. 2002. "Iraq & Just-War Thinking." *Commonweal*. September 27.

Lopez, George A. 2008. "Don't Just Do Something: Getting Sanctions Right." *Commonweal*. June 6.

Luban, David. 2002. "The War on Terrorism and the End of Human Rights." *Philosophy & Public Policy Quarterly* 22 (3): 9-14.

Malinowski, Bronislaw. 2006. "An Anthropological Analysis of War." In *War & Peace in an Age of Terrorism: A Reader*, ed. William M. Evan, 222-26. Boston: Pearson.

Malloy, Edward A., C.S.C. 1982. *The Ethics of Law Enforcement and Criminal Punishment*. Lanham, MD: University Press of America.

Mansfield, Edward D., and Jack Snyder. 2005. *Electing to Fight: Why Emerging Democracies Go to War*. Cambridge, MA: MIT Press.

Mapel, David R. 1996. "Realism and the Ethics of War and Peace." In *The Ethics of War and Peace: Religious and Secular Perspectives*, ed. Terry Nardin, 54-77. Princeton, NJ: Princeton University Press.

Marazziti, Mario. 2012. "Lessons in Peace." *America*. November 19.

Massaro, Thomas J., S.J., and Thomas A. Shannon. 2003. *Catholic Perspectives on War and Peace*. Lanham, MD: Rowman & Littlefield.

Mathews, Jessica. 2009. "This Time, Ban the Test." *New York Times*. October 22.

Mavrodes, George I. 1975. "Conventions and the Morality of War." *Philosophy and Public Affairs* 4 (2): 117-31.

Mayer, Jane. 2009a. *The Dark Side: The Inside Story of How the War on Terror Turned into a War on American Ideals*. New York: Anchor Books.

Mayer, Jane. 2009b. "The Predator War." *The New Yorker*. October 26.

McCarthy, Jeremiah. 1994. "Killing." In *The New Dictionary of Catholic Social Thought*, ed. Judith A. Dwyer, 506-08. Collegeville, MN: Liturgical Press.

McDermott, Terry. 2010. "The Mastermind." *The New Yorker*. September 13.

McFaul, Michael. 2010. *Advancing Democracy Abroad: Why We Should and How We Can*. Lanham, MD: Rowman & Littlefield.

McHugh, John A., O.P., and Charles J. Callan, O.P., trans. 1934. *Catechism of the Council of Trent for Parish Priests*. 2nd rev. ed. New York: Joseph F. Wagner.

McKeogh, Colm. 2002. *Innocent Civilians: The Morality of Killing in War*. New York: Palgrave.

McMahan, Jeff. 1994. "Self-Defense and the Problem of the Innocent Attacker." *Ethics* 104 (2): 252-90.

McReavy, L. L., and F. X. Meehan. 2003. "Pacifism." In *New Catholic Encyclopedia*, 2nd ed., vol. 10, 744-48. Detroit: Gale.

Mead, Margaret. 2006. "Warfare Is Only an Invention, Not a Biological Necessity." In *War & Peace in an Age of Terrorism: A Reader*, ed. William M. Evan, 218-21. Boston: Pearson.

Meehan, Mary. 2012. "In Harm's Way." *America*. January 16 and 23.

Megivern, James J. 1997. *The Death Penalty: An Historical and Theological Survey*. New York: Paulist Press.

Meltzer, Milton. 1993. *Slavery: A World History*. Up. ed. New York: DaCapo Press.

Metaxas, Eric. 2007. *Amazing Grace: William Wilberforce and the Heroic Campaign to End Slavery*. New York: HarperCollins.

Miller, Richard B. 1991. *Interpretations of Conflict: Ethics, Pacifism, and the Just War Tradition*. Chicago: University of Chicago Press.

Miller, Seumas. 1993. "Killing in Self-Defense." *Public Affairs Quarterly* 7 (4): 325-39.

Milne, A. A. 2005. "The Pacifist Spirit." In *Nonviolence in Theory and Practice*, 2nd ed., ed. Robert L. Holmes and Barry L. Gan, 186-93. Long Grove, IL: Waveland Press.

Morgan, Patrick M. 2006. *International Security: Problems and Solutions*. Washington, DC: CQ Press.

Moyo, Dambisa. 2009. *Dead Aid: Why Aid Is Not Working and How There Is a Better Way for Africa*. New York: Farrar, Straus and Giroux.

Mueller, John. 2004. *The Remnants of War*. Ithaca, NY: Cornell University Press.

Mueller, John. 2006. *Overblown: How Politicians and the Terrorism Industry Inflate National Security Threats, and Why We Believe Them*. New York: Free Press.

Mujica, Barbara. 2011. "Don't Look Away." *Commonweal*. March 25.

Murray, John Courtney, S.J. 1959. *Morality and Modern War*. New York: Council on Religion and International Affairs.

Murray, John Courtney, S.J. 1960. *We Hold These Truths: Catholic Reflections on the American Proposition*. New York: Sheed & Ward.

Nadelmann, Ethan A. 1990. "Global Prohibition Regimes: The Evolution of Norms in International Society." *International Organization* 44 (4): 479-526.

Nagel, Thomas. 1974. "War and Massacre." In *War and Moral Responsibility*, ed. Marshall Cohen, Thomas Nagel, and Thomas Scanlon, 3-24. Princeton, NJ: Princeton University Press.

Nardin, Terry, ed. 1996. *The Ethics of War and Peace: Religious and Secular Perspectives*. Princeton, NJ: Princeton University Press.

Narveson, Jan. 1970. "Pacifism: A Philosophical Analysis." In *War and Morality*, ed. Richard A. Wasserstrom, 63-77. Belmont, CA: Wadsworth.

Neufeldt, Reina C. 2007. "Just Policing and International Order: Is It Possible?" In *Just Policing, Not War: An Alternative Response to World Violence*, ed. Gerald W. Schlabach, 153-71. Collegeville, MN: Liturgical Press.

Neuhaus, Richard John. 2003. "The Sounds of Religion in a Time of War." *First Things*. May.

Noonan, John T. Jr. 2002. "Virginia Liberators." In *Before the Law: An Introduction to the Legal Process*, 7th ed., ed. John J. Bonsignore, Ethan Katsh, Peter d'Errico, Ronald M. Pipkin, Stephen Arons, and Janet Rifkin, 241-46. Boston: Houghton Mifflin.

Noonan, John T., Jr. 2005. *A Church That Can and Cannot Change: The Development of Catholic Moral Teaching*. Notre Dame, IN: University of Notre Dame Press.

Norman, Richard. 1988. "The Case for Pacifism." *Journal of Applied Philosophy* 5 (2): 197-210.

Norris, John. 2009. *Pistols at Dawn: A History of Duelling*. Gloucestershire: History Press.

Novak, Michael. 2003. "An Argument that War against Iraq Is Just." *Origins* 32 (36): 593-98.

Obama, Barack. 2009. "Obama's Nobel Remarks." *New York Times*. December 10. http://www.nytimes.com/2009/12/11/world/europe/11prexy.text.html?pagewanted=all&_r=0.

O'Brien, David J. 1980. "American Catholic Opposition to the Vietnam War: A Preliminary Assessment." In *War or Peace? The Search for New Answers*, ed. Thomas A. Shannon, 119-50. Maryknoll, NY: Orbis Books.

O'Brien, William V. 1992. "The Challenge of War: A Christian Realist

Perspective." In *Just War Theory*, ed. Jean Bethke Elshtain, 169-96. New York: New York University Press.

Olsen, Tricia D., Leigh A. Payne, and Andrew G. Reiter. 2010. *Transnational Justice in Balance: Comparing Processes, Weighing Efficacy.* Washington, DC: United States Institute of Peace Press.

Oppel, Richard A. 2010. "Tighter Rules Fail to Stem Deaths of Innocent Afghans at Checkpoints." *New York Times.* March 26.

Oppenheimer, Mark. 2010. "Defender of Waterboarding Hears from Critics." *New York Times.* February 26.

Osborn, Ronald. 2011. "Still Counting." *Commonweal.* February 11.

Pape, Robert A. 2006. *Dying to Win: The Strategic Logic of Suicide Bombing.* New York: Random House.

Pape, Robert A., and James K. Feldman. 2010. *Cutting the Fuse: The Explosion of Global Suicide Terrorism & How to Stop It.* Chicago: University of Chicago Press.

Paskins, Barrie, and Michael Dockrill. 1979. *The Ethics of War.* Minneapolis: University of Minnesota Press.

Patterson, Eric. 2007. *Just War Thinking: Morality and Pragmatism in the Struggle against Contemporary Threats.* Lanham, MD: Lexington Books.

Patterson, Orlando. 1982. *Slavery and Social Death: A Comparative Study.* Cambridge, MA: Harvard University Press.

Patterson, Orlando. 1999. Introduction to *Chronology of World Slavery,* by Junius P. Rodriguez. Santa Barbara, CA: ABC-CLIO.

Paul VI. 1966. "Address of Pope Paul VI to the UN General Assembly." *The Pope Speaks* 11 (1): 47-57.

Paul VI. 1967. *Populorum Progressio.* http://www.vatican.va/holy_father/paul_vi/encyclicals/documents/hf_p-vi_enc_26031967_populorum_en.html.

Paul VI. 1971. *Octogesima Adveniens.* http://www.vatican.va/holy_father/paul_vi/apost_letters/documents/hf_p-vi_apl_19710514_octogesima-adveniens_en.html.

Paul VI. 1975. *Evangelii Nuntiandi.* http://www.vatican.va/holy_father/paul_vi/apost_exhortations/documents/hf_p-vi_exh_19751208_evangelii-nuntiandi_en.html.

Paul VI. 1977. "The Holy See and Disarmament." *The Pope Speaks* 22 (3): 243-59.

Pfeil, Margaret R. 2007. "Whose Justice? Which Rationality?" In *Just Policing, Not War: An Alternative Response to World Violence*, ed. Gerald W. Schlabach, 111-29. Collegeville, MN: Liturgical Press.

Phillips, Robert L. 1990. "Combatancy, Noncombatancy, and Noncombatant Immunity in Just War Tradition." In *Cross, Crescent, and Sword: The Justification and Limitation of War in Western and Islamic*

Tradition, ed. James Turner Johnson and John Kelsay, 179-95. New York: Greenwood Press.

Pinker, Steven. 2011. *The Better Angels of Our Nature: Why Violence Has Declined*. New York: Viking.

Pinkovskiy, Maxim, and Xavier Sala-i-Martin. 2010. "Parametric Estimations of the World Distribution of Income." *Vox*. January 22. http://voxeu.org/index.php?q=node/4508.

Pius XII. 1961. *The Major Addresses of Pope Pius XII*, vol. 2, ed. Vincent A. Yzermans. St. Paul, MN: North Central Publishing.

Polman, Linda. 2010. *The Crisis Caravan: What's Wrong with Humanitarian Aid?* Trans. Liz Waters. New York: Henry Holt.

Pontifical Council for Justice and Peace. 1994. *The International Arms Trade: An Ethical Reflection*. Vatican City: Libreria Editrice Vaticana.

Pontifical Council for Justice and Peace. 2004. *Compendium of the Social Doctrine of the Church*. Washington, DC: United States Conference of Catholic Bishops.

Potts, Malcolm, and Thomas Hayden. 2008. *Sex and War: How Biology Explains Warfare and Terrorism and Offers a Path to a Safer World*. Dallas: Benbella Books.

Power, Samantha. 2009. "The Enforcer." *The New Yorker*. January 19.

Price, Richard, and Nina Tannenwald. 1996. "Norms and Deterrence: The Nuclear and Chemical Weapons Taboo." In *The Culture of National Security: Norms and Identity in World Politics*, ed. Peter J. Katzenstein, 114-52. New York: Columbia University Press.

Prümmer, Dominicus M., O.P. 1957. *Handbook of Moral Theology*. Trans. Gerald W. Shelton, S.T.L. and ed. John Gavin Nolan, S.I.D. Fort Collins, CO: Roman Catholic Books.

Ramsbotham, Oliver, Tom Woodhouse, and Hugh Miall. 2005. *Contemporary Conflict Resolution: The Prevention, Management and Transformation of Deadly Conflicts*. 2nd ed. Cambridge: Polity Press.

Ratzinger, Joseph. 1998. *Milestones: Memoirs 1927-1977*. Trans. Erasmo Leiva-Merikakis. San Francisco: Ignatius Press.

Ray, Jame,s Lee. 1989. "The Abolition of Slavery and the End of International War." *International Organization* 43 (3): 405-39.

Regan, Patrick M. 2000. *Civil Wars and Foreign Powers: Outside Intervention in Intrastate Conflict*. Ann Arbor: University of Michigan Press.

Reitan, Eric. 1994. "The Irreconcilability of Pacifism and Just War Theory: A Response to Sterba (1992)." *Social Theory and Practice* 20 (2): 117-34.

Richardson, John H. 2009. "Acts of Conscience." *Esquire*. September 21. http://www.esquire.com/features/ESQ0806TERROR_102.

Riddell, Roger C. 2007. *Does Foreign Aid Really Work?* Oxford: Oxford University Press.

Ringsmose, Jens. 2008. "When Great Powers Lose Small Wars." *Global Security* 22 (3): 411-18.

Rising, David, and Matt Surman. 2005. "New Pope Made Risky Choices in Bavarian Town during World War II." *Associated Press*. April 23.

Ritchie, Robert C. 1986. *Captain Kidd and the War against the Pirates*. Cambridge, MA: Harvard University Press.

Rodin, David. 2002. *War and Self-Defense*. Oxford: Oxford University Press.

Rodriguez, Junius P. 1997. "Slavery in Human History." Introduction to *The Historical Encyclopedia of World Slavery*, 2 vols., ed. Junius P. Rodriguez. Santa Barbara, CA: ABC-CLIO.

Rodriguez, Junius P. 1999. *Chronology of World Slavery*. Santa Barbara, CA: ABC-CLIO.

Rosenbaum, Ron. 2010. "Ban Drone-Porn War Crimes." *Slate*. August 31. http://www.slate.com/articles/life/the_spectator/2010/08/ban_drone-porn_war_crimes.html.

Rosen, Jeffrey. 2008. "Man-Made Disaster." *The New Republic*. December 24.

Roth, Richard. 2009. *American Homicide*. Cambridge, MA: Harvard University Press.

Rubin, Barnett R. 2008. "The Politics of Security in Postconflict State-building." In *Building States to Build Peace*, ed. Charles T. Call and Vanessa Wyeth, 25-47. Boulder, CO: Lynne Rienner Publishers.

Rummel, R. J. 1997. *Power Kills: Democracy as a Method of Nonviolence*. New Brunswick, NJ: Transaction Publishers.

Ruskin, John. 2008. *The Crown of Wild Olive*. Project Gutenberg. http://www.gutenberg.org/files/26716/26716-h/26716-h.htm.

Russett, Bruce. 1993. *Grasping the Democratic Peace: Principles for a Post-Cold War World*. Princeton, NJ: Princeton University Press.

Russett, Bruce. 2008. "Advance Democracy, Human Rights, and Interdependence." In *Just Peacemaking: The New Paradigm for the Ethics of Peace and War*, new ed., ed. Glen H. Stassen, 116-31. Cleveland: Pilgrim Press.

Russett, Bruce, and John Oneal. 2001. *Triangulating Peace: Democracy, Interdependence, and International Organizations*. New York: W. W. Norton.

Ryan, Cheyney. 1983. "Self-Defense, Pacifism, and the Possibility of Killing." *Ethics* 93 (3): 508-24.

Sachs, Jeffrey D. 2005. *The End of Poverty: Economic Possibilities for Our Time*. New York: Penguin.

Sageman, Marc. 2008. *Leaderless Jihad: Terror Networks in the Twenty-First Century*. Philadelphia: University of Pennsylvania Press.

Sampson, Cynthia. 2007. "Religion and Peacebuilding." In *Peacemak-

ing in International Conflict: Methods and Techniques, rev. ed., ed. I. William Zartman, 273-323. Washington, DC: United States Institute of Peace.

Scahill, Jeremy. 2008. *Blackwater: The Rise of the World's Most Powerful Army*. Rev. ed. New York: Nation Books.

Schall, James V. 2004. "When War Must Be the Answer." *Policy Review* 128 (December/January): 59-70.

Schell, Jonathan. 2003. *The Unconquerable World: Power, Nonviolence, and the Will of the People*. New York: Holt.

Schlabach, Gerald W. 2007a. "Warfare v. Policing: In Search of Moral Clarity." In *Just Policing, Not War: An Alternative Response to World Violence*, ed. Gerald W. Schlabach, 69-84. Collegeville, MN: Liturgical Press.

Schlabach, Gerald W. 2007b. "Practicing Just Policing." In *Just Policing, Not War: An Alternative Response to World Violence*, ed. Gerald W. Schlabach, 93-108. Collegeville, MN: Liturgical Press.

Schlabach, Gerald W., ed. 2007c. *Just Policing, Not War: An Alternative Response to World Violence*. Collegeville, MN: Liturgical Press.

Schroeder, Paul W. 2008. "Work with Emerging Cooperative Forces in the International System." In *Just Peacemaking: The New Paradigm for the Ethics of Peace and War*, new ed., ed. Glen H. Stassen, 154-65. Cleveland: Pilgrim Press.

Schwartz, Mattathias. 2011. "A Massacre in Jamaica." *The New Yorker*. December 12.

Schwellenbach, Nick, and Carol Leonnig. 2010. "Despite U.S. Ban, Tough Battle against Sex Trafficking in War Zones." *Washington Post*. July 17.

Second Vatican Council. 1965. *Gaudium et Spes*. http://www.vatican .va/archive/hist_councils/ii_vatican_council/documents/vat-ii_ const_19651207_gaudium-et-spes_en.html.

Shadle, Matthew A. 2011. *The Origins of War: A Catholic Perspective*. Washington, DC: Georgetown University Press.

Sharp, Gene. 1985. *Making Europe Unconquerable: The Potential of Civilian-Based Deterrence and Defense*. Cambridge, MA: Ballinger Publishing.

Sharp, Gene. 1990a. *Civilian-Based Defense: A Post-Military Weapons System*. Princeton, NJ: Princeton University Press.

Sharp, Gene. 1990b. "Nonviolent Action: An Active Technique of Struggle." In *Nonviolence in Theory and Practice*, ed. Robert L. Holmes, 147-50. Belmont, CA: Wadsworth.

Sharp, Gene. 2005. *Waging Nonviolent Struggle: 20th Century Practice and 21st Century Potential*. Boston: Extending Horizons Books.

Shaw, Joseph. 2005. "Killing in the Catholic Ethical Tradition—II: Self-Defense." *Downside Review* 123 (October): 274-94.

Sheehan, James J. 2008. *Where Have All the Soldiers Gone? The Transformation of Modern Europe.* Boston: Mariner Books.

Sherman, Nancy. 2012. "Hidden Wounds." *America.* May 21.

Shue, Henry. 2010. "Targeting Civilian Infrastructure with Smart Bombs: The New Permissiveness." *Philosophy & Public Policy Quarterly* 30 (3/4): 2-8.

Slim, Hugo. 2008. *Killing Civilians: Method, Madness, and Morality in War.* New York: Columbia University Press.

Smithka, Paula J. 1992. "Are Active Pacifists Really Just-Warists in Disguise?" *Journal of Social Philosophy* 23 (3): 166-83.

Snyder, Timothy. 2010. *Bloodlands: Europe between Hitler and Stalin.* New York: Basic Books.

Sørensen, Georg. 2008. *Democracy and Democratization: Processes and Prospects in a Changing World.* 3rd ed. Boulder, CO: Westview Press.

Sparks, Justin, John Follain, and Christopher Morgan. 2005. "Papal Hopeful Is a Former Hitler Youth." *Sunday Times* (London). April 17.

Spierenburg, Pieter. 2008. *A History of Murder: Personal Violence in Europe from the Middle Ages to the Present.* Cambridge: Policy Press.

Stassen, Glen H. 2007. "War on Terrorism? A Realistic Look at Alternatives." In *Just Policing, Not War: An Alternative Response to World Violence,* ed. Gerald W. Schlabach, 45-65. Collegeville, MN: Liturgical Press.

Stassen, Glen H., ed. 2008. *Just Peacemaking: The New Paradigm for the Ethics of Peace and War.* New ed. Cleveland: Pilgrim Press.

Steinfels, Peter. 1987. "The Heritage Abandoned?" *Commonweal.* September 11.

Stephan, Maria, and Erica Chenoweth. 2008. "Why Civil Resistance Works: The Strategic Logic of Nonviolent Conflict." *International Security* 33 (1): 7-44.

Sterba, James. 1992. "Reconciling Pacifists and Just War Theorists." *Social Theory and Practice* 18 (1): 21-38.

Stillman, Sarah. 2011. "The Invisible Army." *The New Yorker.* June 6.

Stoessinger, John G. 2005. *Why Nations Go to War.* 9th ed. Belmont, CA: Wadsworth.

Syse, Henrik, and Gregory M. Reichberg, eds. 2007. *Ethics, Nationalism, and Just War: Medieval and Contemporary Perspectives.* Washington, DC: Catholic University of America Press.

Taylor, Charles. 1999. *A Catholic Modernity?* Ed. James Heft, S.M. Oxford: Oxford University Press.

Teichman, Jenny. 1986. *Pacifism and the Just War: A Study in Applied Philosophy.* New York: Basil Blackwell.

Tewksbury, William J. 2002. "The Ordeal as a Vehicle for Divine Intervention in Medieval Europe." In *Before the Law: An Introduction to the Legal Process*, 7th ed., ed. John J. Bonsignore, Ethan Katsh, Peter d'Errico, Ronald M. Pipkin, Stephen Arons, and Janet Rifkin, 386-88. Boston: Houghton Mifflin.

Thiessen, Marc A. 2009. "The CIA's Questioning Worked." *Washington Post*. April 21.

Thiessen, Marc A. 2010. *Courting Disaster: How the CIA Kept America Safe and How Barack Obama Is Inviting the Next Attack*. Washington, DC: Regnery.

Thomas, Ward. 2007. "Unjust War and the Catholic Soldier." *Journal of Religious Ethics* 35 (3): 509-25.

Thomsen, Michael. 2011. "Shooting Gallery." *Slate*. September 12. http:// www.slate.com/articles/technology/gaming/2011/09/shooting_gallery. html.

Thomson, Judith Jarvis. 1991. "Self-Defense." *Philosophy and Public Affairs* 20 (4): 283-310.

Tirman, John. 2011. *The Deaths of Others: The Fate of Civilians in America's Wars*. Oxford: Oxford University Press.

Tocqueville, Alexis de. 1969. *Democracy in America*. Ed. J. P. Mayer and trans. George Lawrence. New York: HarperCollins.

Tolstoy, Leo. 2005. "Letter to Ernest Howard Crosby." In *Nonviolence in Theory and Practice*, 2nd ed., ed. Robert L. Holmes and Barry L. Gan, 69-76. Long Grove, IL: Waveland Press.

Toulmin, Stephen. 1992. "The Limits of Allegiance in a Nuclear Age." In *Just War Theory*, ed. Jean Bethke Elshtain, 280-98. New York: New York University Press.

United States Conference of Catholic Bishops. 1983. *The Challenge of Peace*. http://old.usccb.org/sdwp/international/TheChallengeofPeace .pdf.

United States Conference of Catholic Bishops. 1993. *The Harvest of Justice Is Sown in Peace*. http://www.usccb.org/beliefs-and-teachings/ what-we-believe/catholic-social-teaching/the-harvest-of-justice-is-sown-in-peace.cfm.

United States Conference of Catholic Bishops. 1995. *Sowing Weapons of War*. http://www.usccb.org/issues-and-action/human-life-and-dignity/ war-and-peace/sowing-weapons-of-war.cfm.

United States Conference of Catholic Bishops. 2001. *Living with Faith and Hope after September 11*. http://www.usccb.org/issues-and-action/human-life-and-dignity/september-11/a-pastoral-message-living-with-faith-and-hope-after-september-11.cfm.

Victoria, Franciscus de. 1995. *De Indis et de Iure Belli: Reflections*. Ed. Ernest Nys. Buffalo, NY: William S. Hein.

Waldrep, Christopher. 2002. *The Many Faces of Judge Lynch: Extralegal Violence and Punishment in America*. New York: Palgrave Macmillan.

Wallensteen, Peter. 2007. *Understanding Conflict Resolution: War, Peace and the Global System*. 2nd ed. Los Angeles: SAGE Publications.

Walzer, Michael. 1992. *Just and Unjust Wars*. 2nd ed. New York: Basic Books.

Ward, Michael D., and Kristian S. Gleditsch. 1998. "Democratizing for Peace." *American Political Science Review* 92 (1): 51-61.

Weaver, James H., Michael T. Rock, and Kenneth Kusterer. 1997. *Achieving Broad-Based Sustainable Development: Governance, Environment, and Growth with Equity*. West Hartford, CT: Kumarian Press.

Weigel, George. 1987. *Tranquillitas Ordinis: The Present Failure and Future Promise of American Catholic Thought on War and Peace*. Oxford: Oxford University Press.

Weigel, George. 2001. Contribution to *Just War and Counterterrorism: Views from the Catholic Church*. Washington, DC: Faith & Reason Institute.

Weigel, George. 2003a. "Moral Clarity in a Time of War." *First Things*. January.

Weigel, George. 2003b. "The Just War Case for the War." *America*. March 31.

Weigel, George. 2004. "War & Statecraft: An Exchange." *First Things*. March.

Weigel, George. 2005. *God's Choice: Pope Benedict XVI and the Future of the Catholic Church*. New York: Harper Perennial.

Weigel, George. 2006. "Iraq: Then & Now." *First Things*. April.

Weigel, George. 2007. *Faith, Reason, and the War against Jihadism: A Call to Action*. New York: Doubleday.

Weigel, George. 2008. *Against the Grain: Christianity and Democracy, War and Peace*. New York: Crossroad.

Weigel, George. 2009a. "The Just War Tradition." *National Review Online*. December 12. http://www.nationalreview.com/articles/228786/just-war-tradition/george-weigel.

Weigel, George. 2009b. "*Caritas in Veritate* in Gold and Red." *National Review Online*. July 7. http://www.nationalreview.com/articles/227839/i-caritas-veritate-i-gold-and-red/george-weigel.

Weigel, George. 2010. "Through a Glass, Clearly." *First Things*. August/September.

Weigel, George. 2011a. "The Death of Osama bin Laden. *Crisis*. May 18. http://www.crisismagazine.com/2011/the-death-of-osama-bin-laden.

Weigel, George. 2011b. "How Democrats View the World." *National Review Online*. March 25. http://www.nationalreview.com/articles/263126/how-democrats-view-world-george-weigel.

Weigel, George. 2013. "Toward a Just Order." *First Things*. February.

Weil, Simone. 1977. "The Iliad, Poem of Might." In *The Simone Weil*

Reader, ed. George A. Panichas, 153-83. New York: David McKay.

Wendt, Alexander. 1992. "Anarchy Is What States Make of It: The Social Construction of Power Politics." *International Organization* 46 (2): 391-425.

Wendt, Alexander. 1999. *Social Theory of International Politics.* Cambridge: Cambridge University Press.

Whitmore, Todd D. 2005. "The Reception of Catholic Approaches to Peace and War in the United States." In *Modern Catholic Social Teaching: Commentaries and Interpretations*, ed. Kenneth R. Himes, O.F.M., 493-521. Washington, DC: Georgetown University Press.

Winright, Tobias. 1995. "The Perpetrator as Person: Theological Reflections on the Just War Tradition and the Use of Force by Police." *Criminal Justice Ethics* 14 (2): 37-56.

Winright, Tobias. 1999. "From Police Officers to Peace Officers." In *The Wisdom of the Cross: Essays in Honor of John Howard Yoder*, ed. Stanley Hauerwas, Mark Thiessen Nation, Chris K. Huebner, and Harry J. Huebner, 84-114. Grand Rapids: Eerdmans.

Winright, Tobias. 2007. "Community Policing as a Paradigm for International Relations." In *Just Policing, Not War: An Alternative Response to World Violence*, ed. Gerald W. Schlabach, 130-52. Collegeville, MN: Liturgical Press.

Winright, Tobias. 2011. "Predictably Horrific." *Commonweal.* March 25.

Wittes, Tamara Cofman. 2008. *Freedom's Unsteady March: America's Role in Building Arab Democracy.* Washington, DC: Brookings Institution Press.

Woodruff, Paul. 1982. "Justification or Excuse: Saving Soldiers at the Expense of Civilians." In *New Essays in Ethics and Public Policy*, ed. Kai Nielsen and Steven C. Patten, 159-76. Guelph, Ontario: Canadian Association for Publishing in Philosophy.

Woods, Chris. 2011. "Over 160 Children Reported Among Drone Deaths." *Bureau of Investigative Journalism.* August 11. http://www.thebureauinvestigates.com/2011/08/11/more-than-160-children-killed-in-us-strikes/.

World Synod of Catholic Bishops. 1971. *Justice in the World.* http://www.osjspm.org/document.doc?id=69.

Wright, Lawrence. 2006. *The Looming Tower: Al-Qaeda and the Road to 9/11.* New York: Vintage Books.

Wright, Lawrence. 2009. "Captives." *The New Yorker.* November 9.

Wright, Lawrence. 2011. "The Double Game." *The New Yorker.* May 16.

Xenophon. 1998. *Agesilaus.* Trans. H. G. Dakyns. Project Gutenberg. http://www.gutenberg.org/catalog/world/readfile?fk_files=3118548.

Yoder, John Howard. 1984. *When War Is Unjust: Being Honest in Just-War Thinking.* Minneapolis: Augsburg Publishing House.

Yoder, John Howard. 1992a. *Nevertheless: The Varieties and Shortcomings of Religious Pacifism*. Rev. ed. Scottdale, PA: Herald Press.

Yoder, John Howard. 1992b. *What Would You Do? A Serious Answer to a Standard Question*. Exp. ed. Scottdale, PA: Herald Press.

Young, Joseph K., and Michael G. Findley. 2011. "Can Peace Be Purchased? A Sectoral-Level Analysis of Aid's Influence on Transnational Terrorism." *Public Choice* 149 (3/4): 365-81.

Zahn, Gordon. 1993. "Reflections on an Unanswered Challenge." In *Studying War—No More? From Just War to Just Peace*, ed. Brian Wicker, 203-10. Grand Rapids: Eerdmans.

Zakaria, Fareed. 2007. *The Future of Freedom: Illiberal Democracy at Home and Abroad*. New ed. New York: Norton.

Zenit. 2003. "Cardinal Ratzinger on the Abridged Version of Catechism." May 2. http://www.zenit.org/en/articles/cardinal-ratzinger-on-the-abridged-version-of-catechism.

Zohar, Noam J. 1993. "Collective War and Individual Ethics: Against the Conscription of 'Self-Defense'" *Political Theory* 21 (4): 606-22.

Index

Abel and Cain, 110
Abingdon, Earl of, 140
abolition. *See also* abolition of war
  of capital punishment, 153-54, 164,
    166, 181
  of dueling, 3-4, 130-31, 164, 165,
    166, 171
  of lynching, 3-4, 156-59, 164, 165,
    166, 210
  realistic path toward, 171-75
  of slavery, 3-4, 136, 138-47, 164,
    165, 166, 171, 180, 210
  of trials by ordeal and combat, 3-4,
    118-20, 165
abolition of war. *See also* pacifism;
    peacemaking
  concluding comments on, 210-11
  conflict resolution and, 198-200
  decline in warfare, 4, 172-75
  democracy and, 183-87
  development and, 24-28, 175, 191-96
  disarmament and, 200
  European integration and, 195-96
  global norms and, 181-82
  global political authority and, 27-28,
    36, 177-82
  intergovernmental organizations
    (IGOs) and, 179, 185, 195-96
  international sanctions and incentives
    for peacemaking, 180, 199
  John Paul II on, 171
  middle stage of, 210-11
  military interventions and, 201
  and multilateralism, 179-80
  nonviolence and, 187-89
  overview of, 1-4
  prevention of civil wars, 199-200
  prevention of recurrence of war,
    201-03
  "responsibility to protect" and, 200-
    201
  rule of law and, 184-85

  soldiers' role transformed by, 203
  trade and, 194-95
abortion, 32
Abu Ghraib prison, 103
Afghanistan
  British use of poison gas against civil-
    ians in, 48
  casualties from drone strikes in,
    55-56
  civilian casualties in, 55-56, 96
  refugees from, 84
  sex crimes in, 86
  soldier's enjoyment of killing during,
    89
  Soviet invasion of, 46, 84, 98, 102
  Taliban in, 89, 98, 102
  U.S. war against and policing actions
    in, 55-56, 80-81, 86, 206, 207
Africa. *See also specific countries*
  colonization of, 146
  conflict resolution in, 199
  democratization in, 186, 187
  development in, 191-92, 193
  ending of wars in, 200
  exports from, 194
  income levels and quality of life in,
    191-92
  prevention of recurrences of wars in,
    201
  slave trade and, 135-36, 138
  wars in, 98, 99, 174
African Americans. *See* lynching;
  slavery
aid efforts. *See* development
al Qaeda, 55, 103, 208
Alabama, 151, 154
Algeria, 50
Ambrose, St., 8, 15-16, 66
America. *See* United States; *and specific
  states*
American Civil War, 48, 56, 63, 70,
  110, 150

American Revolution, 128, 142, 144
Amistad case, 141
An Lushan Revolt, 45
Anabaptists, 18
animal cruelty, 163, 164
Anscombe, Elizabeth, 17, 53, 60, 95
antilynching movement, 155-59. *See also* lynching
Appiah, Kwame Anthony, 125
Aquinas, Thomas
   just war theory of, 9, 10, 16, 34, 44
   on self-defense, 16, 66-67, 68, 71
   on slavery, 137
arbitration. *See* conflict resolution
Argentina, 62, 198
Aristotle, 136
Asia. *See specific countries*
Association of Southeast Asian Nations, 179
Assyria, 47, 71
atomic/nuclear power, 22, 33, 35, 49, 97, 181, 199
Augustine, St.
   on guilt or innocence of combatants and noncombatants, 43-44, 60
   just war theory of, 8-9, 10, 11, 16, 34, 43-44, 60, 83
   on rape as custom of war, 86
   realism of, 11, 37
   on self-defense, 16, 66
   on slavery, 137, 138
   on tranquility of order, 10, 16, 21, 26, 83, 91, 171
autocracies, 184-85, 188

Bacevich, Andrew, 99-101
Bacon, Francis, 125
Baldwin, Stanley, 48
Balkans, 35, 196
Bangladesh, 46, 186
Bartlett, Robert, 117-18
Benedict XVI, Pope
   Caritas in Veritate by, 25, 26, 28, 33, 178, 192
   on democracy, 186
   on development, 26, 192, 193
   on international law, 27, 28, 180
   on just war theory, 23
   on justice, 20
   military service by, during World War II, 2, 64-65, 74

on peacemaking, 25, 26
on trade, 194
Weigel on, 33
Berman, Eli, 206-7
Biafra, 49
Bilbo, Theodore, 156
bin Laden, Osama, 98, 102
Blease, Cole, 152
Boer War, 48
Bosnia, 198
Botswana, 199
Bourke, Joanna, 51, 69
Brahe, Tycho, 125
Brazil, 135, 136, 142, 145
Britain
   abolitionism in, 136, 141-42, 144, 145
   Boer War and, 48
   colonialism of, in India, 189
   dueling in, 124, 125, 130
   Falkland Islands war and, 62, 71
   killing of Irish Catholics by, in seventeenth century, 88
   poison gas used by, against Afghanistan civilians, 48
   policing in, 78
   slave trade and, 141-42
   trial by ordeal in, 116
Buddhism, 12
Burgundians, 114
Burr, Aaron, 124, 127
Bush, George W., 34-35, 38, 88, 100, 101
Byrd, James, 158-59
Byron, Lord Gordon George, 121

Cahill, Lisa Sowle, 12
Cain and Abel, 110
Calhoun, John C., 142
California, 152, 153
Calley, William, 49
Calvin, John, 9
Cambodia, 200
Cameroon, 199
Canada, 127, 136, 181, 187, 199
capital punishment, 22-23, 153-54, 158, 162, 164, 166, 181
Caritas in Veritate (Benedict XVI), 25, 26, 28, 33, 178, 192
Carthage, 47
Catalonia, 116

Catechism, 43, 45, 109
Catholic Relief Services, 179
Centesimus Annus (John Paul II), 21, 25-26, 32, 94, 97, 178, 188
Central African Republic, 199
Central America. *See* Latin America
Challenge of Peace, The (U.S. Bishops), 32
Chaput, Archbishop Charles, 8
Chase, Salmon, 144
Cheney, Dick, 101
child abuse, 163, 164
child soldiers, 61, 87
Chile, 186, 189, 198
China
    An Lushan Revolt in, 45
    annexation of Tibet by, 97
    foot binding of women in, 161
    Japanese attack on city of Nanking in, 89
    Korean War and, 173
    nonviolent resistance in, 188
chivalry codes, 9, 44, 53
Christiansen, Drew, 195
Church of the Brethren, 11
Churchill, Winston, 48
CIA, 88
Cicero, 8
civil rights movement, 158
civil wars. *See also* American Civil War; Spanish Civil War; war; *and specific countries*
    in Africa, 174
    in Europe, 195
    in Middle East, 98
    prevention of, 199-200
    prevention of recurrences of, 202
    risk of, in poor countries, 191
    statistics on, 173-74
civilians during war
    abuse of, and property destruction by soldiers, 85-86
    atrocities against, 47-50, 53-54, 88, 96
    Augustine on guilt or innocence of, 43-44, 60
    civilian immunity principle of just war theory, 44-45
    deaths of, as unavoidable throughout history, 45-50, 56-57
    deliberate killing of, 43-44

and difficulty in distinguishing combatants versus noncombatants, 54
    double effect principle on killing of, 51-56
    exceptions to civilian immunity principle in just war theory, 50-57
    "gray-area killings" of, 54-55
    impact on, of bombing infrastructure targets, 56
    just war theory on killing of, 43-45, 50-57
    military necessity principle on killing of, 50-51
    neoconservatives on, 56-57
    and prohibition on intentionally killing the innocent, 2, 43, 52, 57, 60
    public's lack of concern for casualties among, 96-97
    statistics on deaths of, 45-46, 97
    and weapons used in modern warfare, 55-56
La Civilta Cattolica, 22
Clark, Tom, 157
Clonard monastery, 200
Code of Hammurabi, 133
Colby, Elbridge, 35, 37
Cold War. *See also* Soviet Union; United States
    autocracies during, 183
    communism during, 33, 37
    end of, 23, 100, 103, 173, 181, 184, 199
    nuclear weapons during, 181
    U.S. policy during, 33, 35, 98, 102
collateral damage, 52-54, 79, 151
Colorado, 157
Colossians, Letter to, 137
combat. *See* trials by ordeal and combat
communism. *See* Cold War
Compendium of the Social Doctrine of the Church, 11, 45, 198
conflict resolution, 175, 198-200, 205
conscientious objection, 23
conscription, 61, 86
Constantine, 8
Costa Rica, 98, 177
Costigan, Edward, 157
Council of Trent, 125-26
courts. *See* judicial system

criminal justice system. *See also* polic-
  ing
  capital punishment, 22-23, 153-54,
    158, 162, 164
  debtors' prisons, 163
  racism in, 158
  against terrorism, 207-10
  torture of criminal suspects, 162, 165
Croatia, 201
Cromwell, Oliver, 48
Cronin, Audrey Kurth, 208
Cushing, Cardinal, 33
Cyprian, St., 83
Cyprus, 201
Czechoslovakia, 199

Dante, 124-25
David and Goliath, 118
Davis, David Brion, 134, 136, 137, 141,
    142-44
Day, Dorothy, 11-12
death penalty. *See* capital punishment
debt crisis (2008), 181
debtors' prisons, 163
dehumanization
  desecration of dead bodies after
    lynching, 149, 150-51
  of slavery, 133-34
  of warfare, 88-91, 96
democracy
  abolition of war and, 183-87
  elections in transitions to, 186
  and fighting terrorism, 208-9
  formula for stable democracies, 187
  John Paul II on, 25, 183, 187, 188
  moral progress and, 166
  nonviolence and, 187-89
  opening up autocratic states to de-
    mocratization, 185-86
  peacemaking and, 24-26, 175, 187-
    89
  political institutions during transi-
    tions to, 187
  postconflict peace process and, 202
  process of democratization, 185-87
  rule of law and, 25, 26, 184-87, 208
  spread of, worldwide, 183-87
  statistics on number of democracies,
    183-84
  strengthening state capacity and
    democratic institutions, 186-87,
    192-93

transition problem for young democ-
    racies, 184
Democratic Republic of Congo, 46
Denmark, 116, 125
Denver, James, 124
desecration of dead bodies
  after lynching, 149, 150-51
  in war, 89-90
development
  Benedict XVI on, 26, 192, 193
  complexity and limits of, 191
  diversion of resources from, for mili-
    tary purposes, 97
  economic fundamentals and, 192,
    194
  guidelines for, 192
  human capital and, 192, 193-94
  international cooperation for, 27,
    180, 192-93
  peacemaking and, 24-28, 97, 175,
    191-96
  progress from, 191-92
  state capacity and, 192-93
  and sustainability and environmental
    protection, 193-94
  trade and, 194-95
  United Nations and, 27
dishonesty. *See* lies
disorder during warfare, 83-91
Disraeli, Benjamin, 142
Doctors without Borders, 179
Donner party, 124
double effect principle
  and killing civilians during war, 51-
    56
  and killing soldiers during war, 67-68
  self-defense and, 66-67
Douglas, Mary, 109-10, 112
Dray, Philip, 151
drug abuse, 80, 85
due process
  democracy and, 25, 186
  in judicial system, 78, 87, 158
  lynching and lack of, 151, 157, 158
  peacekeeping and, 203
  war and lack of, 81, 87
dueling
  abolition of, 3-4, 130-31, 164, 165,
    166, 171
  alternatives to, 130-31
  critics of, 125-26, 127
  honor ethic and, 121, 123, 126-30

as institutionalized violence, 121-31, 177
   just war theory and, 123-24, 129
   lethality of, 124
   motives for, 124-25
   norms of, 123-24
   refusing to duel, 126-27
   rules of, 123
   self-defense and, 128
   social acceptance and moral legitimacy of, 3, 121, 123, 126-30
   social benefits of, 129-30
   social class and, 123, 130
   vendettas as forerunner of, 121-23, 165, 177
   weapons for, 123, 126
"duty to retreat," 68, 69

East Timor, 189, 200, 201
economic development. *See* development
Ecuador, 199
Egypt, 199
El Salvador, 50, 186, 201, 202
England. *See* Britain
environmental protection, 27, 193-94
Erasmus, Desiderius, 44, 72, 84, 95, 110, 172
Estonia, 199
Ethiopia, 102, 200
Ethiopia-Eritrea conflict, 63
ethnic and religious minorities, 25, 163, 164, 199-200, 209-10
euphemisms
   of lynching, 153
   of war, 96
European Union, 179, 195-96
euthanasia, 32
Evangelium Vitae (John Paul II), 43, 67, 188

Falkland Islands war, 62, 71
falsehoods. *See* lies
Feldman, James, 207
Felton, Rebecca, 154
feuds. *See* vendettas
Filkins, Dexter, 81
Finnis, John, 17, 67, 71
First Things, 36, 37, 205
First World War. *See* World War I
Fitzhugh, George, 136, 140
Florida, 142, 150

foot binding of Chinese women, 161
Ford, John, 33, 53, 60
former Soviet bloc countries, 186, 196, 199
Forrest, Nathan Bedford, 150
France
   abolitionism in, 144
   dueling in, 124, 125
   French Revolution, 50
   slavery and, 142, 143
   trial by combat in, 116
   in World War I, 48
Franklin, Benjamin, 125
free trade. *See* trade
frontier lynching. *See* lynching
Fry, Douglas, 112
Fullinwider, Robert, 66

Gandhi, Mohandas, 189
gangs, 85
Gaudium et Spes, 24, 166-67
General Agreement on Tariffs and Trade (GATT), 180
Genesis, Book of, 137
Genghis Khan, 85
George, Robert, 13
Georgia, 150, 151, 152, 154, 155
Germany
   democracy in, 185
   dueling in, 126, 127, 130
   Holocaust in, 64
   reparations by, following World War I, 98
   reunited Germany, 196
   Thirty Years War in, 46, 48
   in World War I, 48, 62
   in World War II, 2, 48-49, 64-65, 74, 80, 86, 88
Ghana, 187
global institutions. *See* development; United Nations; *and* international *headings*
global norms, 180-81, 185
global political authority, 27-28, 36, 103, 177-82. *See also* United Nations
global trade. *See* trade
God's kingdom, 9, 12
Goering, Hermann, 94
Goldstein, Joshua, 201, 203
Goliath and David, 118
"gray-area killings," 54-55

Great Britain. *See* Britain
Greece, 63-64, 196
Greenpeace, 179
Grisez, Germain, 67-68, 71
Grossman, Dave, 55, 62, 70, 90, 96
Grotius, Hugo, 9, 65, 66, 68, 137
Guatemala, 50, 200
Gulf War (1991), 22, 35, 53, 64, 70, 98

Haitian Revolution, 141, 145
Ham, curse of, 137
Hamas, 206
Hamilton, Alexander, 124, 127
Hamm, Mark, 208
Hammond, James Henry, 141
Handel, George Frideric, 125
hate crimes, 158-59. *See also* lynching
Hauerwas, Stanley, 12, 172
Hedges, Chris, 49-50, 85, 94, 96
Hehir, J. Bryan, 9
Hekmatyar, Gulbuddin, 102
Helsinki Accords, 180
Henri IV, Chevalier d'Andrieux, 125
Hezbollah, 206
Himes, Kenneth, 171
Hitler, Adolf, 2
Holland, 123
Holland, Barbara, 129
Holmes, Robert, 47, 86
Holocaust, 64
homosexual persons, 32, 163
honor ethic and dueling, 121, 123, 126-30
Hose, Sam, 103, 152
Howard, Michael, 13
Howes, Dustin Ells, 189
human rights
    Catholic tradition on, 25-27, 166-67, 175
    democracy and, 25
    democratic transitions and, 186-87
    humanitarian concern for, 166-67, 174
    international community and, 4, 192
    modernity and, 166-67
    nonviolence and, 189
    peacemaking and, 210
    United Nations and, 27
    Universal Declaration of Human Rights, 180
    violations of, 86-87, 100, 103, 163, 200
Human Rights Watch, 179

human trafficking, 27, 85, 86-87, 208
humanitarian disasters, 97
humanitarian ethic, 164, 174. *See also* moral progress
hunger, 25
Hussein, Saddam, 102, 103
Hutterites, 11

IGOs (intergovernmental organizations), 179, 185, 195-96, 198
Iliad (Homer), 73, 89
impoverished countries. *See* development; poverty
India, 97, 187, 189, 199
Indonesia, 186, 200
innocent victims. *See* civilians; soldiers
institutionalized violence. *See also* war
    capital punishment, 22-23, 153-54, 158, 162, 164
    debtors' prisons, 163
    declines in, and moral progress, 163-68
    dueling as, 3-4, 121-31, 177
    foot binding of Chinese women, 161
    lynching as, 149-59, 177
    piracy on high seas, 161-62, 166, 177, 180
    slavery as, 133-47
    structural sin and, 109-10, 112, 168
    trial by ordeal and combat as, 3-4, 114-20
intergovernmental organizations (IGOs), 179, 185, 195-96, 198
international community. *See also* development; global political authority; trade; United Nations
    conflict resolution and, 198, 205
    development and, 27, 180, 192-93
    ending of war and, 200-201
    global norms and, 180-81, 185
    peacekeeping efforts by, 80, 175, 201-3
    peacemaking and, 26-28, 36, 201-3
    policing by, 181
    prevention of recurrence of war by, 201-3
    "responsibility to protect" and, 200-201
    rule of law and, 178, 192
    sanctions by, and incentives for peacemaking, 180, 199
International Court of Justice, 198

International Criminal Court, 179
international law
  Benedict XVI on, 27, 28, 180
  G. W. Bush administration and, 101
  on humanitarian and peacekeeping
    operations, 80
  John Paul II on, 27
  just war theory and, 9
  on killing of soldiers in self-defense
    during wars, 65
  mediation and arbitration mecha-
    nisms in, 198
  and military force for defense against
    terrorism, 101, 205
  on military interventions, 201
  neoconservative critics on, 36, 102-3
  peace and, 27
  on terrorism, 205
International Monetary Fund, 185
International Peace Operations Association, 101
Iowa, 153
Iran, 35, 188
Iraq, 48. *See also* Gulf War (1991);
  Iraq war (2003)
Iraq war (2003)
  American sniper in, 71
  as breach of international law, 201
  Catholic opposition to, 32-33, 34,
    36, 45
  civilian casualties during and after,
    46, 54, 55, 101
  dehumanizing impact of, 91
  failures of, 103
  families and, 87-88
  increase of terrorism due to, 207
  innocence of soldiers in, 60-61
  neoconservatives on, 102-4, 207
  Neuhaus on, 36
  refugees after, 84
  sex crimes and, 86
  soldier's enjoyment of killing during,
    89
  terrorist activity at beginning of, 206
  torture at Abu Ghraib prison, 103
  U.S. callousness about, 88
  U.S. justifications for, 100-103
  war-fighting and policing activities in,
    80-81
  Weigel on, 32-33, 35, 103
Ireland, 48, 88, 126, 130, 200, 208, 209
Islam

jihadism/terrorism and, 36-38, 97,
  102, 206, 207
slavery in Muslim communities, 135
Israel, 49-50, 88, 199
Italy, 124-25

Jackson, Andrew, 128-29
Jainism, 12
Jamaica, 80
James, William, 203
Japan
  atomic bombs dropped on, 49
  attack on Chinese city of Nanking
    by, 89
  democracy in, 185
  refugees from, 84
  refusal of use of firearms in, 111-12
  renunciation of war by, 177
  in World War II, 49, 62, 70, 86, 90
Jefferson, Thomas, 140
Jervis, Robert, 173
Jesus, 7, 11, 84
John, Gospel of, 7
John of Salisbury, 16
John Paul II, Pope
  on abolition of war, 171
  Centesimus Annus by, 21, 25-26, 32,
    94, 97, 178, 188
  on democracy, 25, 183, 187, 188
  on development, 24, 25-26
  Evangelium Vitae by, 43, 67, 188
  on families, 87
  on fighting terrorism, 208-9
  Guadium et Spes by, 166-67
  on Gulf War (1991), 98
  on human dignity, 166-67
  on international community, 26, 27-
    28, 178, 179
  on international integration, 195
  on Iraq War (2003), 32-33
  on justice, 24
  mediation by, of border dispute be-
    tween Chile and Argentina, 198
  on moral progress, 166-68
  on nonviolence, 23
  on original sin, 167
  on peacemaking and pacifism, 21, 24,
    26, 27, 32, 87, 187
  on sacredness of human life, 43, 57
  on self-defense, 67, 68, 69, 71
  Sollicitudo rei Socialis by, 26, 167,
    195

on structural sin, 109, 112, 168
on terrorism, 205
on United Nations, 27
on violence justified by deceit, 94
on war, 22, 84, 85, 90, 97, 98, 104
John XXIII, Pope, 22, 26, 168, 175
Johnson, James Turner, 13, 34, 36
Johnson, James Weldon, 156-57
Johnson, Samuel, 128
Jones, Seth, 207
judicial system
  due process in, 78, 87, 158
  dueling and, 126, 130
  lynching and, 153, 158
  policing versus, 78-79
  and trials by ordeal and combat, 119
  vendettas and, 122
jus ad bellum principles, 9-10, 35, 51,
    61, 62-63
jus in bello principles, 10, 22, 35-37,
    43, 51, 62-63
just war theory. *See also* war
  Augustine on, 8-9, 10, 11, 16, 34,
    43-44, 60, 83
  Catholic doctrine on, 1-2, 8-11, 15-
    17, 20-28, 33-38
  civilian immunity principle of, 44-45
  double effect principle of, and killing
    civilians, 51-56
  dueling and, 123-24, 129
  and exceptions to civilian immunity
    principle, 50-57
  features of, 9-11, 35-36
  on innocence and moral equality
    among combatants, 60-65, 72
  jus ad bellum principles of, 9-10, 35,
    51, 61, 62-63
  jus in bello principles of, 10, 22, 35-
    37, 43, 51, 62-63
  on killing innocent civilians, 43-45,
    50-57
  on killing soldiers, 60-74
  and license to kill soldiers, 72-74
  in Middle Ages, 44
  military necessity principle of, and
    killing civilians, 50-51
  neoconservatives' support of, 2, 4,
    32-38, 53, 56-57, 83, 94, 102-4,
    137, 156, 171
  parallel between domestic security
    and war, 1, 2, 3, 15-18
  political authority and, 9-11

popes on, after Second Vatican Coun-
    cil, 20-28
  presumption against war and, 23,
    34, 37
  proponents of, 1-2, 10-11, 32-38
  Protestantism on, 9, 17-18
  and punitive justification for killing
    soldiers and civilians, 43-44, 60,
    63
  Second Vatican Council and, 2, 20-
    28, 32
  and self-defense justification for kill-
    ing soldiers, 65-72
  slavery and, 138, 143
  on terrorism, 205
  and threat-based preventative justi-
    fication for killing of soldiers,
    65, 68
justice
  Benedict XVI on, 20
  development and, 24-28
  Erasmus on, 95
  peace and, 24-28, 36
  United Nations and, 27

Kahn, Paul, 79
Kant, Immanuel, 183
Kaplan, Fred, 102
Kavanaugh, John, 96
Keegan, John, 50, 110-11, 133, 174
Kenny, Charles, 193
Kentucky, 151, 152
Kenya, 186, 199
Key, Francis Scott, 125
Khatchadourian, Raffi, 54
Kiernan, V. G., 127, 129
Korean War, 46, 49, 85, 96, 173
Krauthammer, Charles, 13
Ku Klux Klan, 150
Kurdistan Workers Party (PKK), 207,
    209
Kuwait, 98

Las Casas, Bartolomé de, 139
Lateran Council (1215), 119
Latin America
  border dispute between Chile and
    Argentina, 198
  democracy in, 186
  ending of wars in, 200
  Falkland Islands war in, 62, 71
  nonviolent resistance in, 189

prevention of recurrences of wars in, 201

slavery in, 135, 136, 141, 142, 145

U.S. Cold War policy on, 35, 103

War of the Triple Alliance in, 46

warfare of Yanomamo in, 47

law. *See* international law; rule of law

law enforcement. *See* criminal justice system; policing

lawlessness during warfare, 83-91

least development nations. *See* development; poverty

Lebanon, 198

LeBlanc, Steven, 45

LeMay, Curtis, 49

Lepanto, battle of, 63

libel laws, 130

Liberia, 200

Libicki, Martin, 207

Lichtenberg, Judith, 53

lies

    of slavery, 134

    of war, 1, 3, 94-104

Lindbergh, Charles, 70

Lithuania, 189

Lombards, 117, 118

Luitbrand, King of Lombard, 117, 118

Luke, Gospel of, 7

Luther, Martin, 9

lynching

    abolition of, 3-4, 156-59, 164, 165, 166, 210

    criticisms of antilynching efforts, 155-56

    defense of, 152-56

    definition of, 149

    desecration of dead bodies following, 149, 150-51

    euphemisms of, 153

    frontier lynching, 149-50, 153

    innocence of victims of, 151, 156

    as institutionalized violence, 3-4, 149-59, 177

    laws against, 153, 156, 157-58

    media coverage of, 152-53, 156-57

    middle phase of abolition of, 210

    motives behind, 149-51

    origin of term, 149

    public nature of and popular participation in, 151-52

    social acceptance and moral legitimacy of, 3, 149-56

    social purpose of, 151-52

    Southern racial lynching, 149-58

    statistics on, in U.S., 149

Lyon, archbishop of, 117

Macedonia, 199

male-only priesthood, 32

Mao Tse-Tung, 71

Mark, Gospel of, 7

Martino, Archbishop Renato, 22-23

Maryland, 157

Mather, Increase, 48

Matthew, Gospel of, 7

McKeogh, Colm, 44, 73

McVeigh, Timothy, 53

Mead, Margaret, 110

media coverage

    in autocracies, 185

    of lynching, 152-53, 156-57

    and moral progress in response to suffering, 164

mediation. *See* conflict resolution

medieval period. *See* trials by ordeal and combat

Mennonites, 11

Metaxas, Eric, 146, 164

Middle Ages. *See* trials by ordeal and combat

Middle East, 98, 102, 135, 184. *See also* Gulf War (1991); Iraq war (2003); *and specific countries*

military coups, 181

military interventions for ending wars, 201

military necessity principle, 50-51

military training, 90-91

Miller, C. J., 151, 152

Milne, A. A., 18

Mississippi, 150, 153, 156

modernity, 164-67

Mohammed, Khalid Sheikh, 110

Mongols, 47

moral progress

    and declines in institutionalized and interpersonal violence, 163-68

    humanitarian ethic and, 164, 174

    John Paul II on, 166-68

    John XXIII on, 168

    modernity and, 164-67

    moral perfection versus, 165, 166

    politics and, 166

    as realistic, 165-68

reality of sin and, 166, 167-68
Mozambique, 200, 201, 202
Mueller, John, 174, 184, 187
multiculturalism, 36, 38
multilateralism, 179-80
murder rates, 163
Murray, John Courtney, 10, 33, 83
My Lai massacre, 49, 88, 96

Nagel, Thomas, 66
Namibia, 199, 201
Napoleon, 63, 73, 128
Narveson, Jan, 17-18
National Security Strategy of the United States (2002), 34-35
Native Americans, 47, 48, 89
natural law, 11, 84, 144
neoconservatives
    on civilians during war, 56-57
    on international law, 36, 102-3
    on international political authority, 178
    on Iraq war (2003), 102-4, 207
    on just war theory, 2, 4, 32-38, 53, 83, 94, 102-4, 137
    on peacemaking, 36-38, 156, 171, 175, 188
    on September 11 terrorist attacks, 34, 207
    on terrorism, 205
    on United Nations, 36, 102-3
Neuhaus, Richard John, 33-36, 103
New Testament. *See* Jesus; *and specific books of New Testament*
New Zealand, 203
NGOs (nongovernmental organizations), 179, 185, 186, 189
Nicaragua, 200, 201
Nigeria, 49, 199
9/11 terrorist attacks, 33, 34, 88, 100-103, 110, 205-7
noncombatants. *See* civilians during war
nongovernmental organizations (NGOs), 179, 185, 186, 189
nonviolence, 23, 175, 187-89. *See also* pacifism; peacemaking
Norris, John, 124
North American Free Trade Agreement, 179
North Carolina, 150
North Korea, 101, 185

Northern Ireland, 200, 208, 209
Norway, 115
nuclear power. *See* atomic/nuclear power

Obama, Barack, 110
Oklahoma federal building bombing, 53
Old Testament, 8, 137. *See also specific books of Old Testament*
On the Duties of the Clergy (Ambrose), 15-16
Oneal, John, 196
ordeal. *See* trials by ordeal and combat
organized crime, 174, 208
Origen, 8
original sin. *See* sin
Otto I, 117

Pacem in Terris (John XXIII), 26, 168, 175
pacifism. *See also* abolition of war; nonviolence; peacemaking
    Catholicism and, 11-12, 17, 23
    Christian pacifism, 11-12
    criticisms of, 12-13, 17-18, 36, 37, 155, 156
    engaging and healing impulse within, 12
    of Erasmus, 84, 95, 110, 172
    non-Christians and, 12
    and opposition to use of military force for ending wars, 201
    and parallel between domestic security and war, 15-18
    peacekeeping and, 203
    policing and, 18
    presumption against war and, 23, 34, 37
    "sectarian withdrawal" and, 171
    self-defense and, 18
    separatist impulse within, 12, 18
Pakistan, 46, 55-56, 81, 97, 199
Palestinian refugees, 49-50
Pape, Robert, 207
Paraguay, 46
Patterson, Eric, 34-37
Patterson, Orlando, 133
Patton, George, 71
Paul, St., 7, 8, 137
Paul VI, Pope
    condemnation of war by, 21, 98

on development, 24, 84
on free trade, 194
on international cooperation, 26, 179
on police measures against terrorism, 208
Peace of God, 117
Peace of Westphalia, 50
peacekeeping operations, 80, 175, 201-3
peacemaking. *See also* abolition of war; nonviolence; pacifism; rule of law
   Catholic doctrine on, after Second Vatican Council, 23-28, 175, 187
   conflict resolution and, 175, 198-200
   democracy and, 24-26, 175, 187-89
   development and, 24-28, 175, 191-96
   ending of war through international efforts, 200-201
   international cooperation for, 26-28, 36, 201-3
   justice and, 24-28, 36
   neoconservative critics of, 36-38, 156, 171, 175, 188
   poverty as threat to, 25-26, 84, 191
   "responsibility to protect" and, 200-201
   United Nations and, 27
   women involved in, 202
Peel, Sir Robert, 78
Pennsylvania, 152
Peru, 186, 199
Philippines, 186, 189
Pinker, Steven, 163, 164, 165
piracy, 161-62, 166, 177
Pius XII, Pope, 16-17
PKK (Kurdistan Workers Party), 207, 209
Plato, 136
Poland, 186, 189
policing
   in Britain, 78
   differences between war and, 77-81, 203
   functions of, 77-78, 83
   goal of, 79
   international coordination of, 181
   judicial system versus, 78-79
   lynching and, 153, 157
   modernity and, 165
   moral legitimacy of, 77, 81
   pacifists on, 18

   parallel between war and, 1, 2, 3, 15-18
   peacekeeping and, 80, 201-3
   physical force/deadly force and, 77-78, 79, 80
   relationship between citizens and police, 77
   rule of law and, 77, 83
   by soldiers, 80-81
   of spousal abuse, 163
   against terrorism, 207-10
   weapons used in, 79-80
Policraticus (John of Salisbury), 16
political authority. *See also* democracy; global political authority
   Catholic tradition on, 9-11
   global political authority, 27-28, 36, 103, 177-82
   just war theory and, 9-11
   moral progress and, 166
   pacifism and, 12-13
   and prevention of recurrence of civil war, 202
Pontifical Council for Justice and Peace, 22-23
Portugal, 196
poverty, 25-26, 84, 191, 192. *See also* development
preventative justification for killing of soldiers, 65, 68
prevention of war. *See* abolition of war
prisoners of war, 63, 70, 138
propaganda, 94. *See also* lies
Protestantism
   on just war, 9, 17-18
   pacifism and, 11-12
Punic Wars, 47
punitive justification for killing soldiers and civilians, 43-44, 60, 63
Pyle, Ernie, 64

Quakers, 11, 18, 143

racism, 146, 158. *See also* lynching; slavery
Ramsay, James, 144
Ramsey, Paul, 9, 11
RAND Corporation, 202
rape. *See* sex crimes
Ratzinger, Cardinal Joseph. *See* Benedict XVI, Pope
Raynal, Abbé, 143

refugees, 84
Register, Katherine, 45
"responsibility to protect," 200-201
Roman Empire, 8, 18, 47, 135
Romans, Letter to, 16
Roosevelt, Franklin, 157, 158
Rousseau, Jean-Jacques, 125
rule of law
    abolition of war and, 4, 184-85
    breakdown of, in war zones, 85
    democracy and, 25, 26, 184-87, 208
    and fighting terrorism, 208-9
    international community and, 178,
        192
    peacemaking and, 210
    policing and, 77, 83
Rummel, R. J., 188
Rush, Benjamin, 162
Ruskin, John, 174
Russett, Bruce, 196
Russia, 127, 184. *See also* Soviet Union
Rwanda, 198

same-sex marriage, 32
sanctions, 180, 185, 199
Sant'Egidio Catholic Community, 200
Scandinavian countries, 177
Schall, James, 32, 34, 35, 37, 38
Schlabach, Gerald, 15, 78
Scotland, 126
Second Vatican Council, 2, 20-28, 32,
    167, 179
Second World War. *See* World War II
"sectarian withdrawal," 171
self-defense
    Ambrose's prohibition against, 15-16,
        66
    Aquinas on, 16, 66-67, 71
    and asymmetry between victim and
        attacker, 69, 71-72
    Augustine's prohibition against, 16, 66
    conditions for justifiable self-defense
        by individuals, 66-69, 72
    double effect principle and, 66-67
    dueling and, 128
    "duty to retreat" and, 68
    John Paul II on, 67, 68, 69, 71
    as justification for killing soldiers
        during war, 65-72
    "no-fault" account of individuals'
        right of, 65-66, 69
    pacifists on, 18

parallel between war and, 1, 2, 3, 15,
    16-17, 65-72
Pius XII on, 16-17
Sennacherib, 71
September 11 terrorist attacks
    G. W. Bush administration on, 88,
        101, 103
    Iraq war following, 33, 88, 100-101,
        103, 205, 207
    neoconservative critics on, 34, 207
    planner of, 110
    rates of terrorist attacks following,
        206
    war on terrorism following, 33, 35,
        98, 100, 102
Serbia, 50, 189
sex crimes
    decline in rape rates, 163, 164
    fear of, as justification of lynching,
        153, 154-56
    war and, 85-86, 89, 96
Shalmaneser III, 47
Sharp, Gene, 188
Sheehan, James, 95, 196
Sherman, William T., 48, 56, 110
sin
    original sin, 167
    reality of, 166, 167-68
    slavery associated with, 137, 139-40,
        143
    structural sin, 109-10, 112, 168
    war as, 109-10, 112
slander laws, 130
slave revolts, 141, 145
slave trade, 135-38, 141, 143, 145
slavery
    abolition of, 3-4, 136, 138-47, 164,
        165, 166, 171, 180, 210
    in Americas, 135-42, 144, 145
    Bible on, 137
    chattel slavery, 133
    Christianity's defense of, 137-39
    classical philosophers on, 136
    common dynamics of, throughout
        history, 133-35
    defense of, 136-42
    dehumanization of, 133-34
    families of slaves, 135
    history of globally, 133-36
    as institutionalized violence, 3-4,
        133-47, 165
    Jefferson on, 140

just war theory and, 138, 143
lies of, 134
middle phase of abolition of, 210
moral contradiction of, 134
root word for slave, 135
sin associated with, 137, 139-40, 143
social acceptance and moral legitimacy of, 3, 136-42
social control required for, 134
violence and brutality against slaves,
134-35, 139, 143-44
Slim, Hugo, 50, 85-86
Smith, Lillian, 157
Smithka, Paula, 17
soldiers during war
abuse of civilians and property destruction by, 85, 86
ambushes and surprise attacks
against, 70-71
atrocities against civilians by, 47-50,
53-54, 88, 96
child soldiers, 61, 87
compared with police, 77-81
conscription of, 61, 86
dehumanization of the enemy by,
88-91, 96
desecration of dead bodies by, 89-90
double effect principle on killing of,
67-68
enjoyment of killing experienced by,
88-89
and failure to uphold formal rules of
engagement, 54
innocence and moral equality among
combatants, 60-65, 72
job of, as killing and being killed, 71,
73, 78, 79, 90-91
jus in bello principles on, 62-63
just war theory on killing of, 60-74
license to kill soldiers and just war
theory, 72-74
and low threshold for killing, 54-55,
78-79
military training of, 90-91
physical and psychological wounds
of, 91
policing by, 80-81
as prisoners of war, 63, 70, 138
and prohibition on intentionally killing the innocent, 2, 60, 74
psychological impact of war on,
90-91

punitive justification for killing of,
60, 63
rape of female soldiers by their comrades, 86
reasons for military service of, 61
refusal to kill by, 62
self-defense justification for killing of,
65-72
statistics on deaths of, 63-64, 70
surrender by, 63, 70
threat-based preventative justification
for killing of, 65, 68
transformation of role of, with abolition of war, 203
voluntary versus forced military
service by, 61, 86
wounded soldiers, 63, 70
Sollicitudo rei Socialis (John Paul II),
26, 167, 195
Somalia, 102, 198
South Africa, 186, 189
South America. *See* Latin America
South Carolina, 138-39, 141, 152, 155
Southern racial lynching. *See* lynching
Soviet Union. *See also* Cold War
Afghanistan invasion by, 46, 84, 98,
102
nuclear weapons of, 181
Ukraine's break with, 199
in World War II, 48, 86, 87
Spain, 46, 51, 137, 142, 181, 196
Spanish Civil War, 46, 51
Spierenburg, Pieter, 121, 122, 163
spousal abuse, 163, 164
Sri Lanka, 96
Stephenson, James, 150
Sterba, James, 17
Stiltner, Brian, 17
Stroessinger, John, 97
structural sin, 109-10, 112, 168. *See
also* sin
Suárez, Francisco, 9, 44, 45, 60, 137
Sub-Sahara Africa, 191-92
Summa Theologia (Aquinas), 16
"sunk-cost fallacy," 95
surrender of soldiers, 63, 70
sustainability, 193-94
Switzerland, 122

Taliban, 89, 98, 102
Tamil insurgency, 96

Tamil Tigers, 207
Tennessee, 150, 152, 154
terrorism
  al Qaeda and, 55, 103
  as asymmetrical warfare, 206
  Catholic teaching on, 205, 208-10
  characteristics of terrorists and ter-
    rorist groups, 206-7, 209
  criminal justice strategies against,
    207-10
  decline in, 206
  development targeting causes of, 24
  failure of, 206
  funding for, 206, 208
  hard-core members of terrorist
    organizations versus affiliated
    sympathizers, 206-7, 209
  ineffectiveness of war as response to,
    206, 207-8, 210
  Islamic jihadism, 37-38, 97, 102, 206,
    207
  against Israel, 88
  military force for defense against, 205
  military occupation as motivation
    for, 207
  neoconservatist critics on, 205
  9/11 terrorist attacks, 33, 34, 88,
    100-103, 110, 205-7
  nonmilitary approaches for fighting,
    208-10
  in Northern Ireland, 208, 209
  organized crime and, 208
  rule of law in fighting, 208-9
  suicide attacks as, 206-7
  torture of suspected terrorists, 36, 53,
    87, 88, 103
  underlying causes of, 209
  war on terrorism, 33, 35, 98, 100,
    102
Texas, 142, 149, 150, 152, 153, 155,
  158-59
Thiessen, Marc, 36, 38, 53, 103
Thirty Years War, 46, 48
Thomson, Judith Jarvis, 65-66, 69
Tibet, 97
Tirman, John, 81, 96-97
Tocqueville, Alex de, 174
Tolstoy, Leo, 18
torture
  at Abu Ghraib prison, 103
  of criminal suspects, 162, 165

laws against, 207
  of lynching's victims, 149, 150
  of suspected terrorists, 36, 53, 87,
    88, 103
trade, 179, 180, 185, 194-95. *See also*
  slave trade
tranquility of order, 10, 16, 21, 26, 83,
  91, 171
Tranquillitas Ordinis (Weigel), 83
trials by ordeal and combat
  abolition of, 3-4, 118-20
  criticisms of, 117-18
  description of, 114-16
  as institutionalized violence, 3-4,
    114-20
  participants in, 115
  prayers before, 114-15
  regulations for, 115-16
  social acceptance and moral legiti-
    macy of, 3, 116-18
  social class and, 115
Truce of God, 117
Truman, Harry, 49
Tunisia, 189
Turkey, 96, 209
Turner, Mary, 151

Ukraine, 189, 199
United Nations. *See also* global political authority; International community
  autocracies and, 185
  critics of, 36, 102-3, 178
  decline of war and, 179
  development and, 27
  International Court of Justice and,
    198
  John Paul II on, 27
  and Paul VI on condemnation of war,
    21
  peacekeeping efforts by, 202
  peacemaking and, 27, 200, 201
  terrorism and, 208
  workforce of, 202
United States. *See also* American Civil
  War; American Revolution; Cold
  War; lynching; slavery; terrorism;
  *and specific states, presidents, and
  wars*
  dueling in, 124-28, 130
  militarism in, 33, 35, 99-104, 202

nuclear weapons and, 181
U.S. Bishops
  on civilian immunity during war, 45
  on double effect principle of just war
    theory, 52
  on just war theory, 23
  on modern warfare, 22, 104
  on pacifism and peacemaking, 20, 23,
    26, 32, 33
  on terrorism, 205
  on United Nations, 27
Universal Declaration of Human
  Rights, 180
Upshur, Abel P., 142
utopianism, 1-4, 10, 15, 36-37, 97, 137,
  171, 188, 205

Vardman, James K., 152
Vatican Council, Second. *See* Second
  Vatican Council
Vatican's Pontifical Council for Justice
  and Peace, 22-23
Vattel, Emmerich de, 65
vendettas, 3-4, 121-23, 165, 177
Verdun, battle of, 63
video games, 97, 99
Vietnam War
  Agent Orange in, 56
  atrocities against civilians in, 49, 88,
    96
  Catholic support for, 33
  civilian casualties of, 46, 49, 56
  criticism of and public opposition to,
    33, 56, 96-97
  deaths of soldiers in, 88
  dehumanization of the enemy during,
    88
  desecration of dead bodies during,
    89-90
  failure to uphold formal rules of
    engagement in, 54
  landmines from, 56
  outcome of, 98
  soldier's enjoyment of killing during,
    89
  Weigel on, 35
violence. *See* civil wars; dueling;
  institutionalized violence; lynching; slavery; trials by ordeal and
  combat; war
Virginia, 135, 144, 149, 153

Vitoria, Francisco de, 9, 16, 34, 44, 45,
  60

Waldrep, Christopher, 149
Walzer, Michael, 17, 51, 61
war. *See also* abolition of war; civil
  wars; civilians during war; just war
  theory; soldiers during war; *and
  specific wars*
  American militarism and, 33, 35, 99-
    104, 202
  "carnivalesque spirit" of, 89-90
  collateral damage during, 52-54, 79,
    151
  conflict resolution for prevention of,
    175, 198-200
  cycle of violence caused by, 98, 99
  decline in, 4, 172-75, 181-82, 183,
    195, 201
  as development in reverse, 84-85
  differences between policing and,
    77-81, 203
  disarmament and, 200
  ending of, 200-201
  Erasmus on, 84, 95, 110, 172
  euphemisms of, 96
  families and, 87-88
  global efforts against generally, 4
  history of, 8, 110-12
  human rights violations during, 86-
    87
  involuntary labor during, 86-87
  lawlessness, disorder, and dehuman-
    ization as features of, 83-91
  lies and illusions of, 1, 3, 94-104
  military interventions for ending, 201
  motives for, 94-95, 98-100, 103
  objectives of, 111
  organized crime and, 174
  outcomes of, 97-98
  parallel between policing and, 1, 2,
    3, 15-18
  and prohibition on intentionally kill-
    ing the innocent, 2, 43, 52, 57,
    60, 74, 81
  recurrence of, 201-2
  refugees and, 84
  reveling in violence of, 88-90
  ritualism and ceremonialism in,
    111-12
  romantic belief in goodness of, 174

sex crimes and, 85-86, 89, 96
statistics on casualties of, 45-46, 63-
64, 70, 97, 173
as structural sin, 109-10, 112
"sunk-cost fallacy" and, 95
twentieth-century popes on condemnation of, 21-23
utopianism and, 3, 97, 137, 171, 205
weapons of, 55-56, 71, 79-80, 111-12
War of the Triple Alliance, 46
Washington, Jesse, 149, 155, 158
weapons. *See also* atomic/nuclear
power
civilian casualties from, 55-56
for dueling, 123, 126
of mass destruction, 103, 181
policing and, 79-80
in warfare, 55-56, 71, 79-80, 111-12
Weigel, George, 32-38, 65, 83, 91, 103,
178, 205
Weil, Simone, 73
Wellington, Lord, 124
Wells, Ida B., 156
Wendt, Alexander, 180, 195
White, Walter, 156
Wilberforce, William, 146, 164
Wilhelm II, Kaiser, 51
Wilson, John Lyde, 128
Wilson, Woodrow, 97
Winright, Tobias, 77
Wisconsin, 153-54
women
deaths of, from childbirth, 193
foot binding of Chinese women, 161
lynching of, 151
peacemaking and, 202
protection of Southern white women
from purported black violence,
153-55, 157
rights of, 25
as slaves, 141
spousal abuse against, 163, 164
in U.S. armed forces, 86
World Bank, 179

World War I
bombing during, 48
casualties of, 46, 63, 70, 87, 195
genocide of Armenians by Turkish
government during, 96
justification for killing civilians during, 51
long-term impact of, 98, 131
orphans and widows following, 87
reparations by Germany following,
98
soldier's enjoyment of killing during,
88-89
soldiers' refusal to kill during, 62
"sunk-cost fallacy" and, 95
trench warfare in, 90-91
World War II
aerial bombing of cities during, 33,
48-49, 53, 80, 97
atomic bomb during, 49
casualties of, 46, 56, 173, 195
dehumanization of Germans during,
88
desecration of dead bodies during, 90
Japan in, 49, 62, 70, 86
long-term impact of, 98
military casualties in, 62, 64
military leader in, on deaths of soldiers, 73
Patton in, 71
prisoners of war during, 70
Ratzinger in German army during, 2,
64-65, 74
refugees and, 84
sex crimes during, 86
siege of Leningrad during, 48, 87
soldier's response to killing in, 90
Weigel on U.S. involvement in, 35

Xenophon, 63-64

Yemen, 55
Yoder, John Howard, 18, 97

Zohar, Noam, 61, 68